Pioneers or Pawns?

Gender, Culture, and Politics in the Middle East

miriam cooke, Suad Joseph, *and* Simona Sharoni, *Series Editors*

Other titles in Gender, Culture, and Politics in the Middle East

Pioneers

WOMEN HEALTH WORKERS AND THE

or Pawns?

POLITICS OF DEVELOPMENT IN YEMEN

Marina de Regt

Syracuse University Press

First Edition 2007
09 10 11 12 13   6 5 4 3 2

The paper used in this publication meets the minimum requirements of American National Standard for Information Sciences—Permanence of Paper for Printed Library Materials, ANSI Z39.48-1984.∞™

All photographs except on page 13 were taken and provided by author.

ISBN-13: 978-0-8156-3121-7   ISBN-10: 0-8156-3121-9

Library of Congress Cataloging-in-Publication Data

De Regt, Marina.
   Pioneers or pawns? : women health workers and the politics of development in Yemen / Marina de Regt. — 1st ed.
      p. cm. — (Gender, culture, and politics in the Middle East)
   Includes bibliographical references and index.
   ISBN-13: 978-0-8156-3121-7 (cloth : alk. paper)
   ISBN-10: 0-8156-3121-9 (cloth : alk. paper)
   1. Economic development projects—Yemen (Republic) 2. Women—Yemen (Republic) 3. Medical personnel—Yemen (Republic) I. Title.
HC415.34.Z9E443 2007
338.9533—dc22   2007019307

This book is dedicated to the spirit of three women:

My mother Jannie de Regt-Gohres

(1928–2001)

My colleague Thera de Haas

(1935–1999)

My friend Marjan Rens

(1960–1999)

Marina de Regt is a Dutch anthropologist specializing in gender, labor, migration, and development in the Middle East, and in particular Yemen. She worked for six years in development projects in Yemen, after which she returned to academia. She received her Ph.D. from the University of Amsterdam. Currently, she is working at the International Institute for Social History in Amsterdam.

Contents

Illustrations

Acknowledgments

WHEN I WAS AN ADOLESCENT I dreamed of adventure and travels to faraway countries, bored by my life at home in the Netherlands. I had already made up my mind: I wanted to learn Arabic and become an anthropologist. My mother, however, was trained as a nurse and wished that one of her children would share her interest in medical issues and take up work in health care. None of her three children did. But, as the stories in this book show, lives can take surprising turns, affected by circumstances, by the initiatives we take, and by other people. And whether one calls it "coincidence," "fate," or "God's hand," sometimes these turns seem to fit a larger plan. This book is the outcome of a number of surprising turns, which in the end happen to fit neatly together: an anthropological study of women health workers in an Arabic country, whose stories and interests sometimes bear re-markable similarities to those of my mother. Both my mother and the Yemeni women health workers had been longing for education and en-tering health care gave them the opportunity to develop themselves. In chapter 1 I describe the circumstances and my own initiatives that led to writing this book. Here I want to acknowledge the numerous people that, in addition to my mother, have inspired and supported me.

Not surprisingly this book would not have come into being without the support of many women in Hodeida, health workers as well as oth-ers. They succeeded in turning Hodeida into a second home for me: I enjoyed living and working with them and had great difficulty leaving. The idea of starting a Ph.D. after six years working in development projects in Yemen was not only intellectually inspired but also based on practical considerations: it offered me the possibility of continuing to stay in touch with my friends and former colleagues in Hodeida, albeit from a different angle and a different location. I am greatly indebted to them. It is impossible to mention all their names, also for reasons of privacy, yet I feel a great need to thank by name Aicha, Bilqis, Bouthaina, Hanaan, Jamila, Jamila, Morjana, and Na'ma. I promise that the finishing of this book will not be the end of our friendship.

In addition to the Yemeni women in Hodeida, there were many other people in Yemen who supported me. One of the most important persons was Thera de Haas, my Dutch colleague in Hodeida and the "mother" of the women trained and employed as health workers. From my very first visit to the project, Thera helped me wherever she could, and she became a close friend. I will never forget the many evenings at her house, when she would cook for me and tell me about her life and about the project. Thera was strongly interested in my research because she loved her Yemeni colleagues and was proud of their achievements. Her death came far too early, and I feel very sorry that she is not able to read the final result. Other people that supported me in Yemen are, amongst many others, Mohamed Aideroos, Joke Buringa, Debbie Penney, Khalid al-Dubai, Ali M. Ghailan, Sam Loli, Abdalla al-Siyari, and Saeed al-Sha'arani. I want to thank Arwa Ahmed Abdu al-Izzi for transcribing many tapes.

When I decided to gather material for a dissertation, in the last year of my employment in Hodeida, I received the enthusiastic and inspiring support of Annelies Moors, who had supervised my MA thesis and with whom I stayed in contact during the years that I lived in Yemen. Without her support this book may not have seen the light at all, or, in any case, it would have been of a different nature. Her genuine interest in my research, her close reading of everything I wrote, and her efforts to encourage me to improve my work have been of immense importance for the final result. I am very grateful to her. I also want to thank Sjaak van der Geest for his support. Although he did not know me at all, he accepted me as a Ph.D. student at the time that Annelies was not yet a full professor. I appreciate his help and am thankful to him for introducing me to medical anthropology.

Returning to the Netherlands after six years living in Yemen, and making a comeback in the academic world, was greatly facilitated by a number of people. I want to thank in particular Ellis Jonker, whom I met in the first month of my return and with whom I shared a lengthy absence from academia. Together we established the Oral History Club, which turned into an important support group for young feminist researchers working with life stories. I want to thank all its members, as well as the members of the Ph.D. club of the Medical Anthropology Unit and the Anthropology Ph.D. club of the Amsterdam School for Social Science Research at the University of Amsterdam. The meetings of these groups were very important to me, not only as a source of intellectual inspiration but also as a source of social contacts.

In addition to the members of these clubs, many other people read and commented upon my writings or supported my work in other ways. I want to thank in particular Marjo Buitelaar, Janine Clark, Rineke van Daalen, Margaret von Faber, Marloes Janson, Reinhilde König, Wendy Lee, Eileen Moyer, Frits Muller, Karin van Nieuwkerk, Marta Paluch, Mathijs Pelkmans, Nathalie Peutz, Caroline Roset, Chrisje van Schoot, Rachel Spronk, Ali de Regt, Ada Ruis, Ahmed Saleh al-Amery, Lidwien Scheepers, Willem van Schendel, Seteney Shami, Delores Walters, and Vazira Zamindar. With my friend Marjan Rens I was only able to share my first ideas and writings. We had discovered feminist anthropology together and shared an ambition to combine academic research with activism, but I was able to realize this ambition while she was not. Her tragic death in 1999 brought an end to her ambitions.

I want to thank the Amsterdam School for Social Science Research (ASSR) and the Netherlands Foundation for the Advancement of Tropical Research (WOTRO) for financing important parts of the research. The ASSR offered an inspiring environment and its administration provided the necessary support to facilitate my work. I also want to thank the Yemeni Centre for Research and Studies (YCRS) and the Centre Français d'Archéologie et de Sciences Sociales de Sana'a (CEFAS) in Yemen for supporting my research. Marta Paluch was responsible for checking and editing the English text during two of her precious holidays and even came over from London to discuss the changes she made, for which I am very grateful. I owe my gratitude to Syracuse University Press, in particular to Mary Selden Evans and Amy Barone, and to the two anonymous reviewers of my manuscript. I really enjoyed working together with them on preparing the manuscript for publication.

Before publishing the book in English, I was able to publish it in Arabic. I elaborate on the backgrounds of that translation in the epilogue, but here I want to thank the many people that helped me to realize the translation, in particular the people who donated money, the Department of Central Programmes and Institutes of the Dutch Organization for Scientific Research (NWO) for funding the translation, and Mohamed 'Abdelhamid, who translated the book.

Last but not least I want to thank my family and friends for their continuous support. A special word of thanks goes to my father, who always has a great interest in everything I do and who reads almost everything I write. My concern for people in less privileged circumstances is definitely inspired by him. I am also grateful to my brothers and their respective families and to my numerous friends. Although they often heard me express my wish for more time to work and less distraction, they continued to contact me and invite me for lunches, dinners, movies, parties, and much more. Writing a book about my beloved Yemeni colleagues in the surrounding of equally beloved relatives and friends in the Netherlands was a perfect way to come to terms with an important part of my life.

Abbreviations

DGIS	Directoraat Generaal Internationale Samenwerking (General Directorate for International Cooperation)
GAD	Gender and development
GAVIM	Good Governance, Armoede, Vrouwen, Institutionele Ontwikkeling en Milieu (Good governance, poverty, women, institutional development, and environment)
HEMIS	Health Information System
HMI	Health Manpower Institute
HPHSS	Hodeida Primary Health Systems Support Project
HUPHC	Hodeida Urban Primary Health Care Project
ICD	International Cooperation for Development
ICPD	International Conference on Population and Development
ID	Identity card
IUD	Intra-uterine device
IMF	International Monetary Fund
LCCD	Local Council for Cooperative Development
LDA	Local development association
LDC	Least developed country
MCH	Mother and child health
NGO	Nongovernmental organization
OXFAM	British development organization (lit. Oxford Committee for Famine Relief)
PDRY	People's Democratic Republic of Yemen
PGC	People's General Congress

PHC	Primary health care
RIRDP	Rada' Integrated Rural Development Project
SAP	Structural Adjustment Program
SNV	Stichting Nederlandse Vrijwilligers (Society of Dutch Volunteers)
SWAp	Sector-wide Approach
UN	United Nations
UNFPA	United Nations Population Fund
UNICEF	United Nations Children's Fund
USAID	United States Agency for International Development
WHO	World Health Organization
WID	Women in Development
YAR	Yemen Arab Republic
YEMDAP	Yemen Drug Action Program
YSP	Yemeni Socialist Party
YWA	Yemeni Women's Association

PART ONE

Introduction

1

From Academic Research to Development Work and Back Again

THIS BOOK IS ABOUT a group of women in Yemen who were first colleagues, then friends, and only in the end research subjects. It is a book about an important part of their lives in which they were employed as health-care workers in a Dutch-Yemeni development project, a book that analyzes the different ways in which their training and employment introduced new opportunities as well as new forms of social control. But it is also a book about an important part of my own life, as I worked for the same development project for years. My own experiences in Yemen are thus closely linked to the experiences of the women about whom I write. Because this way of working goes against the grain of more conventional ways of doing academic research, in which people are in the first place research subjects, then might become friends, and in rare cases even might become colleagues, the background to my research project deserves some extra attention. The story of my own involvement in Yemen, and the various phases I went through, are important to understanding why and how this study came about.

Rada': First Encounter with Development Work

In June 1991, I noticed a vacancy for a job in a rural development project in Yemen. A Netherlands development organization was looking for a handicrafts adviser whose main task would be the development

of a marketing channel for carpets made by rural women in Yemen. I
felt attracted to this job, even though I had trained as an anthropologist and not as a handicrafts adviser. During my master's studies I had
done research among women carpet workers in Morocco, and I was
interested in taking up work abroad. My commitment to working with
Arab women, the fact that I spoke Arabic (albeit the Moroccan dialect), and the fact that I was acquainted with the production of carpets
led to my employment. I obtained a three-year contract, and within a
short period of time I found myself preparing to go to Yemen, a country about which I knew very little.

When I arrived in Yemen at the end of 1991, one of the first Yemeni women I met was Zahra.[1] Zahra was working as a rural extension
agent (f. sing., *murshida zira'iyya;* f. pl. *murshidat*) in the Rada' Integrated Rural Development Project (RIRDP).[2] Rada' is a rural town
to the southeast of Yemen's capital, Sana'a, two hours away by car and
located in what is considered a highly tribalized and conservative area.
The Rada' Integrated Rural Development Project had started in 1978
and was supposed to run until 1994. The main aim of the project was
to improve the living standards of the population of Rada' District by,
among other things, constructing roads, building dams, improving irrigation techniques, and introducing new agricultural methods. Zahra
was one of the five *murshidat* in the Rural Women's Extension Section, and she was going to be my counterpart in the following years.
The function of a *murshid* can be described as guide, instructor, or
educator. In the Yemeni context, *murshidin* and *murshidat* inform and
educate people about new ways of living and working.[3] There are, for

1. Owing to the sensitive and personal nature of the information provided I
have used fictitious names for the people involved in this study, with the exception of
Thera de Haas, to whom this book is dedicated.

2. The Rada' Integrated Rural Development Project was a bilateral project of
the Dutch General Directorate of International Cooperation of the Ministry of Foreign Affairs and the Yemeni Ministry of Agriculture.

3. The terms *murshidin* and *murshidat* are also used for Boy Scouts and Girl
Scouts. The use of the term for extension agents is recent, linked to the establishment of foreign development projects. I will continue to use the Arabic words

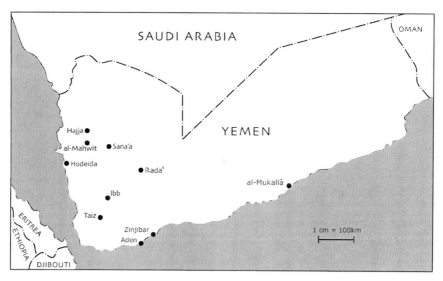

Yemen

example, *murshidin* and *murshidat* working in agricultural extension, in water and sanitation activities, and in health education. *Murshidin* and *murshidat* have attended a minimum of six years of primary school and then completed a one-year training course, mostly financed by foreign development agencies. The project in Rada' provided the training for the *murshidat,* while the Yemeni Ministry of Agriculture employed them. They were working alongside five expatriate advisers: a Sudanese adviser for agricultural extension, a Sudanese adviser for livestock, a Dutch adviser for health education, a Dutch adviser for nutrition, and a Dutch adviser for handicrafts. Every adviser worked together with one of the *murshidat,* implementing one of the extension programs directed at rural women.

---

murshida (singular) and *murshidat* (plural), and not the English translation of "guide" or "educator." Although the use of local terms may give rise to a certain exoticism, I have decided to stick to the words *murshida* and *murshidat* because Yemeni as well as non-Yemeni development workers use these words. For some words I use the third-person plural, as used in Yemeni dialect and not the Modern Standard Arabic form (e.g., *murshidin* instead of *murshidun*).

The strength and motivation of Zahra and the other four Yemeni women working for the project immediately impressed me; they were young, ambitious, and willing to improve their own livelihoods and those of other women. Together with their foreign counterparts, but sometimes also on their own accompanied by a driver, they went into the villages to inform women about new agricultural and livestock techniques, to give health and nutrition education, and to teach women how to make knotted carpets from sheep's wool. They stood out in Rada', where very few women had salaried work or were active in the public domain. The other Dutch women working for the project told me how difficult it had been to find women willing to do this type of work and how happy they were with their counterparts. I was intrigued by the relationship between the foreign advisers, with their colorful clothes and bare heads,[4] driving their four-wheel-drive cars, and the young Yemeni women, dressed in black *sharashif*,[5] with veiled faces, who were restricted in their mobility. The contrast could hardly be greater, but the cooperation between these two parties seemed to be strong.

In the previous five years, Zahra and my Dutch predecessor had trained a group of fifty rural women in three villages to produce handmade woolen carpets, and my task was to find a sustainable marketing channel for these carpets. In the past, Yemeni men used to weave rugs on horizontal looms, but this craft had almost disappeared with the migration of the male population to other parts of Yemen, to Saudi Arabia, and to the Gulf States. In addition, imported factory-made carpets had replaced homemade ones because of the increased

---

4. The majority of female Dutch development workers in Yemen do not cover their hair, even when working in conservative areas. The explanation they give is that Yemenis have gotten used to the presence of foreign women with uncovered hair. Although prepared to wear a headscarf, I adapted to the social norms among Dutch development workers and did not cover my hair during my stay in Yemen.

5. The *sharshaf* (pl. *sharashif*) is a black three-layered garment, including a face veil, worn by women when they go into public. For details on Yemeni women's clothing see Makhlouf (1979, 30–38), Carapico (2001), and Moors (2003).

availability of money. From then on wool was discarded. In 1986, two Moroccan women visited the project as advisers and suggested that rural women learn to make carpets on vertical looms, which (contrary to horizontal looms) could be placed inside the houses. Rural women in the villages around Rada' were interested in learning a new skill that would enable them to obtain an independent income. In the following years, fifty rural women were trained in knotting carpets, yet the only people interested in buying these carpets were expatriates residing in Yemen.[6] Yemenis preferred colorful factory-made carpets to white carpets made from sheep's wool. The gap between the producers in the villages and potential consumers was enormous; the women were unable to leave the villages to sell their carpets in town, as women selling in the market were looked down on, and their male relatives were not interested in marketing the carpets. I was the only one able to bridge the gap, trying to sell the carpets in Sana'a, just as my predecessor had done. Our search for a sustainable solution failed and, in view of the coming end of the entire project, it was decided that the carpet program had to stop, leaving fifty rural women without an income.

In this first experience in a development project, I was immediately confronted with the overly optimistic attitude and ill-considered ideas of expatriate development workers who introduce new activities without foreseeing their long-term impact. I also wondered what was going to happen to the female extension agents when Dutch funding came to a halt. Although they were employees of the Yemeni Ministry of Agriculture, and their salaries did not depend on foreign funding, the context of their work depended to a large extent on the presence of expatriate advisers. The expatriate advisers were the ones who supported and promoted the work of the female extension agents, and almost all of the activities were financed with Dutch funds. During

6. There was a relatively large expatriate community in Yemen in the 1990s, consisting of embassy personnel, development workers, employees of oil companies, and businessmen. Since the events of September 11, 2001, the size of the expatriate community has decreased.

the one and a half years that I worked for the project, almost all the expatriate project members left because the project was coming to an end, and the number of female extension agents working for the project also gradually decreased, as two of the five *murshidat* married and stopped working. After November 1994, when Dutch technical and financial assistance to the RIRDP stopped completely, the activities of the Rural Women's Extension Section came to an end as well. There was no money to pay for gasoline for the cars to go to the villages, and the three remaining *murshidat* stayed in the office without work. Soon afterwards the head of section left for a better position, and the two female extension agents, one of whom was Zahra, stayed at home. There was no reason to go to work anymore because there were no cars available and no funds to finance the activities of the section. This was also the case for other sections of the project. The Rada' Integrated Rural Development Project collapsed, despite its ambitious plans to be the focal point of rural development in the district.

Hodeida: A Second Experience

In August 1993, I moved from Rada' to Hodeida, Yemen's main port on the Red Sea coast. The end of the carpet program in Rada' had made my presence in the project unnecessary, and I was offered a job as an anthropologist in a Dutch-financed health-care project.[7] I jumped at the chance to work somewhere else, as I enjoyed living and working in Yemen. The fact that I easily found a new job whereas the Yemeni women with whom I had worked in Rada' were unable to move on to more fulfilling work was a clear sign of the unequal positions we occupied. Although their government salaries continued, they lost their work and had no choice but to stay at home.

The Hodeida Urban Primary Health Care Project (HUPHC), which started in 1984, was a bilateral project of the Dutch General Directorate of International Cooperation and the Yemeni Ministry

7. My contract with SNV ended, and I became an employee of DGIS, the Dutch General Directorate of International Cooperation of the Ministry of Foreign Affairs.

of Public Health. In the early 1960s, Hodeida had been only a small coastal town, but it developed in a short period of time into one of Yemen's main cities. The commercial activities of the port attracted large groups of migrants from other Yemeni cities, the highlands, and rural villages in the Tihama, the coastal plain along the Red Sea coast, as well as migrants returning from abroad. The high influx of people in a relatively short period of time resulted in the creation of large squatter areas on the outskirts of town, areas without electricity, water and sanitation facilities, or educational and health-care services. Whereas the health-care activities of foreign development agencies had been directed at rural areas in the 1970s, in the mid-1980s health experts worldwide became increasingly aware of the need for primary health care in poor urban areas (see Rossi-Espagnet 1984). The Hodeida Urban Primary Health Care Project was a result of this new way of thinking. The project was set up as a pilot, and on the basis of its results urban primary health-care activities were to be extended to other parts of Hodeida, and even to other parts of Yemen. Dr. Cees van Oordt, the Dutch team leader; Dr. Mohamed Ibrahim, a Tunisian public health expert; Thera de Haas, a Dutch public-health nurse; Veronica Thijssen, a Dutch midwife; and Joyce Bakker, a Dutch anthropologist, formed the first expatriate team. Together with Yemeni counterparts from the Ministry of Public Health, they were responsible for carrying out the project activities.

The first activity of the project was the opening of a small health center for mother and child health-care (MCH) services in one of the squatter areas of Hodeida. Because there were few female health workers in Yemen, the health center was initially staffed by the Dutch nurse and the Dutch midwife. Another important activity of the project was the training of women as health-education workers, in Arabic known as *murshidat sihhiyyat* (f. sing. *murshida sihhiyya*). *Murshidat sihhiyyat* are women with at least six years of primary education who have attended a one-year training course in preventive health-care services, in particular in mother and child health care. At first it was not easy to find women for the *murshidat* training course, owing mainly to the low educational level of women but also to the negative notions concerning women's paid work in general, and in health care in particular. Men were (and still are) considered to be the main providers for their families, and practices of gender segregation limited women's access to paid work. Moreover, certain types of health-care work were perceived to have a low status because they implied contact with bodies and bodily fluids. Traditionally, only people of low social status performed this type of work (see Gerholm 1977, 131).

Despite these obstacles, within a couple of years more than twenty *murshidat* had been trained and employed in Hodeida. The *murshidat* divided their time between offering preventive health services in the center and giving health education to women in the area by way of home visits. In 1989, a second health center in another squatter area became part of the project. When I arrived in Hodeida in August 1993, the project had just expanded to all thirteen government health centers in the city. There were more than one hundred *murshidat* working in the centers, trained by different donor organizations, and some of them were responsible for the management of the health centers. I was immediately impressed by the large presence of Yemeni women working in health care, and in particular by the *murshidat*. Compared with Rada', the situation with regard to women and paid labor in Hodeida seemed very different.

In Hodeida I moved into a small independent house in one of the better-off areas of the city. In view of the extremely high temperatures in Hodeida,[8] I was advised to arrange good housing with air-conditioning, where I could relax after working. Although at first I had qualms about my housing situation, as it contrasted sharply with the poor living conditions of the squatters and the *murshidat* with whom I spent most of my time, I gradually began to see the advantages, in particular in view of the long period of time I intended to live in Hodeida. Living in poorer conditions may have been possible for a shorter period of time, but I doubt that I would have been able to live for four

8. From April until October the average temperature is around forty-five degrees Celsius with a very high degree of humidity, and the other six months the temperature is only ten degrees lower.

years without the comfort and privacy of a good house. I had access to a project car, which I shared in the beginning with one of the Yemeni team members, and that facilitated my mobility in the city. Whereas Rada' was a small town of thirty thousand inhabitants, Hodeida was a big and busy port in which more than three hundred thousand people lived. I used the car to go to work, visit the health centers, and go into the various areas for work purposes, but also to visit colleagues and friends outside working hours and on the weekends.

What was an anthropologist doing in a primary health-care project? In the mid-1970s, it had become clear that technological interventions did not lead automatically to better living conditions for the majority of the population, and that social and cultural factors had to be taken into account as well. From that point onward, an increasing number of anthropologists began to be employed in development projects. In particular, primary health-care projects have made extensive use of anthropologists because of the importance attributed to local notions of health and health care and community participation. In Hodeida, foreign anthropologists had been involved in the project from the very beginning, employed on long-term and short-term contracts. Together with the *murshidat*, they carried out baseline studies of the areas, did short applied research analyses, and provided advice on the establishment of literacy and sewing programs for women in the health centers.[9] My responsibilities were more or less the same. In addition, I was responsible for establishing a community participation program. In the thirteen catchment areas of the health centers, "local health committees" had to be formed. These committees consisted of five well-respected community members who would represent the interests of the community in the health center of each area, and who would be responsible for

9. Illiteracy rates among Yemeni women are very high: in 1999, 76.1 percent of the women were illiterate (UNDP 2002, 151). It has been shown worldwide that literacy has a positive effect on women's health-care behavior, and primary health-care projects have often included literacy programs. Sewing classes were included because they offer women in poor urban areas an opportunity to earn an income.

the management of the money recovered via user fees. Training the committee members and monitoring the activities of the committees was also part of my job. I had to carry out all my responsibilities in close cooperation with the women health workers present in the project—the *murshidat*, midwives, and nurses working in the health centers and in the regional Health Office.[10]

In the next four and a half years, I worked closely with the *murshidat* in training and supervising the health committees as well as in several small-scale research efforts. We studied nutrition habits and child feeding practices among the poor of Hodeida, the impact of literacy and sewing classes for women, the attendance of poor people at the health center, and the practices of traditional birth attendants in the city. All this research was based on the information needs of the health center staff and of the project management and was designed, carried out, analyzed, and reported in cooperation with the *murshidat*, nurses, and midwives involved in the health centers. My main task was to train and supervise female health staff during the research process, not to do research on my own, so that the Yemeni health-care staff would learn how to investigate problems or issues they encountered during their work. Together with the *murshidat* and the supervisors of the *murshidat*, I designed a procedure for the selection of local health committees, based on focus group discussions, home visits, and in-depth interviews with possible candidates.[11] We established thirteen local health committees, consisting of male and female community members, and set up a system to monitor their activities.

I enjoyed my close relationships with the *murshidat* and visiting community members or interviewees at home. But I also began to see the limitations of applied research. Every research project needed to result in immediately applicable recommendations. Moreover, the

10. The Health Office is the regional office of the Ministry of Public Health in Hodeida.

11. For a detailed description of the community participation program in Hodeida, see de Regt (1997).

The author in the company of some of her colleagues, 1997. Photographer unknown.

female health workers suffered from a heavy workload, running the health centers, delivering health education in the areas, and often carrying out additional tasks, leaving them little time to do research. My own time was restricted as well, and gradually I began to long for in-depth and academic research again. In the last year of my employment, I decided to use my leisure time to gather material for a dissertation. Selecting a topic for my Ph.D. research was not difficult: I wanted to know more about the backgrounds and motivation of the *murshidat*, something that I had been interested in since my first experiences in Rada'.

From Development Work to Academic Research

In the four years that I lived and worked in Hodeida, I built up close contacts with a number of *murshidat*. We were not only colleagues but also friends, and we often came together on Thursday afternoons to chew *qat*[12] and smoke a water pipe. I went with them to parties and weddings, or I visited them at home after work. I met their families and shared in the ups and downs of their personal lives, as they did in mine. Through my daily contacts with the *murshidat* I had picked up bits and pieces of their backgrounds and their motivations to become *murshidat*, but I was longing to hear more about their lives. The Dutch staff of the project protected and promoted the *murshidat*, seeing them as agents of change. In their eyes the *murshidat* were able to change the health-care situation and the living conditions of the squatters in general, while bringing about changes in their own lives at the same time. They put them on a pedestal and presented them as the first group of locally trained professional women with close contacts in the community and with an enormous capacity to bring about change. But what was the social position of the women trained as *murshidat?* How had their status changed because of their training and employment? And how did they themselves evaluate these changes?

Although I was worried about the sustainability of many of the project activities, I was also convinced that the training of *murshidat* was beneficial in some way. The *murshidat* strengthened my convictions by telling me time and again that their training and employment was of the utmost importance to them, that they loved their work, and that they could not imagine what their lives would be like if they had not become *murshidat*. If the other project activities did not last, at least a group of one hundred women had been trained and

---

12. *Qat* is a shrub whose leaves have a mildly stimulant effect when chewed. A large part of the Yemeni adult population, in particular men, chews *qat* in the afternoon, alone or with others. *Qat* sessions are the most important pastime in Yemen and excellent opportunities for meetings and discussions. For detailed studies of *qat* and its social function in Yemen see Weir (1985) and Kennedy (1987).

employed. Like Delores Walters (2001), an American anthropologist researching *murshidat* in the Tihama town of 'Abs, I saw the *murshidat* as pioneers challenging social boundaries in Yemen. But while Walters emphasizes the impact of the *murshidat* on race relations, delivering health care to the lowest social-status group in Yemen,[13] I wanted to focus on the ways in which the employment of women as *murshidat* shifted gender boundaries. They were salaried state employees, active in the public domain, and moving out of their houses to go to work and to pay home visits to unrelated families, managing health centers, and dealing with unrelated men in community affairs. In view of the negative values attached to women's wage labor, in particular in health care, the main question of my research was therefore: How and why did large numbers of women in Hodeida enter this new type of paid work? And what does the training and employment as *murshidat* tell us about changing gender relations in Yemen?

In 1997, the last year of my employment in Hodeida, I gathered twenty topical life stories of *murshidat* (in Arabic) on tape. I call these interviews "topical" because the focus was on the training and work as *murshidat*; I did not intend to gather integrated life stories.[14] The interviews were done on the basis of a checklist covering family and educational background, reasons for entering the *murshidat* training course, experiences working as a *murshida*, and future ambitions. The selection of the *murshidat* was based on when they started their training, their marital status, their position in the project, and their family background. The interviews were mostly done on Friday afternoons, when the *murshidat* and I had our day off. I visited them at home and we would spend a pleasant afternoon together. All the *murshidat* I approached were willing to be interviewed, and most of them were

13. Yemen has a hierarchical system of social stratification, based on people's ancestry and the work they perform. In chapter 3 I elaborate on this system of social stratification.

14. For the particular use of "topical life stories" see Bertaux (1981, 8) and Moors (1995, 8). For the use of life stories in feminist research see Gluck and Patai (1991) and the Personal Narratives Group (1989).

enthusiastic when I told them about my intention to write a book about them. They had always been positioned as intermediaries between the community and the project management and had taken up the roles of health educator, community worker, researcher, or interviewer. In my study they became interviewees themselves, and they clearly enjoyed the attention that I was giving them. They interpreted the fact that I was going to write a book about them as an important recognition of their work. In addition, I gathered project documents and policy papers and took notes of relevant observations, meetings, and discussions. Yet the main research source for this book is what can be called "experiential knowledge," the insights I obtained during the years that I lived and worked in Yemen.

In the interviews, the *murshidat* spoke openly about their frustrations at work, the lack of possibilities to upgrade their qualifications and their worries about the future when Dutch funding to the health centers would come to a halt. With the integration of the Hodeida Urban Primary Health Care Project into the Yemeni Ministry of Public Health from 1993 onward, the *murshidat* gradually lost the protection of the foreign project and became more dependent on changes in local and national policies. Local health administrators in Hodeida did not share the project's view of the importance of preventive mother and child health services and made a plea for the inclusion of curative care in the health centers. Moreover, in 1996, the Yemeni Ministry of Public Health decided to stop training *murshidat* and to train community midwives instead. These women had completed nine years of education and attended a two-year training course in midwifery. Obviously the *murshidat* were afraid to lose out. Gradually I started to question my previous convictions. Were the *murshidat* really pioneers, shifting gender boundaries in Yemen, as foreign development workers saw them? Or were they merely pawns, deployed to realize the agendas of international donor organizations and Yemeni state institutions?

Back in the Netherlands I found an important source of inspiration in critical approaches to development, providing a theoretical framework for my own experiences with the ambiguities and contradictions of "development." One of the main articles that inspired me was Fahmy's analysis of the Egyptian School of Midwives (1998), which was established in the early nineteenth century. In the next chapter I will elaborate on the ambiguous character of the school, as a point of departure for a discussion of the relationship between gender, labor, development, and modernity. Here it is important to mention that, following Fahmy, I decided to study the Hodeida Urban Primary Health Care Project as "a site of contestation," paying attention to the different, and sometimes contradictory, discourses of development of the actors involved in the project—Dutch development workers, Yemeni state officials, and the women involved as *murshidat*.

The fact that I was closely involved in the project and shared many of the convictions of my Dutch team members automatically raises the question of how that involvement influenced the study. Feminist researchers were among the first to show that all knowledge is "situated" (Mies 1983; Haraway 1991). The background and position of the researcher also affects the data and therefore the outcomes of the research. In the past twenty years, discussions about objectivity and partiality in the social sciences, and in particular in anthropology, have become increasingly part of mainstream thinking. The argument that ethnographic representations are always "partial truths" (Clifford 1986, 6) has become more accepted, and a reflexive stance, in which the researcher reflects (briefly) upon his or her role in the production of data, has become almost standard in ethnographic studies.

In addition, it has become increasingly clear that the boundaries between being an insider and an outsider are not always clear-cut. In my case, I started as a partial insider because of my position as an active member in the development project that is the subject matter of this study. I was employed by the Dutch Ministry of Foreign Affairs, I formed part of the team of (Dutch) development workers, and I shared many of their notions on gender, labor, and health-care development. I worked closely with the *murshidat*, and some of them became friends; I had my own opinions about the position of the *murshidat*, and I played an active role in protecting, supporting, and promoting them. Only in the last year of my employment in Hodeida did I decide to gather data for a book.

The fact that I followed an unusual trajectory required a special way of working. As mentioned before, my analysis of the different practices and discourses of the actors involved in the project—Dutch development workers, Yemeni state officials, and the women involved as *murshidat*—is mainly built on the knowledge I gathered during my stay in Hodeida. In order to make this "experiential knowledge" explicit, and to put my experiences and insights in perspective, I needed distance, geographically as well as mentally, and early in 1998 I went back to the Netherlands. In 2002, I returned to Yemen for a field-work period of six weeks to fill information gaps and to discuss the preliminary outcomes of my study with as many people as possible. I met many of the *murshidat* and former project team members. I gave a number of chapters to Yemeni colleagues working in health care and development, including former project team members. Moreover, I translated the four life stories that are presented in the book verbatim for the four *murshidat*. Their reactions were reassuring; while I had been a bit anxious that they would not approve of the presentation of their life stories, they expressed pride because I had selected them.

An important part of the book is based on the interviews with the *murshidat*. Their detailed narratives bring to the fore the individual motivations and strategies of women but also demonstrate the ways in which their space for maneuver is limited by social structures. Because I use the stories to give insight into social relations and not for detailed narrative analysis,[15] I have opted for extensive editing so as to facilitate reading. My main ambition was to write a readable book: a book in which the *murshidat* would be able to recognize their experiences (after it had been translated into Arabic),[16] a book in which I would describe my own experiences, a book nonacademics would be able to

15. This does not mean that I do not acknowledge that the stories are representations of reality, first of all constructed by the women involved, and second, constructed by me for the sake of analysis (see Moors 1995, 12).

16. In 2005 the Arabic translation of this book was published in Cairo and distributed among the *murshidat* and all the other people who participated in the research.

read and understand, an ethnography about a group of women in a Yemeni city, but also an ethnography of a development project.

Outline of the Book

In this book I unravel the politics of development behind the training and employment of women health workers in a foreign-funded development project in Yemen, in particular through the eyes of the women involved. My main argument throughout the book is that while women's training and employment as *murshidat* offered new opportunities for self-development, simultaneously new forms of social control were introduced, at the level of the state, the project, and the family. In order to analyze the politics of development at these different levels, and to show the enabling and the disciplining side of women's training and employment as *murshidat* at different levels and at different periods, I have divided the book into five parts: the introduction, in which I introduce my research and the theoretical framework, and four parts in which I focus on different levels and different periods. Every part consists of two chapters.

In the next chapter, which is still part of the introduction, I discuss the main theoretical debates related to my study. I start the chapter with a description of the Egyptian School of Midwives established in the nineteenth century, a project that also focused on the training and employment of female health-care workers. I draw connections with the Hodeida Urban Primary Health Care Project and discuss debates on development, the politics of health care, and the implications for women. My main argument in this chapter is that critical perspectives of development and modernization projects have tended to neglect the ways in which these projects may also be enabling, and suggest that an actor-oriented approach leaves more room for agency. At the end of the chapter I formulate an approach for my study of women health workers in Hodeida.

In part 2 ("Yemen and the Politics of Development") I discuss the politics of development at the level of the state and at the level of the project. I first describe processes of Yemeni state formation and their links with development and modernization programs, in particular concerning women and health care. I argue that political interests mainly inspired the Yemeni government's support of education and employment projects for women and primary health-care projects, and explain this argument by reference to the country's heavy dependence on foreign aid. I describe the history of the Hodeida Urban Primary Health Care Project, emphasizing the different discourses of development of the Dutch government reflected in the different phases of the project. One of my main conclusions is that the link with Dutch development policies was rather weak and that instead local, national, and international events affected the course of the project to a large extent. In addition, I highlight the importance of individual people in the development of the project.

In the following three parts of the book I focus on the *murshidat* and elaborate on the developments in the project. In every part I present the life stories of a different group of *murshidat*. On the basis of these stories I analyze their backgrounds, motivations, and strategies. The three parts are structured in chronological order; in each part a certain cohort is the center of attention.

In part 3 ("Shifting Boundaries") I focus on the first group of *murshidat*, trained in 1985–86. Although the intention of the project was to train adult women from the squatter areas as health workers, the first group of *murshidat* consisted mainly of young and unmarried women from families living outside the squatters. These young women were longing for education, but education and paid employment of women were negatively valued in their families. Becoming *murshidat* was not so much inspired by the need for income but more by an interest in obtaining new knowledge and skills. The focus in this part is on the ways in which the first group of *murshidat* gradually shifted the boundaries of dominant gender ideologies, while simultaneously, new forms of social control came into being.

In part 4 ("New Positions and Identities") I introduce the second and the third groups of *murshidat*, trained in 1988–90. The backgrounds of the *murshidat* changed, and the implications of this change for the status of the profession are analyzed. While the first *murshidat* came from outside the squatter areas, the groups of *murshidat* that followed were predominantly coming from poor families living in the squatter areas. The women of the second cohort were mainly daughters of rural migrants and of returning migrants who had lived for considerable periods in Africa. They had benefited from the increased educational opportunities in the 1980s but often had stopped schooling in order to provide for their families. Becoming *murshidat* was one of the few ways to state employment and offered the opportunity to combine work with study. Developments that took place in the project resulted in a higher status for the *murshidat*. Through their training and employment as *murshidat*, these young women from poor families obtained new positions and identities.

In part 5 ("Other Modernities") the focus of attention is the period after 1990. Developments on the national and international level affected the *murshidat* profession, and other categories of women made their entry. One of the main developments was the influx of thousands of returnees from Saudi Arabia and the Gulf States after the outbreak of the Gulf crisis in 1990. As a result, large groups of young and educated women born and brought up in Saudi Arabia were trained and employed as *murshidat*. Although these women might not have entered a health-care profession in Saudi Arabia or taken up paid work at all, they felt forced to leave school and get employed. Their employment as *murshidat* sometimes offered them new opportunities but sometimes also introduced new forms of social control, for example from the side of their male relatives. In addition, changes at the level of the project led to a greater say for new (male) health managers who did not share the project's history. Other notions of modernity were introduced affecting the positions of the *murshidat*.

In the conclusion I return to the theoretical debates discussed in chapter 2. While critical studies of development and modernization projects inspired me, my analysis of the Hodeida Urban Primary Health Care Project shows the importance of agency and the ways in which power constellations continuously change. Development projects have both enabling and disciplining aspects for different groups of people at different periods of time. The *murshidat* were therefore both pioneers, changing their own lives as well as the lives of others, and pawns used in the politics of other actors involved in the project.

2

Women, Health-Care Work, and the Politics of Development

Two Projects of Modernity

IN 1832, EGYPT'S FIRST School of Midwives was opened, established by Antoine-Barthélemy Clot, a French doctor, following a request from Mohamed 'Ali, the governor of Egypt at that time. The European involvement in setting up a health-care system in Egypt had started in the early nineteenth century when the Egyptian government tried to avert plague and cholera by introducing a European maritime quarantine system (Kuhnke 1990, 2). Dr. Clot was one of the main contributors to the introduction of Western medicine in Egypt. He first established a Western-style medical school attached to a hospital and in 1832 founded the School of Midwives. The midwifery training lasted six years. Two years of Arabic literacy were followed by four years of training, including obstetrics, pre- and postnatal care, dressing wounds, vaccinations, and the identification and preparation of most common medicines. The *hakimat*,[1] or female doctors, were government employees and were housed, fed, clothed,

---

1. Although most studies refer to this newly trained group of midwives as *dayat* (the local term for birth attendant; sing. *daya*), Kuhnke prefers to call them *hakimat* (female doctors; sing. *hakima*) in order to distinguish this group from the not formally trained folk midwives (Kuhnke 1990, 123).

and instructed at state expense. After finishing their studies, the *hakimat* worked in the maternity wards of the military and civic hospital in Cairo. Gradually, the *hakimat* received other assignments including vaccinating children against smallpox, examining women at quarantine stations, and verifying the causes of death for women, first in Cairo and later in the entire country. Because of the controversial character of the profession, it was not easy to find women willing and able to become *hakimat* but the school continued to function in the Egyptian public health establishment well into the twentieth century (Tucker 1985, 120; Kuhnke 1990, 132).

From its establishment, the School of Midwives attracted the attention of European travelers and historians. At a time when educational opportunities for women in Egypt were limited and few women were involved in government employment, the school offered women the opportunity to train as midwives. According to Kuhnke, who studied the introduction of European medical theory and organization to Egypt, the School of Midwives was remarkable for two reasons: "it was the first governmental educational institution for women in the Middle East, and it was an unprecedented experiment in drawing into social service women who appeared to be more secluded from public activity than women in any other part of the world" (1990, 122). Kuhnke adds that the employment of the *hakimat* was doubly remarkable in view of the military context in which they functioned. They were employed by the Ministry of War and subject to army regulations (125). European travelers and historians were amazed to see Egyptian women working in a modern health-care establishment, with their faces uncovered, and ascribed this remarkable phenomenon to the enlightened character of Mohamed 'Ali's regime. The School of Midwives was in their eyes an important step on the road toward modernity and away from medieval customs and beliefs.

In his article "Women, Medicine, and Power in Nineteenth-Century Egypt," Khaled Fahmy takes a closer look at the School of Midwives and deconstructs the image of the school as an example of the development and emancipation of Egyptian women. He argues that the school was "a site of contestation" where various battles about modernity and science were fought (1998, 37). Fahmy reveals these battles through an analysis of the aims of the school, the backgrounds of the young women who entered the school, and the position of the newly trained midwives. In his view, the main aim of the school was to create a healthy climate for the army because the high risks of smallpox and syphilis were threatening the availability of military personnel. The education and emancipation of women was merely a side effect of the school. Moreover, difficulties in finding women willing and able to undertake this lengthy, rigorous, and unorthodox training resulted in the recruitment of women from low-class backgrounds, such as enslaved, orphaned, and homeless girls. In addition, the *hakimat* occupied the lowest positions in the newly founded medical establishment, with local and foreign administrators above them. They were the most vulnerable component of this new structure and the easiest to attack (59). Summing up, Fahmy argues that despite the opportunities for empowerment, which the women may have used avidly, the state also intentionally used the *hakimat* as agents of discipline and regulation (63).[2]

Fahmy's analysis of the School of Midwives as a "project of modernity" is a source of inspiration for my own analysis of the Hodeida Urban Primary Health Care Project (HUPHC). The project in Hodeida was seen as one of the most successful attempts to improve basic health care in Yemen. The fact that a large number of young women were trained and employed as health-care workers contributed to this image of a successful project. In addition, the project was a joint effort of European and local authorities, with the European administration occupying the dominant position in the health establishment. A closer look at the Hodeida Urban Primary Health Care Project shows that it can also be regarded as a site of contestation. In the first place, the project aimed to improve basic health services in Yemen based on a Western concept of health care. Second, training and employing Yemeni

2. Although Fahmy does not explicitly refer to Foucault, his analysis of the School of Midwives is clearly inspired by Foucault's *Birth of the Clinic: An Archaeology of Medical Perception* (1975).

women as health educators was seen as emancipatory by the Dutch donor organization, as women would move out of their houses to take up paid work. These external views on health care and on women's place in society had to be translated and negotiated with local authorities and the women involved. Yet whereas the *murshidat* benefited from the opportunities that were offered to them in the form of training and employment, new forms of social control also came into existence. A striking similarity with the School of Midwives is that in the Hodeida Urban Primary Health Care Project little attention was paid to the backgrounds of the young women trained as *murshidat* and to the ways in which their backgrounds might affect the status of the profession. Likewise the duties of the *murshidat* contain elements that challenged gender boundaries, such as home visits to unrelated families. And finally, the *murshidat*, like the *hakimat*, occupy the lowest positions in the medical establishment in Yemen, with a heterogeneous hierarchy consisting of local and foreign administrators above them.

Despite the interesting similarities between the School of Midwives and the Hodeida Urban Primary Health Care Project, there are also a number of important differences. First of all, the School of Midwives was established during Egypt's colonization in the nineteenth century, while the Hodeida Urban Primary Health Care Project came into being in the late twentieth century in Yemen, a country that had never been colonized by a European power. In the next section I argue, however, that there are similarities between modernization projects established in the colonial period and development projects in the postcolonial period. Second, the project in Hodeida did not have any importance for military aims, and the training and employment of women health workers was not so much a side effect of the project as a means to achieve a better health situation in the squatter areas. While this may definitely have had political aspects, as I will discuss later in this chapter, the relationship with political interests of people in power was not that obvious.

One of the main differences between Fahmy's analysis of the School of Midwives and my study of the Hodeida Urban Primary Health Care Project is that whereas Fahmy had to base his analysis

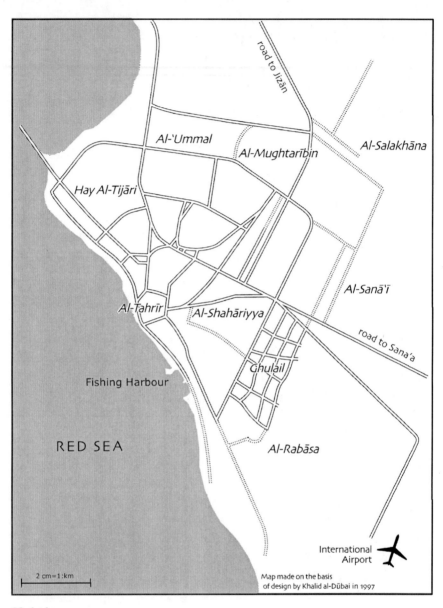

road to Jizān

Al-'Ummal

Al-Mughtaribin

Al-Salakhāna

Hay Al-Tijāri

Al-Sanā'ī

Al-Tahrīr

Al-Shahāriyya

road to Sana'a

Ghulail

Fishing Harbour

RED SEA

Al-Rabāsa

International
Airport

2 cm=1:km

Map made on the basis
of design by Khalid al-Dūbai in 1997

Hodeida

on archives, I was able to meet and interview the *murshidat* and the other actors in the project. Instead of a historical study, my study is of an anthropological nature, and that allowed me to get a fuller account of the different backgrounds, motivations, experiences, and views of the women trained and employed as health workers on the project. A particularly important asset of an anthropological approach is that it leaves ample space for agency and prevents us from drawing over-simplified conclusions about the working of projects of development and modernity. It can give better insight into how these projects are shaped by the everyday practices of the actors involved but also how interventions or development activities are positioned in their political context, both in the local situation of a country and in the politics of development agencies (see Crewe and Harrison 1998; Hilhorst 2003). In this chapter I introduce the main theoretical concepts and debates of relevance to my research. The main argument throughout the chapter is that projects of development and modernity may have both enabling and disciplining aspects and that an actor perspective is essential to understanding the working of these projects. I will first discuss differ-ent anthropological approaches toward the study of development and modernity and introduce the actor-oriented approach that I employ. I will move on to a discussion of the politics of health-care development and make a plea for a multilevel perspective to unravel the different notions of development and the different interests of the actors in-volved in a health-care project. I will then discuss different approaches toward women's paid labor, in particular in the Middle East, and argue that it is necessary to revisit the debate about the possible emancipa-tory effects of women's employment. In the last section of the chapter I outline the main elements of the approach of my study.

Discourses of Development

Fahmy's article on the School of Midwives is part of Lila Abu-Lughod's edited volume *Remaking Women: Feminism and Modernity in the Middle East*. In this book Abu-Lughod introduces a new approach to the study of women and gender in the Middle East and, in particular, to the historical study of projects that focused on "remaking women" (projects aimed at modernizing Middle Eastern women in the nineteenth and twentieth centuries). In her view, previous studies on women and gender in the Middle East have not paid enough attention to the dynamics and subtleties of the debates at particular historical moments nor to the significance of links between reforms for women and the "politics of modernity" (1998a, 5). The ambiguities and contradictions of these projects can only come to the fore when the ways in which different notions of modernity have been produced and reproduced are analyzed. Inspired by Foucault, Abu-Lughod makes a plea for unraveling the assumptions about women's place in society that form the basis of many of these projects. She emphasizes the importance of studying the "politics of modernity" critically, the ways in which new ideas and practices considered modern and progressive have not only ushered in forms of emancipation but also new forms of social control (6). Second, attention should be paid to what she calls "the politics of East/West relations": the discourses that were borrowed from Europe, supported by Europeans, or shaped in response to colonial definitions of the "backwardness" of the East (6). She stresses that there is a need to pay more attention to the actual dynamics of cultural hybridization in order to question rigid concepts of culture and to move beyond the dichotomies of East and West (16). Third, she asserts that the role of class should be studied in relation to the politics of modernity and of East/West relations. Who became involved in debates about women, and what relationship does their involvement have to consolidating class projects and identities? (6).

Although the articles in Abu-Lughod's book all focus on modernization projects during the nineteenth and early twentieth centuries, I find her approach also very helpful for the analysis of contemporary modernization projects, such as development projects in the South. Modernization and development are both concepts used in particular discourses of modernity, linked to the history of capitalism, colonialism, and the emergence of particular European epistemologies from the eighteenth century onwards. And while colonial projects were part of "the politics of East/West relations," modernization and development projects in the postcolonial period are part of "the politics of North/ South relations." Development is one of the key concepts of postwar modernization theories, when Western countries became concerned with the modernization of colonial and postcolonial states. An evolutionary perspective, in which various levels of development were distinguished, is the basis of the idea that countries in the south represented earlier stages of development. In order to achieve the modern condition of Western countries (Western modernity) they needed assistance and modernization and development projects could help them to "catch up." Although modernization theories have been widely criticized and rejected, the basic assumptions of what development implies remain part of current development discourses.

In the past two decades, an increasing body of scholarship has deconstructed the claims of knowledge that are part of dominant development discourses and formulated critiques of the working of the development industry. Escobar (1984, 1995) argues that development discourses have *produced* the "Third World" through the use of a specific corpus of techniques organizing knowledge and power. First, development was preceded by the creation of "abnormalities," social phenomena that were different from the West, and that were given a label such as the "underdeveloped," the "malnourished," and the "illiterate." These phenomena were presented as problems that needed to be solved. Second, a whole range of development disciplines and subdisciplines emerged allowing experts to remove these problems from the political realm and to recast them in the apparently more neutral realm of science (1984, 387). The creation of "development economics" was very important in this strategy. Industrial and economic growth was presented as the way to achieve a status similar to that of Western countries, and development economics was designed to assist non-Western countries in achieving this status. Third, development became professionalized and institutionalized, with its own professionals, institutions, and practices, at local, national, and international levels (1984, 388).

Development projects, initiated, financed, and managed by Western donor agencies, can be defined as the embodiment of development discourses. While development projects have been the objects of anthropological study ever since their conception, anthropologists initially tended to focus on the impact of development activities, the reasons for their failure, and the ways in which these projects could improve their effectiveness. The increased attention to social and cultural factors in development even led to the employment of anthropologists in development projects, and a specific "development anthropology" came into being (see Escobar 1991). The assumptions on which the development enterprise is based are accepted in principle, instead of being scrutinized and refuted, as Escobar suggests. In the past ten years an increasing number of anthropologists have made development itself their object of study, aiming to deconstruct the ideas and practices that form the basis of development activities (see Sachs 1992; Hobart 1993; Crush 1995). These studies are sometimes categorized as "the anthropology of development."[3]

One of the first anthropological studies that looked at the discourse of development played out at the level of a development project is Ferguson's *Anti-Politics Machine: "Development," Depoliticization, and Bureaucratic Power in Lesotho.*[4] Ferguson focuses in this study on a rural project in Lesotho and analyzes the unintended consequences of this project through an analysis of the ideas and discourses that formed the basis of the project and the effects of these ideas and discourses in practice. Ferguson speaks of development as a conceptual "apparatus" in order to emphasize the fact that it "is not an abstract set of philosophical or scientific propositions, but an elaborate contraption that *does* something" (1990, xv). The project in Lesotho was set up with the intention of improving the economic situation of the rural poor, which was seen as a technical problem, not a political one. Yet

3. The dividing line between development anthropology and an anthropology of development is not clear-cut, and some prefer not to use this distinction at all (Grillo 1997, 2; Crewe and Harrison 1998, 16).

4. Other book-length studies that have analyzed a development project from a critical perspective are, for example, Porter, Allen, and Thompson (1991) and Villareal (1994).

while most of the project activities "failed" (that is, the activities did not have the intended effects), the side effects of the project were much more important and led to the expansion and entrenchment of (bureaucratic) state power. The project thus had important political effects, but they were denied "under the cover of a neutral, technical mission to which no one can object" (256). That is why Ferguson calls development "the anti-politics machine": in his view, the development apparatus on the one hand denies the political effects of its activities, while on the other hand it promotes a colonizing bureaucratic power and expands its reach and extends its distribution (173).

Ferguson presents his study as an anthropological one but adds that he focuses on the apparatus that does the "developing" and not on the people to be "developed" (unlike many other anthropological works on development) (1990, 173). In his view, developers, beneficiaries, and government representatives are all part of this all-embracing development machine. The only way to escape dominant development discourses is to resist and form countermovements. Both Escobar and Ferguson use a Foucauldian interpretation of the notion of discourse, viewing it as an all-encompassing scheme of thought that exists outside of people's agency, and they emphasize the production and reproduction of development discourses. Although their studies have led to important new insights into the workings of development discourses, they leave little space for agency and negotiation (see also Crewe and Harrison 1998, 19; Hilhorst 2003, 9).

The idea that development knowledge is a single set of ideas and assumptions, "a monolithic enterprise heavily controlled from the top" (Grillo 1997, 20), is not shared by all anthropologists of development (see for example the contributions in Grillo 1997). Grillo (21) calls this "the myth of development" and criticizes this myth as ill informed, ethnocentric, and grounded in a victim-culture in which there are "developers" and "victims of development." Just as "the people being developed" do not exist, there is also no singular group of "developers." The groups of people involved in development are heterogeneous, and their ideas and practices may change over time. Moreover, people do not just adapt to or resist development but have much more complicated strategies and reactions. Long (1992) introduced an actor-oriented approach to development that "recognizes the "multiple realities" and the diverse social practices of various actors." The actor-oriented approach is based on the idea that social change can only be understood by analyzing the relationship between social structures and human agency. Social structures and social changes do not determine the life worlds of individuals and social groups but are mediated and transformed by these same actors. The actor-oriented approach follows Foucault in his notion that all social actors have access to power, even those actors occupying subordinate positions. Yet while Foucault emphasizes the power of discursive regimes, the actor-oriented approach stresses the power of social actors to influence and transform these regimes by employing alternative ways of formulating their objectives and deploying specific modes of action, however restricted their choices (Long 1992, 25).

Applied to the field of development research, an actor-oriented approach requires "a full analysis of the ways in which different social actors manage and interpret new elements in their life-worlds, an understanding of the organizing, strategic and interpretive elements involved, and a deconstruction of conventional notions of planned intervention" (Long 1992, 9). Interventions are not the simple outcome of a value-free and linear planning process, but rather the changing and negotiated manifestation of diverse and sometimes competing interests (Crewe and Harrison 1998, 19). Most studies of development that use an actor-oriented approach focus on the meaning of interventions for the intended "beneficiaries" of a project (see for example Long and Long 1992; Villareal 1994; Arce and Long 2000). In my study I shift the attention to the women trained and employed on the project as health workers, a group of social actors that has received little attention in actor-oriented studies.[5] Crewe and Harrison (1998,

---

5. Most studies on community health workers have focused on their impact on health-care delivery and not on what it means to become a health worker (see for example Bastien 1990; Robinson and Larsen 1990; Hoodfar 1998). Exceptions are Stark (1985) and Ramirez-Valles (1997).

19) stress the importance of studying development organizations and projects from within in order to understand the power hierarchies involved and the politics behind development. Hilhorst's study of a Philippine NGO (2003) is one of the few in-depth studies of a development organization. She unravels the everyday politics of this seemingly successful NGO by using an actor-oriented approach and also pays attention to the different backgrounds and views of people working in the organization. Just like me, Hilhorst worked for a number of years for the organization about which she is writing. According to Arce and Long (2000, 27) a reflexive ethnography in which the practices and experiences of local actors are analyzed alongside the researcher's own encounters and experiences is necessary for a sound anthropology of development. Only then is it possible to give up one-dimensional notions of development and acknowledge the different notions of development and modernity people may have, as well as the practices and strategies they employ to live up to these notions.[6]

The Politics of Health-Care Development

The fact that the Egyptian School of Midwives and the Hodeida Urban Primary Health Care Project are both health-care projects is not accidental. Whereas health care was for a long time seen as apolitical and per definition good, it has increasingly become clear that health care, and in particular Western health care, is an important vehicle for the spreading and consolidation of state power (Van der Geest 1986). Owing to the high costs and technology involved in the provision of Western medicine, the state is one of the few organizations able to provide it, which is very much in its favor. By providing Western health care, the state establishes a positive image of its regime, while people's increasing dependency of these services underlines the state's

---

6. In this study I will follow Arce and Long (2000) by using the terms "development" and "modernity" in a discursive way and not as analytical concepts. Notions of development refer to people's notions of societal progress, while notions of modernity refer to people's sense of belonging to the present.

authority and guarantees social cohesion (Van der Geest 1986, 246). Political and economic interests first and foremost inspire health-care interventions. In the case of the School of Midwives, creating a healthy climate for the military was Mohamed 'Ali's main goal. Only those parts of the local population that were of use for the (colonial) state, such as the army and people working at production sites, "benefited" from health-care interventions. The rest of the population was excluded from Western health care. "Health was not an end in and of itself, but rather a prerequisite for development" (Packard 1997, 94). In this section I look more closely at the politics behind health-care development and in particular behind the support for primary health care. As mentioned before, the training and employment of women health workers in the Hodeida Urban Primary Health Care Project was not as clearly related to political and economic interests as in the School of Midwives, but these interests did also play a role. Yet instead of only emphasizing the political interests of the Dutch donor organization and the Yemeni state, I argue that it is more useful to take the interests of all social actors involved in the project into account. This means that we should also analyze the interests of women trained and employed as health workers. I therefore use a multilevel perspective in my study of the Hodeida Urban Primary Health Care Project.

Packard argues that after World War II, political and economic interests continued to determine health-care interventions in "developing countries." Although health-care development was then put under the banner of "working toward a better world," many of the characteristics of the colonial period remained: inequality in the distribution of health resources, the tendency to see health as a prerequisite for social and economic development, the view of health as the absence of disease, and the continuation of colonial attitudes toward local populations as ignorant and in need of technical knowledge (1997, 102–11). Health care was seen as a purely technical solution, and local social and economic dynamics were neglected. Ensuing from the dominant Western medical model of the early twentieth century, in which the body was seen as a machine to be repaired when it broke down, curative care was favored over preventive care. While there had been

considerable attention to public health in Europe in the early nineteenth century, gradually public health was separated from the work
of doctors, and the "engineering model" started to dominate the world
of health and medicine (Macdonald 1994, 32). The power of the "engineering model" is closely linked to notions of Western modernity,
in which science, knowledge, and technology master the human body.
This also explains the attractiveness of the "engineering model" in
developing countries: highly sophisticated curative care is a powerful
symbol of modernity.

Only in the late 1960s, after the failure of many health-care interventions in developing countries, did awareness grow that health
was not a purely technical affair but linked to social and economic
circumstances. It was in this context that primary health care gained
importance, with its emphasis on prevention, community participation, equity, appropriate technology, and intersectoral cooperation.
Health care had to be comprehensive, not selective, combating the
social and economic causes of ill health. The international conference
on Primary Health Care, organized by the World Health Organization in Alma-Ata (former USSR) in 1978, was an outcome of this shift
in (Western) development thinking. Health education, pre- and postnatal care, immunization, and the distribution of contraceptives and
basic drugs were seen as essential activities to fight infant, child, and
maternal mortality rates and to reduce population growth. The training of primary health-care workers, or community health workers, was
an important part of the primary health-care approach as developed
in Alma-Ata. Local people with little or no formal education would be
trained during a short period of time in health education and preventive health services and afterwards would work voluntarily in their
own communities. They would give, for example, basic health care
and health education on hygiene and nutrition and would vaccinate
children and distribute contraceptives.[7]

7. The idea of training community health workers was largely based on the experiences of the public health movement in Western Europe and the United States
with the rise of the welfare state at the end of the nineteenth century. Women from

Governments of almost every country in the world signed the declaration of Alma-Ata and included the concept of primary health care in their health policies. The reasons most governments were willing to endorse the primary health-care approach were mainly political. Primary health care was seen as a way to expand medical facilities, push back mortality and morbidity rates, increase governments' political credibility, and reduce health-care expenditures (Van der Geest, Speckmann, and Streefland 1990, 1028). Moreover, primary health care is often used to guarantee donor support. International development organizations have taken the lead in promoting primary health-care activities in "developing" countries. It is important to note that the primary health-care approach as developed in Alma-Ata, with its five basic principles of equity, prevention, community involvement, appropriate technology, and an intersectoral approach, had never been part of Western health-care systems (see Macdonald 1994, 13). The approach was clearly created *for* "developing" countries but on the basis of Western concepts. Ramirez-Valles (1997, 75) argues that donor organizations have encouraged, pressured, and guided national governments to take community-oriented approaches in delivering health-care services to the poor. Yet very few states have paid serious attention to the basic elements of primary health care. What was meant by these concepts was often not congruent with local notions.[8]

---

the middle classes became so-called "health visitors," visiting working class women at home and educating them about good motherhood, hygiene, and nutrition, as part of a more general civilization mission with the aim of increasing population growth (Ramirez-Valles 1997, 72). At a later stage, working-class women were asked to do this type of work themselves, as it was argued that they would be better able to reach and influence other poor women. Teaching and educating women, and in particular poor women, about "good motherhood" was seen as the main solution for high infant mortality and low birth rates, and for leading to population growth and a healthy nation. Another source of inspiration for primary health-care programs were the experiences with barefoot doctors in China, part of China's health-care policy in the second half of the 1960s (Sidel and Sidel 1975).

8. Examples of studies that have analyzed the discrepancies between different notions of development and health care are Justice (1986), L. Stone (1986; 1989) and Pigg (1997).

Although primary health care was intended to increase local people's self-reliance in health care, it has in many cases been imposed by the state and carried out by professionals working for the government or for foreign donor organizations. Primary health care has become an important political instrument of state institutions as well as of donor organizations. This is to a large extent due to its vague meaning. "Primary health care can mean all sorts of things to different people in different positions in the political hierarchy" (Van der Geest, Speckmann, and Streefland 1990, 1025). It is for this reason that Van der Geest et al. make a plea for the use of a multilevel perspective in the study of primary health care. A multilevel perspective means that the object of research is not studied in isolation but in relation to other levels of society. The word "level" refers in particular to international, national, regional, and local tiers of social organization (Van der Geest, Speckmann, and Streefland 1990, 1026). Primary health care lends itself in particular to a multilevel perspective: it is a concept that was launched at an international conference organized by the World Health Organization, and it was adopted by national governments, promoted by international donor organizations and nongovernmental organizations, and implemented at local levels of "developing countries." The fact that many primary health-care projects failed could be a result of the different views and interests of the various actors involved (see Justice 1986). My study of the Hodeida Urban Primary Health Care Project also requires a multilevel perspective, as the different notions of development of the Dutch donor organization, Yemeni state officials, and in particular the women trained and employed as *murshidat* are of crucial importance to understanding their ambiguous position. In addition, a multilevel perspective leaves space for agency.

Women and the Cultural Politics of Paid Labor

I started the previous section with the statement that it was not accidental that both the School of Midwives and the Hodeida Urban Primary Health Care Project focused on health care because health care is an important political tool. Another common element of these two projects is that they were both directed at women, and that is also not accidental. Women play an important role in the cultural politics of nation-states and political movements and often function as signs and symbols of the identity of a nation or ethnic group (Yuval-Davis and Anthias 1989; Moghadam 1994). Yet women's symbolic function is highly ambiguous. Women may be seen as the repositories and pre-servers of tradition, while they also may be used as the benchmark for the level of modernity of a country. In both cases, be it as preserv-ers of tradition or as paragons of modernity, women are symbolically employed in contestations between government institutions, local pressure groups, and international organizations. The training and employment of women health workers in the School of Midwives is a very clear example of the political, economic, and symbolic interests of the Egyptian state. In the Hodeida Urban Primary Health Care Project these interests were not so clear. I argue, however, that the training and employment of women as *murshidat* should be viewed as part of the cultural politics of the Yemeni state and the Dutch donor organization. I also emphasize the importance of agency by looking at the motivations and strategies of women trained and employed as health workers.

As mentioned before, women's employment not only has economic effects but is also part and parcel of the cultural politics of nation-states. For progressive governments, women's employment often sym-bolizes development and modernity. Increasing women's participation in the labor market is put forward as an essential step to modernize the country. In former South Yemen, for example, emphasizing the need for women to enter the labor force was not only inspired by economic factors but was also seen as part of the struggle to help women to eman-cipate themselves from traditional forms of subordination through acquiring a measure of economic independence (Molyneux 1982, 37). The fact that women's formal labor-force participation has become an indicator of the level of development of a country is another example of this way of thinking (see UNDP 2002). Conservative governments, on the other hand, are often less in favor of women's employment because they are afraid that it may lead to changes in gender relations and to a weakening of family ties, and hence to cultural and moral decline.

Even though conservative governments may see the necessity of educating and employing women, they try to do it within the boundaries of what is culturally acceptable.

Governments in Muslim majority states are often confronted with the dilemma of promoting socioeconomic change or preserving cultural authenticity. The "woman question" therefore was, and still is, a particularly important topic in the search for identity and legitimacy of Muslim majority states (see the contributions in Kandiyoti 1991). Their governments have to respond to the sometimes contradictory pressures of internal constituencies or external forces, such as international organizations (Kandiyoti 1991, 14). This need for response has particularly become clear in the 1990s, a period in which the increasing influence of religious fundamentalism on state policies coincided with economic and political liberalization processes and other neo-liberal policies resulting from structural adjustment programs imposed by the World Bank and the IMF. In addition, international donor organizations pushed governments to pay attention to gender issues. The result is that governments are caught in "the cross-fire of conflicting demands, attempting at times to comply with international conventions, and at others to placate internal constituencies opposing an expansion of women's rights" (Kandiyoti 2001, 55).

One of the main questions that has determined the debate about women and development in the Middle East is why women's labor force participation is among the lowest in the world (see Youssef 1974; Abu-Nasr, Khoury, and Azzam 1985; Hijab 1988, 2001; Moghadam 1993, 1995). The Arab Human Development Reports 2002 again underlined this fact (UNDP 2002). According to these reports, Arab states are "lagging behind" on numerous levels, and one of them is the formal labor participation of women.[9] Yet the use of women's formal

9. The highest female labor participation in the Middle East was found in Kuwait: in 1998 24.7 percent of the women were active in the labor force, and the lowest percentage in Oman: 8.6 percent of the women were counted as economically active. In Yemen, 17.7 percent of the women were part of the formal labor force in 1998 (UNDP 2002, 158).

labor force participation as a measurement of development has been criticized (see, for example, Moghadam 1995, 6; Hoodfar 1999, 103; Olmsted 2005). First, statistics in many Arab countries are often not reliable and there are numerous chances of undercounting. Second, the majority of women in the Middle East are economically active, but they are not included in the statistics because they work in agriculture, in the domestic sphere, or in the informal labor market. These activities remain largely "invisible" when using women's formal labor participation as a benchmark. Third, women's formal labor market participation may be an indicator of economic growth, but it is not a very useful measurement to gauge "development" and in particular "women's development." Women's employment does not necessarily lead to more independence for women but can instead lead to new forms of social control. The challenge is, therefore, "to be skeptical of modernity's progressive claims of emancipation and critical of its social and cultural operations and yet appreciate the forms of energy, possibility, even power that aspects of it might have enabled, especially for women" (Abu-Lughod 1998a, 12). Paying attention to women's own notions of development and modernity is crucial to understanding both the disciplinary and the liberatory aspects of "projects of modernity."

In order to understand the disciplinary and the liberatory aspects of projects of modernity, I want to look at a development project that focused on training and employing women health workers. I am interested in the cultural politics of women's paid labor. Although earlier studies emphasized the economic aspects of women's employment, in recent studies more attention is being paid to other aspects that play a role. I will first of all look at the political projects that formed the basis of the different notions of development and modernity of the actors involved in the project. How have these different political projects, of the nation-state as well as of international donor organizations, affected the notions of development and modernity of the women employed as *murshidat?* In this regard I am inspired by Lisa Rofel's study of women workers in the silk industry in China. According to Rofel, "gender differentiation—the knowledges, relations, meanings, and identities of masculinity and femininity—operates at the heart of modernity's power" (Rofel 1999, 19). While modernity is often presented as a unified project that produces a homogeneous form of subjectivity, Rofel emphasizes the presence of "other modernities." She compares three different cohorts of women workers who came of age in three important periods in China's recent history (the socialist revolution, the Cultural Revolution, and the Deng era) and concludes that each period produced its own "imaginary of modernity" with very different implications for women workers.

Second, I am interested in what motivates women to take up and continue in particular types of paid labor. The women in my study often presented their decision to become *murshidat* and to continue their work, for example after marrying, as an individual choice, but a closer look at their life stories shows the importance of their positions within their families. In addition, their choice to become *murshidat* was not influenced only by economic factors. Cultural practices and political ideas also played a role. The fact that women sometimes decide to enter certain types of paid labor, which do not necessarily bring greater economic rewards than other types of work, comes clearly to the fore in Freeman's research (2000) on female data processors in Barbados. While the work of the data processors is comparable to the work of blue-collar workers, as it is repetitive, tedious, and semiskilled, the setting of their work resembles that of white-collar workers, as it is clean, cool, and officelike. The women in Freeman's study are able symbolically to construct a middle-class status, mainly through dress and appearance, while working long days, earning relatively little, and dealing with surveillance, discipline, and their structurally subordinated status (Freeman 2000, 257). The women's ability to represent themselves as middle-class workers made this job highly desirable.

Third, I am interested in the strategies women employ to enter or continue in paid employment. Also in this respect individual strategies and family strategies intersect; women may present their actions as individually taken, but they are often a result of family dynamics and vice versa. Macleod (1991), for example, describes the ambiguous position of working women from the lower middle classes in Cairo and the strategies they employ to deal with this ambiguity. These women continue their paid work mainly because their salaries are important to sustain their families. Yet they are at the same time subjected to a gender ideology in which women are supposed to stay at home fulfilling their roles as wives and mothers. One way that women have found of dealing with this dilemma is to opt for a new version of Islamic dress developed in the 1980s. Macleod argues that this new type of veiling should be seen as a form of "accommodating protest": the veil helps women to accommodate their role as workers in the public sphere with dominant gender ideologies, expressing that they are good Muslim women working for the benefit of their families. The case studies of women and paid labor in China, Barbados, and Cairo inspire me because they show both the disciplining and the enabling aspects of women's paid labor. They describe in detail the ways in which economic, cultural, and political factors intersect, producing different outcomes at different times, and emphasize the different ways in which women judge, negotiate, and accommodate their employment. In so doing these studies eloquently intertwine the importance of social structures with human agency and avoid oversimplified conclusions.

Relevance and Approach of the Study

The above-mentioned debates about women, health-care work, and development form the basis for my own study of the training and employment of women health workers in the Hodeida Urban Primary Health Care Project in Yemen. Using an actor-oriented approach, I intend to provide a nuanced view of the history, organization, interests, and outcomes of the project for the women involved as health workers. As mentioned before, instead of looking at the interventions and the impact for the so-called beneficiaries, I focus on the women working on the project, an approach that is new to the anthropology of development. Very few ethnographic monographs have looked at women in institutions, in anthropology in general but particularly in Middle Eastern studies. In addition, there are few anthropological studies about the working of foreign aid and foreign-funded development projects in the Middle East, even though countries such as Egypt and Yemen are to a large extent depending on foreign aid. Two early analyses of development projects in the Middle East are Tony Barnett's study of the Gezira Scheme in Sudan (1977) and Annika Rabo's study of the Euphrates Scheme in Syria (1986). A recent analysis of the development industry in Egypt is provided by Timothy Mitchell (2002). However, none of these studies pays particular attention to gender issues. The anthropological studies on gender and development in the Middle East tend to focus on women in rural areas and on women in the informal economy, and there are relatively few studies that have studied women in the formal labor market. This particularly applies to studies about women in Yemen (see for example Dorsky 1986; Mundy 1995; Meneley 1996).

In addition to the actor-oriented approach, I use a historical perspective, both in the analysis of the discourses of development of the Yemeni state, the Dutch donor organization, and the history of the project and in the study of the backgrounds and motivations of the women trained as health workers. The case study of the Hodeida Urban Primary Health Care Project is a diachronic case study in which a detailed description is given of what happened when, with the aim of unraveling the various notions of development of the Yemeni state, the donor organization, and the women involved. I see the project as a microcosm in which relationships and inequalities of central importance in Yemen (social status, class, gender, and ethnicity) and the changing values attached to these categories intersect.

In order to study the backgrounds and motivations of the women health workers and their experiences throughout their training and employment, I use a life-story approach. Life stories give insight into the individual motivations and strategies of people but also show the ways in which their room to maneuver is limited by social structures. The gathering and analysis of life stories are in my view very suitable methods for an actor-oriented approach to development. I study three cohorts of women taking up work as *murshidat* in Hodeida, at different moments in Yemen's sociopolitical history. I pay attention to the time at which they entered the profession as a specific period in the history of Yemen with specific social and economic conditions and producing specific discourses on gender, labor, and health-care development. Next, I address the changing positions of the *murshidat*, and the local discourses linked to these changing positions. Age, marital status, social class, and ethnicity are among the factors that were important in these changing discourses.

The last element of my approach is a multilevel perspective. Through an analysis of the various notions of development of the Yemeni state, the donor organization, and the women involved, with the emphasis on the local level of the project, I intend to show how different discourses intersected, engendering new opportunities and experiences for women as well as new forms of social control.

PART TWO

Yemen and the Politics of Development

3

Developing the Nation

SCATTERED VILLAGES on high mountain peaks, men with daggers chewing *qat*, and heavily veiled women are the most common images of Yemen seen in the West. These images often go hand in hand with statements that Yemen can be compared to a medieval country, isolated from the rest of the world until it started to "develop" after the revolution of 1962. Yet the implications of these statements are misleading and contain normative values about what "development" implies. They have contributed to the idea that prerevolutionary Yemen was an isolated and backward country where no changes took place. Although that idea may be partly true for a particular period in Yemen's history, it ignores hundreds of years of economic and political change. Yemen has had periods of international importance at various points in its history. Overseas connections, through trade and migration, have affected the Yemeni population in various ways, not least of which is the resulting ethnic diversity. Moreover, these statements endorse the view that contact with Western countries is the only avenue to "development," recognizing only Western notions of development. In this chapter I take a closer look at Yemeni discourses of development, first by describing the formation of the Yemeni nation-state and second by analyzing development discourses regarding women and health care. My main argument is that the Yemeni government's support of women's education, women's employment, and primary health care is mainly politically inspired and related to the heavy dependence on foreign aid. Although gender issues and health-care development are important priorities on paper, little is done to put these priorities into practice.

A Short History of Modern Yemen

Yemen was for centuries an Imamate, ruled by religious leaders, and it is the period under the rule of Imam Yahiya (1904–48) and under Imam Ahmed (1948–62) to which people refer when they speak of Yemen as an isolated country.[1] Both imams intentionally isolated Yemen from the rest of the world, particularly from Western countries, in order to preserve their own positions. Yemenis were discouraged from traveling abroad; education was limited to religious schools attached to mosques; and contractual relationships with foreign agencies, whether governments or private enterprises, were avoided. Yet active and enterprising Yemenis, frustrated by the economic and political situation, succeeded in migrating to Aden, Saudi Arabia, East Africa, Southeast Asia, Great Britain, and the United States. Many migrants adopted modernist views on society and politics, emphasizing a strong state that would ensure better living conditions for the population. An important source of inspiration was Egypt's president Gamal 'Abdul Nasser, who called for a unified Arab movement against foreign occupation and oppression in the Arab world (see Zabarah 1982). In South Yemen, intellectuals started to revolt against British occupation, while in North Yemen progressive reformers inspired by Nasserite ideology, as well as conservative traditionalists who resented the autocracy of the imam, criticized the Imamate. In 1962, a group of army officers were able to seize power and declare independence, naming the state the Yemen Arab Republic. A seven-year civil war followed between supporters of the imam, financially backed by Saudi Arabia, and republicans supported by Egyptian forces. In 1970, the Yemen Arab Republic was officially recognized by Saudi Arabia, after which recognition by other countries such as Britain and the United States followed.[2]

1. As this study focuses on a development project in Hodeida, located in former North Yemen, I will exclude developments in former South Yemen, unless they are of relevance for the subject matter of this study.

2. For detailed overviews of Yemen's political history see Halliday (1974), Peterson (1982), Zabarah (1982), Stookey (1978), Burrowes (1987), and Dresch (2000).

Immediately after 1962, foreign companies and donor organizations started to show an interest in Yemen. Both Arab and Western countries were willing to invest in North Yemen, mainly because of its strategic position on the edge of the Arabian Peninsula. For other Arab governments, such as Saudi Arabia and Kuwait, it was important that the Yemen Arab Republic should not become too independent, with republican policies challenging the authority of the conservative elite in power in the other countries of the Arabian Peninsula. The governments of Western countries saw North Yemen as an important ally to counterbalance the power of the ruling elites of Saudi Arabia and the Gulf States. In addition, during the oil crisis of 1973 Western countries realized that in order to obtain a regular flow of oil, they needed to maintain stability and good relations on the Arabian Peninsula, and investing in Yemen was seen as a way to strengthen their position in the region. The Dutch government was among those countries that started funding development programs and projects in the Yemen Arab Republic and became one of its biggest Western donors.

While in the 1950s and 1960s Yemeni development discourses were mainly inspired by Nasserite notions of development, emphasizing Arab nationalism, anti-imperialism, and self-reliance, in the late 1970s Western notions of development, consisting of a belief in the free market, foreign investment, and assistance from abroad, gained importance. Yet the practical aims of these different ideologies were the same: the creation of a strong economy, educational and health-care facilities for the people, and the eradication of poverty. In 1975, North Yemen was officially named a Least Developed Country (LDC), a designation used by the United Nations for countries with a gross national product per capita lower than US$300 per year. In the following decades a wide range of international and regional donors became involved in North Yemen's "development." In addition to infrastructure projects, the World Bank, the United Nations, and European donors supported the strengthening of the major ministries and trained Yemeni administrators in management and institution building. Kuwait and a number of other Arab donors assisted in developing a public education system by building schools and employing foreign teachers to work in them (Carapico 1998, 41).[3]

Just as foreign companies and donor agencies started to show an interest in Yemen, many Yemenis left the country. The establishment of the Yemen Arab Republic coincided with the "oil boom" in Saudi Arabia and the Gulf States, caused by a sudden increase in oil prices. There was a high demand for cheap and unskilled labor in the oil-producing countries of the Arabian Peninsula, and many Yemenis decided to try their luck there. Within a short period of time, the remittances sent home by the migrants became an important source of income for the new republic. However, there was a shortage of specialized skills in Yemen, and foreigners coming from a wide variety of countries filled this need. Moreover, Yemeni emigrants residing overseas, who were considered to be more educated, were enticed to return home with a promise of better living conditions, so they could assist in "developing" the country. The changing political climate in the countries of migration was an additional reason to come home. Despite the many presidential changes, the overall atmosphere in the country during the 1970s was characterized by optimism. Labor remittances and foreign aid were increasing, and businesses and national and international development projects were mushrooming.

Thus, from the early years of the Yemen Arab Republic, foreign aid and labor migration were the two main pillars of the economy. This heavy reliance on external financial sources had several consequences. The first consequence was that because of the availability of foreign currencies, the import sector grew and many new consumer goods, such as cassette players, radios, televisions, batteries, cigarettes, and powdered milk, entered the country. The government did little to prevent the breakdown of the agricultural sector, and this laissez-faire attitude was also apparent in the limited efforts made

3. There was a shortage of male and female Yemeni teachers. Large numbers of Egyptian, Sudanese, and Syrian teachers started working in Yemen, often religious conservatives paid by Saudi Arabia to enforce its religious ideology (Carapico 1998, 41).

to establish an industrial sector; merchants were more interested in buying land and building houses than in investing in local industries, and nothing prevented them from doing so (Dresch 2000, 137). A second consequence of the heavy reliance on external financial sources was its vulnerability. In the mid-1980s, employment opportunities in Saudi Arabia and the Gulf States diminished because of declining oil prices, and increasing numbers of migrant workers returned home. The population grew, and one of the country's main financial resources, remittances of migrant workers, decreased. A third consequence was the heavy influence of foreign donors on Yemen's state formation. Bilateral and international organizations stressed "institution building"; large ministries were established and the number of government employees multiplied (Dresch 2000, 133, 159). In the 1970s, almost anyone possessing a primary-school certificate could become a government employee. The government had become the main employer in the country, offering its employees a life-long contract with important social benefits such as the right to sick leave, maternity leave, and health insurance.

In a short period of time, the state had become a cumbersome apparatus that worked mainly top-down. The revolutionary slogans of the 1960s and the early 1970s, in which local "development" for the Yemeni people had been promised, had lost their value because the People's General Congress (PGC), the ruling party of President 'Ali 'Abdullah Saleh, who has been in power since 1978,[4] controlled almost all the local initiatives by incorporating them into government programs. Yet over half of the government budget went to the army and the police, and development projects were mainly funded with foreign grants or loans (Carapico 1993a, 13; Dresch 2000, 157). Global recession in the second half of the 1980s caused an increase in population size owing to the return of migrants, and diminishing

4. The People's General Congress was established in 1982 and designed to be the instrument of political mobilization and participation. In effect, the PGC became a rudimentary political party (Wenner 1991, 158) and was the only official political party in North Yemen until unification in 1990.

remittances and foreign aid[5] forced the government to cut down on its expenditures.

The unification of North and South Yemen in May 1990 ushered in a new period in Yemen's history. Both countries had followed different political trajectories since the end of the 1960s, one a conservative capitalist republic, the other a socialist state. Hostility had dominated their relationship, but the end of the Cold War led to a changing political climate. Unification became negotiable after years of tension and conflict. A transitional government was installed for a period of three years, after which free elections were to be held for a multiparty parliament in April 1993. Democracy saw the light, with a flourishing press and political parties, nongovernmental organizations, committees, and platforms mushrooming everywhere (see Carapico 1998, 135–69).

However, the optimistic attitude in the country disappeared within a couple of months. In August 1990, Iraq invaded Kuwait, and the Gulf crisis had dramatic consequences for the newly formed republic. As a result of Yemen's position in the United Nations Security Council, in which it argued for an Arab solution to the problem and stood against military attacks on Iraq, the governments of Saudi Arabia and the Gulf States changed the residence rights of Yemeni migrants.[6] Around 800,000 Yemeni emigrants and their families left Saudi Arabia and the Gulf States. The government lost one of its main economic resources, namely the remittances of migrant workers, and suddenly had to take care of a large group of people in need of housing, work, food, and health care. Moreover, the position Yemen took in the Gulf crisis also led to the withdrawal of many Western companies and donor organizations, at a time when their support was very much needed.

5. Development aid to North Yemen was in 1981 over US$1 billion; it declined to half that amount in 1985 and to less than US$100 million in 1988 (Carapico 1993a, 13).

6. While other foreign guest workers in Saudi Arabia and the Gulf States had needed a Saudi sponsor *(kafil)* to obtain a residence permit, Yemenis had always been allowed to work without a *kafil* and a residence permit. From September 19, 1990, Yemenis lost this special status.

A slum in the city of Hodeida.

The Gulf crisis and the subsequent economic problems Yemen faced resulted in immediate tensions between the two ruling parties of President 'Ali 'Abdullah Saleh and Vice President 'Ali Salem al-Bid (who had been the president of the former South Yemen).[7] There was lack of agreement about how to rule the country and solve its problems, and little of what had been promised at the time of unification was realized. Moreover, it became increasingly clear that northern laws and customs were prevailing over southern laws, leading to increasing frustration for the socialists. In April 1993, the first democratic elections took place. Yet the coalition formed between the conservative People's General Congress (PGC), the Yemen Socialist Party (YSP), and the Islamist Islah party[8] came to an end a year later. In May 1994,

7. The government of the Yemen Arab Republic had been an ally of Iraq, while the government of the People's Democratic Republic of Yemen had been opposed to Iraq's regime.

8. The Islah Party, or the Yemeni Congregation for Reform, was established

a civil war broke out between northern and southern armies, which ended in a victory for the northern army on July 7, 1994. The socialists disappeared from the political arena, and the Islamist Islah party filled the gap. A conservative government was back in place, now controlling both North and South Yemen.

The economic situation was disastrous after the civil war because of costly war efforts but also because oil prices had decreased and Western donor agencies had withdrawn their aid. The new government announced several plans for reform to "build up" the country and reorganize its economy (Carapico 1998, 58). Direct measures taken as part of this Structural Adjustment Program (SAP) were, among other things, the devaluation of the Yemeni riyal, the removal of government subsidies on primary necessities such as flour and oil, and a freeze on government employment.[9] For the majority of the Yemeni population, the economic reforms meant a worsening of their living conditions, with increased costs of living, low salaries, and high unemployment rates. In order to soften the impact of the structural adjustment program, the World Bank initiated a Social Fund for Development, financing projects that were meant to alleviate the impact of these economic measures.

Yet instead of poverty alleviation, existing patterns of inequality have largely been reproduced. Not only are personal and political relations increasingly being merged, but also the dividing line between politicians and merchants has become blurred. Encouraged by the call for privatization, many politicians have acquired shares in important

---

in 1990 and can be seen as a coalition of northern-based conservatives who share a common pro-Saleh regime stance and conservative social objectives (Clark 2004, 120). Islah is often mistakenly regarded as a fundamentalist party sharing characteristics with the Muslim Brotherhood, yet the political agenda of Islah and its position in the Yemeni political establishment is more complicated (see also Dresch and Haykel 1995).

9. As part of the structural adjustment program, 30,000 government employees out of a total of 700,000 were to be dismissed (Detalle 1997, 27), but resistance led to the scrapping of this policy.

companies, safeguarding their access to hard currency. International donors do little to fight the Janus-faced attitude of the government because that would mean dismantling the entire state (Dresch 2000, 208). In 1997, new elections were held, but they did not lead to significant changes in the distribution of seats; the president's PGC continued to be the biggest party.[10] The same applies to the elections of 2003.

Yemeni Women and the Politics of Development

Women figured in different ways in Yemeni development discourses. Promoting equality and democracy for all Yemeni citizens had been an essential element of the discourse of the republicans, and explicit reference had been made to improving the position of women. The government followed Egypt's president Gamal 'Abdul Nasser in his promotion of women's emancipation, but little was do   put the revolutionary slogans into practice (Molyneux 1995, 4   vague and inadequate government policies with regard to wo   lted in what Badran (1998, 503) calls "piecemeal feminism": women in former North Yemen had to stake out new roles and claim public space themselves and were quietly assisted by the state. In the 1960s and 1970s particularly, the government was relatively liberal, and women made strategic use of the available space for maneuvering. In 1965, for example, a group of women established the Yemeni Women's Association, offering a social program including literacy classes, health education, and practical skills such as sewing and typing (Badran 1998, 503). In addition, a number of women from the middle and upper classes benefited from the increased educational opportunities and sometimes took up paid work in teaching or radio broadcasting.

The government considered education to be one of the main ways to develop and modernize the country. Education was important to

10. During the first presidential elections in 1999, 'Ali 'Abdullah Saleh obtained 96.3 percent of the votes, which obviously raises questions about Yemen's democratic system. In 2006 the second presidential elections were held. See for interesting studies of Yemen's elections Carapico (1993b), Detalle (1993), and Wedeen (2003).

make the transition from "backwardness" (takhalluf) to civilization (hadara) and progress (taqaddum). Large-scale efforts were made to expand the educational sector through the building of schools and the training of teachers, with the financial and technical assistance of foreign donors. Numerous schools were built in both rural and urban areas, and curricula and teaching methods were developed. Radio and television messages encouraged people to send their children to school. Being educated (muta'allim) increasingly became synonymous with being developed (mutatawwur), and this trend continues today. Education became a free right for everybody, stipulated by law, but it is not yet compulsory. As late as 1999, adult female illiteracy was still 76.1 percent (UNDP 2002, 151), and although an increasing number of girls in urban areas attend school, in rural areas school enrollment of girls remains low.[11] Although the government has put a lot of effort into building the educational sector, the system has favored males and urban areas, and little has been done to encourage the education of rural girls. Social, economic, and cultural factors, such as women's workload, early marriage, lack of separate girls' schools and female teachers, and the idea that women do not need schooling, continue to affect women's education, particularly in rural areas. The government had no special policies to increase women's education in rural areas. Only recently has there been a move to build more girls' schools and train women teachers, again with the financial and technical support of foreign donors.

Mobilizing women to take up paid employment became an important part of the effort to build up a modern nation-state. A lot of work was needed to establish government institutions such as ministries, hospitals, and schools, and there was an urgent need for labor because a large part of the male population had migrated to Saudi Arabia and the Gulf States. The shortage of labor was one of the main reasons the government promoted women's paid employment. The government

11. In total, only 37 percent of girls aged six through fifteen years are enrolled in school. According to the 1994 census, 14 percent of the six-year-old girls of in rural areas attend school (UNICEF 1998, 4).

wished to integrate women into the labor force but did not want to harm so-called traditional social structures, afraid of the power of conservative groups. The result was that women were caught in what Seif (1995, 294) calls "double-edged discourses," which on the one hand encouraged them to take up paid labor outside the home and on the other hand stressed their traditional roles as wives and mothers.

The education, training, and employment of women became urgent national priorities. Yet as only a limited number of women had a chance to attend primary school, even fewer women were able to enter professional training. According to the 1975 census, only 4 percent of the formal urban labor force consisted of women. Women working in private enterprises were mainly doing unskilled manual work (Myntti 1985, 45). More than two-thirds of working women were government employees. The Ministry of Education, the Ministry of Health, and the Ministry of Municipalities were the main employers of women; these ministries employed women as teachers, nurses, paramedic professionals, or cleaners. Women working in government-owned factories, such as the textile factories in Sana'a, the plastics and biscuit factories in Taiz, and the cigarette factory in Hodeida, were also considered government employees (Myntti 1985, 45).

Although government employment was in general highly valued because civil servants had the benefits of a tenured contract, a monthly salary, sick leave, and maternity leave, there were important differences in the status of jobs performed by women in the civil service. Teaching was one of the most respectable jobs open to women. First, women teachers worked in girls' schools and had relatively little contact with unrelated men, so their employment did not challenge gender segregation. Second, knowledge is highly valued in Islam, and women were seen as the transmitters of religious values through their role as mothers. Teaching was seen as an extension of this role. Yet, owing to the limited number of women who had finished secondary school, few women were employed as teachers in the 1970s, and the Ministry of Education often employed foreign female teachers. The status of nursing and midwifery was lower than that of teaching, resulting in even more serious shortages of female health cadres. Many foreign women, including Sudanese midwives and Indian and Filipino nurses, were employed by the Ministry of Health. The least valued types of government employment were factory work and cleaning, even though these jobs guaranteed a monthly salary. Only women of low-status groups were involved in this type of work (Myntti 1985, 46; Lackner 1995, 89).

The unification of North and South Yemen in May 1990, and the subsequent coalescence of two different political systems, affected Yemeni women in different ways. Yemeni women activists were initially optimistic about the consequences of unification for women. In former South Yemen women's issues had been taken more seriously, and women activists hoped that southerners could influence policies in North Yemen. Moreover, after unification large numbers of professional women from South Yemen moved to Sana'a, where there was a high demand for educated women. They were employed as civil servants in junior- and middle-management positions (see Lackner 1995, 90). In addition, women's issues received a great deal of attention from foreign donor organizations, and Yemeni women were needed as counterparts for development projects and programs. However, although unification had only been possible because the governments of both North and South Yemen had agreed to establish a legal system based on northern and southern elements, as mentioned before, northern laws and customs very soon prevailed over southern laws (see Würth 2003). In the new constitution the *shari'a* became the main source of legislation, which had important implications for the personal status law, and thus for women. While interpretations of the *shari'a* were largely conservative, women did have the right to vote and could also stand for parliament.

The coalition government that was formed after the 1993 elections did very little to improve the position of women in the country. After the civil war in 1994, the socialists left the political arena and the Islah party gained importance. Women's issues were an important element in Islah's political program, used in their fight against moral decay. Islah declared that they were not against women's paid work but emphasized that domestic activities were women's primary responsibility and that women's paid work was only acceptable as long as a woman's husband approved of it (Badran 1998, 426). Yet the impact of Islah on government policies remained relatively limited, and despite the conservative attitude of the government, changes have taken place in women's access to education and employment. Social attitudes toward women's education and employment are changing, partly because of economic recession and impoverishment after the return of 800,000 migrants and their families from Saudi Arabia and the Gulf States in 1990–91 and the introduction of Structural Adjustment Programs in 1995. Formal employment of women increased from 5.6 percent in the early 1980s to 13 percent in 1990 (Lackner 1995, 88) and to 17.7 percent in 1997 (UNDP 2002, 158). Although these percentages are still not very high compared to other countries, they have increased rapidly in a relatively short period of time. In addition, a larger variety of jobs are now open to women, and women have entered these jobs with great enthusiasm. The status of the type of paid work open to women as well as the categories of women taking up certain types of paid labor are shifting, a change that will become clear when we look at the *murshidat* profession.

The Politics of Health-Care Development in Yemen

In addition to education, health care is an important public policy issue in Yemen. As mentioned before, there were hardly any formal health-care facilities in North Yemen at the end of the civil war in 1970. Foreign doctors and nurses had taken care of the health needs of the imam and his kin,[12] while local communities had sometimes established clinics but lacked professional staff. Infant and maternal mortality rates were very high, one of the main reasons that Yemen was, and is still, seen as a "developing" country.[13] In 1971, after the civil war, the

12. For accounts of foreign doctors in Yemen during the Imamate see Fayein (1955) and Hoeck (1962).

13. In 1970, the infant mortality rate was 177 per 1,000 live births, and the under-five mortality rate 293 per 1,000 live births (UNICEF 1993). These numbers

Ministry of Health was established and health care became a funda-mental right of every citizen (Stephen 1992, 208).[14] There was a large program for the expansion and improvement of health-care facilities. These facilities were mainly curative oriented, with the government concentrating on building hospitals and clinics and on training medi-cal personnel such as doctors and nurses.[15] In 1972, there were thirty-three hospitals and two hundred doctors in the country, with more than two-thirds of the hospitals and 90 percent of the doctors located in the three main cities of Sana'a, Taiz, and Hodeida (Bornstein 1974, 1). In 1972, the nursing schools were incorporated into the Health Manpower Institutes, which provided training for a wider range of health personnel (Stephen 1992, 216).[16] Foreign assistance, technical as well as financial, was deemed inevitable, and foreign development agencies were quickly involved in the Yemeni health-care sector. In-ternational organizations such as the World Bank, WHO, and UNI-CEF, but also bilateral donors and NGOs, became involved in the formulation of health-care policies. They emphasized the importance of preventive health care in fighting high infant and maternal mor-tality rates, in particular in rural areas. In 1976, at least twenty-four foreign development agencies were providing a major portion of the

---

had decreased to 83 and 110 in 1998, which is significantly lower than the average for so-called least developed countries, but still very high in comparison to other coun-tries in the Middle East and North Africa (UNICEF 1998, 19). Maternal mortality rates are much harder to estimate, as the cause of a woman's death is often not regis-tered. The Yemeni Ministry of Public Health estimates maternal mortality rates at 1,000 per 1,000,000 births, while UNICEF and WHO give a much higher rate of 1,400 per 1,000,000 births, making it one of the highest maternal mortality rates in the world (UNICEF 1998, 30).

14. The Ministry of Health was later named the Ministry of Public Health.

15. According to Hermann (1979, 59), in 1976 only six of the available doctors in the country specialized in public health.

16. The Health Manpower Institutes (HMI) provide a three-year training for nurses and midwives, medical assistants, pharmacists, sanitarians, laboratory tech-nicians, radiological technicians, and anesthetic technicians. Students entering the HMI must have completed intermediate school, that is, nine years of education.

preventive services, especially mother and child health (MCH) services (Hermann 1979, 69). A Department of Basic Health Services and Primary Health Care was established within the Ministry of Health in 1977. A three-tier system consisting of health units, health centers, and hospitals was established, with each level responsible for providing care to a larger number of people. Yet despite prioritizing basic health care on paper, little was actually done to encourage the running of health facilities, particularly in rural areas. North Yemen's health sector remained largely curative and urban oriented.

The international conference on Primary Health Care, organized by the WHO in Alma-Ata in 1978, had an important impact on the health-care policies of North Yemen, inspiring Yemeni health-care managers as well as staff of foreign donor organizations. Health education, pre- and postnatal care, immunization, and the distribution of contraceptives and basic drugs were seen as essential activities to combat infant and maternal mortality rates and to reduce population growth. In 1980, the government initiated a national primary health-care project in cooperation with WHO and UNICEF, aimed at extending primary health-care services to the rural population (Stephen 1992, 208). The building of rural health clinics and the training of primary health-care workers were the main activities of the project. Rural community leaders selected primary health-care workers from within their own communities (*murshidin* and *murshidat*).[17] They had to have six years of primary education, as reading and writing skills were necessary, and they had to be at least eighteen years of age. The training courses took place in the nearest health center with training facilities.[18] Contrary to community health programs in other countries, Yemeni primary health-care workers did not work on volunteer

17. In practice this often meant that the *shaykh* of a village selected eligible men and women.

18. The first training courses for primary health-care workers were six months, but this period was soon extended to nine months. As foreign donor organizations created and funded the training courses, the length, contents, and structure of the courses were in the beginning not uniform.

basis. Rather the costs of their training and their annual salary were divided between the rural community and the government.

One of the most remarkable features of the formal health-care system of both North and South Yemen is the fact that the large majority of trained health workers were male. The reason is that very few women had the necessary school certificates to enter vocational training centers and institutes in the early 1970s. However, professional health care continued to be a male-dominated sector even when women's educational achievements had improved. In 1992, 90 percent of nurses were still male (Stephen 1992, 216). Although women were involved in informal health-care practices, as healers and midwives, professional health care did not seem to be an attractive option for them. "Work in the health sector suffers from traditional prejudices: whereas to be a doctor is to have a high-status occupation even for women, nursing and other paramedic activities are of very low status" (Lackner 1995, 88).[19] Primary health-care projects also encountered difficulties in recruiting women as community health workers. The lack of women health workers was a major problem because improving MCH services was at the heart of these projects. The low status of certain health-care professions, the low level of education of girls and women in the villages, the heavy workload of women, and cultural notions about women's waged labor, such as the ideology of the male breadwinner and gender segregation, affected the recruitment of women as *murshidat*. The fact that training courses were often organized in health centers in small rural towns where trainees had to stay for six months to one year also limited women's participation.

As a result, in the majority of rural health centers there were only male primary health-care workers, who focused on vaccinations and small curative services and neglected MCH services. In order to recruit women, health-care projects in rural areas changed their selection criteria for female health workers by dropping the condition of

19. Nursing has a low status in many countries of the world because cure is valued over care (see Pizurki et al. 1987).

six years of primary education.[20] Women and girls with limited basic education or no education at all were trained. These women were not called *murshidat* but local birth attendants *(daya sha'biyya.)*[21] In addition, women who worked as traditional birth attendants *(jadat)* received training to improve their skills and knowledge, which was also part of the primary health care (PHC) approach as formulated in Alma-Ata. The number of women working as local birth attendants was very limited, and the fact that often lower-class women and illiterate women were doing this work affected the status of the work negatively. People had no confidence in the services provided by women of low social status. Moreover, the contents of the local birth attendant training varied considerably. While there was a national curriculum available for *murshidin,* there was none for local birth attendants or for *murshidat* and every project developed its own course. Foreign development workers stressed the need to train local women as healthcare workers, on the assumption that women's health care would not improve unless female health cadres were available. However, they did not always pay attention to the reasons women were not interested in working in health care.

Despite these obstacles, an increasing number of women have trained as *murshidat,* in both rural and urban areas, in the past twenty years. The first groups of *murshidat* were trained in the mid-1980s.[22] *Murshidat* training courses have been funded and organized by foreign donor organizations, such as USAID, OXFAM, and bilateral donors. The national Health Manpower Institutes (HMI), which were

20. In the vivid but cynical account of his experiences in a primary health project in Yemen, Morris (1991, 118) describes the difficulties the project encountered in recruiting women willing and able to be trained as local birth attendants.

21. The word *daya* was introduced by Sudanese midwives training Yemeni women as local birth attendants.

22. In 1983, the training of *murshidat* started in ten governorates under the auspices of the World Health Organization. A team of Sudanese midwives was employed as trainers/supervisors. In the beginning a Sudanese curriculum was used, and literacy classes were part of the training because many of the trainees were illiterate. Later a national curriculum was designed, but it was only approved in 1996.

responsible for the training of paramedical staff in Yemen, lacked the capacity to train and supervise health cadres in rural areas and therefore left the training of *murshidin* and *murshidat* to foreign development organizations. The HMI was responsible for approving the curriculum, monitoring and evaluating the course, and signing the certificates. Although primary health care was a priority on paper, the Yemeni Ministry of Public Health did not take full responsibility for its development, and the promotion of primary health-care activities remained largely a "foreign affair."

After unification, southern health-care administrators took up important positions in the Ministry of Public Health in Sana'a and began to influence policy making. The health-care system in former South Yemen had been more primary health care oriented,[23] and southerners introduced new concepts and strategies in the health-care system of former North Yemen. As a reaction to the economic recession following the Gulf crisis, a national population strategy was approved in August 1991. Improving the social and economic status of women was central to this strategy, as it assumed a positive relationship between the enhanced access of women to health and education services, the integration of women into the labor market, reform of family law, and the hoped-for decrease in fertility rates (Worm 1998, 8). Worm (1998) gives a very interesting analysis of the debate over women's health in unified Yemen. In the transitional period, the Islah party regularly blamed the government for the deterioration of medical services in the country. The poor quality of the services, financial and administrative mismanagement, the lack of motivated health staff, the absence of essential drugs, and bad maintenance were the main complaints. Women were seen as the main victims of a weak health-care policy—there was

---

23. In former South Yemen the basis for a primary health-care system was already established prior to 1978 (see also Segall and Williams 1983). Physicians were encouraged to specialize in public health, and a committed team of public health experts was established who set up a well-organized primary health-care system. However, this system was almost completely destroyed after the civil war in South Yemen in 1986.

a shortage of well-trained female health staff who could treat women in health centers and hospitals, and women suffered as a result of poor conditions in health-care facilities. In the election campaign of 1993, the three main parties, the PGC, the YSP, and the Islah, all promised to improve the health-care system in Yemen by developing primary health-care services, training health cadres, and promoting private investment in the curative sector.

When Islah entered the coalition government in April 1993, it took control of the Ministry of Public Health, and the resulting power struggle between health administrators with different political backgrounds led to the gradual paralysis of the ministry. Despite these conflicts, an important document was issued in 1994 under the title "Forward Looking Policies and Strategies for Health Development in the Republic of Yemen" as a follow-up to the National Population Strategy approved in 1991. Health, and in particular women's health, was put in a broader social and economic context, and the need to link health services with other developmental efforts was recognized (Worm 1998, 11). After the civil war and the defeat of the socialists, Islah was able to strengthen its position in the health administration. Yet there were no major changes in policy; Islah health administrators followed a pragmatic approach in the international debates on population, health, women, and development. In August 1994 Yemen participated in the International Conference on Population and Development (ICPD) in Cairo, and in July 1995 in the Fourth World Conference on Women in Beijing, and the final resolutions and action programs of both conferences were approved. As a result of the ICPD, reproductive health became the new focus of the Yemeni Ministry of Public Health, replacing the former focus on maternal and child health care.[24] The reproductive health-care approach links population issues to the improvement of socioeconomic conditions, in particular that of women. Demographic targets and a focus on family planning

24. In April 2001, the Ministry of Public Health changed its name to Ministry of Public Health and Population Affairs (Martin 2001, 13). The Mother and Child Health Departments had earlier been renamed the Reproductive Health Departments.

services were replaced by a much broader approach to health care, including the promotion of women's access to education, employment, and legal rights. Although Islah health administrators had a pragmatic attitude toward international debates on health care, in the Population Action Plan that was drafted in 1996 the concept of reproductive health was adapted to the Yemeni context. The right to abortion and the provision of sexual health education to adolescents were, for example, omitted. The influence of Islah was also clearly visible in the "Shari'a Guidelines for Family Planning" which were issued in the same year. Social problems existing in Yemen were linked to the availability of contraceptives, and early marriage was encouraged as a way to preserve moral integrity on an individual and societal level (Worm 1998, 15). Yet very little of what Islah policy makers proposed with regard to improving health services and the restrictive guidelines for family planning was implemented.

One of the few issues in which Islah administrators were successful was the promotion and training of female health-care workers. Worm (1998, 21) mentions that the Minister of Public Health himself, in an interview with the newspaper *al-Sahwa* in December 1994, urged young Yemeni women to become nurses and emphasized that "practicing this noble profession was fully in accordance with Islamic values." A number of new nursing colleges were established, and the Community Midwife Program was initiated in 1995–96. It was presented as a way to train a large number of young women as midwives in rural areas.[25] The Community Midwife Program envisaged the training of four thousand community midwives, young women with nine years of basic education and two years training in reproductive health and child health care. The Ministry of Public Health would employ some of the community midwives, while the rest had to earn an income with private practice in their communities. A wide range of foreign donor organizations supported this Community Midwife

25. An additional reason was that these young women could also function as possible ways into local communities and gain support for the Islah party (interview with Frits Muller, Apr. 3, 2000).

Program. The Dutch government, for example, financed the training of fifteen hundred community midwives.

After the 1997 elections, a PGC Minister originally from former South Yemen replaced the Islah Minister of Public Health. Under his auspices, a national health-care policy was formulated in the form of a Health Sector Reform Program. It was an ambitious program aimed at reorganizing the public health sector following the recommendations of the World Bank and IMF.[26] The main elements of the health sector reform strategies are decentralization, a redefinition of the role of the public sector, a district health system approach, community participation, cost recovery, an essential-drugs policy, intersectoral collaboration, and a sector-wide approach to donor funding and programming.[27] It also calls for a stronger role for the Ministry of Public Health in coordinating donor assistance. Yet the fact that only 4 percent of the national budget is allocated to health care,[28] compared to 20 percent to education and 32 percent to defense (Al-Dubai 2000, 6), shows the low priority of health care for the Yemeni government, despite the commitment of some individuals.

In short, the ways in which health-care policies were developed in Yemen show its particular politics of development: although health-care development is on paper a priority, in practice only a very small

26. Health Sector Reform Programs (HSR) have been imposed on other developing countries as well and are often put forward as ways to bring about fundamental changes in the health sector in order to make it equitable, efficient, and effective (see Cassels 1995).

27. In the late 1990s, the so-called "sector-wide approach" (SWAp) was adopted, also at the instigation of the World Bank. The basic idea of the sector-wide approach is that foreign donor organizations financially support governments of developing countries with activities aimed at public-sector reform and leave the technical implementation of these activities to the national government. The aim of the sector-wide approach is to increase the level of "ownership" and to decrease the power of donor organizations in order to guarantee sustainability of development activities.

28. Eighty-one percent of the budget for health care is used to pay the salaries of personnel, leaving little for the running costs of the health facilities (Al-Dubai 2000, 7).

percentage of the national budget is allocated to health care. Most of this money is used for infrastructure and the purchase of high technology, while the promotion of primary health care is largely left to foreign donors. Yemen's support for primary health care can to a large extent be interpreted as paying lip service to foreign donors. Just as in health care, gender plays an important role in the politics of development; the government has used women as identity markers of development and modernity. Yet despite the verbal promotion of women's education and employment, little has been done to improve the conditions for women's education and to facilitate women's entrance into the labor market. The fact that very few women were interested in taking up professional work in health care such as nursing was a result of the limited attention paid to the particular position of women workers. Only recently, as a result of the economic recession, are an increasing number of women interested in being trained and employed as health-care workers.

4

A Dutch-Yemeni Project

A CLOSE-UP of two veiled women with beautiful dark eyes appeared on the front cover of "International Cooperation,"[1] the monthly magazine of the Dutch Ministry of Foreign Affairs, in June 2001. Their white veils indicated that they are health-care workers, but that may only be clear to insiders. "Yemen: The Poverty-Stricken Pearl of the Middle East" is the caption under the picture. I quickly glance through the magazine, looking forward to an article on women health workers in Yemen. In vain. The three articles on Yemen are about democracy, the shortage of water, and a distribution program for essential drugs. Even in this last article, there is no reference to women health workers. The women on the front page are clearly used as symbols of Yemen and therefore a clear example of Yemeni women's ambiguous symbolic function. On one hand, they are "pearls": mysterious and attractive, confirming Orientalist notions about Arab women represented by their veiled faces showing only their beautiful dark eyes. On the other hand, the women, and in particular their veils, symbolize a traditional country, which is a very common Orientalist image as well. The fact that these images are used in a magazine about Dutch development aid gives rise to questions about Dutch development discourses, in particular with regard to women and health care in Yemen. How are Yemeni women presented in the development discourses of the Dutch government?

---

1. *Internationale Samenwerking* 6, June 2001.

Which policies have been designed to focus on women and health care? And how have these policies been included in the Hodeida Urban Primary Health Care Project?

Dutch Discourses of Development

In the past thirty years the Netherlands has become one of the biggest foreign donors to Yemen.[2] Numerous development projects and programs in the fields of health care, agriculture, water and sanitation, education, industry and enterprise, and infrastructure have been financed by Dutch development aid. Although the Dutch government has been involved in Yemeni development efforts since the establishment of the Yemen Arab Republic, the official development relationship between the two countries started in 1978. In that year North Yemen was identified as a "target country"[3] of Dutch development aid, based on its low income per capita (US$90) and the social orientation of Yemeni government policies (DGIS 1975, 49). But a political motive also inspired Dutch interest in Yemen. During the oil crisis of 1973, and the subsequent problems in obtaining gasoline, the Dutch government realized that it had little contact with governments in the Middle East. Establishing a development relationship with Yemen was one of the ways in which the government tried to strengthen its position on the Arabian Peninsula. In addition, development aid to Yemen was presented as a way of encouraging the peace process in the Middle East and supporting regional stability.

2. In 1996, the Dutch share of total bilateral assistance was 40 percent, followed by Germany (29 percent), Japan (17 percent), and France (5 percent) (UNICEF 1998, 15).

3. Target countries were identified on the basis of "the degree of poverty, the specific uncovered need for aid (distinct from the need for expansion of trade opportunities), and the extent to which a social and political structure is present which will make possible a policy truly designed to improve the situation within the country itself and will provide a guarantee that the aid will benefit the whole community." Particular attention would be paid to human rights (DGIS 1975, 45).

In the Agreement on Technical Cooperation, signed in 1978, the basic arrangements between the governments of the two countries were laid down. The General Directorate for International Cooperation (DGIS) of the Dutch Ministry of Foreign Affairs would be responsible for Dutch compliance, the Yemeni Ministry of Planning for compliance from the Yemeni side. Dutch development aid to Yemen would be given in the form of grants and not as loans, so that Yemen's foreign debt would not increase, and mainly as project aid. Capital investment and technical assistance, mainly in the form of bilateral development projects carried out by Dutch organizations or consultancy firms in cooperation with Yemeni ministries, formed the core of Dutch-Yemeni development relations. Rural development was the main focus of attention and projects in urban areas were only supported on a limited scale (DGIS 1988, 6). In the early years of Dutch development aid in Yemen, infrastructural improvements formed a major part of the activities, but in the second half of the 1970s more socially oriented development projects were introduced. Rural projects, in which infrastructural improvements were combined with extension services, were established. The Rada' Integrated Rural Development Project, which I described in the introduction, was an example of this approach.

Following the first UN conference on women in 1975, women's issues gained increasing importance in Dutch development policies. Integrating women into development activities by acknowledging their economic roles was the primary aim of the newly identified Women in Development (WID) approach. Although modernization theories as developed in the 1950s and 1960s propagated women's domesticity, in the 1970s women's paid labor was seen as development. This shift was partly due to the realization that large groups of people, including women, had failed to benefit from modernization projects. Women in the South had been approached primarily in their reproductive roles, as mothers and housewives, and particular forms of domesticity, based on Western notions of modernity, had been introduced. Development projects that had been directed at women were mainly mother and child health-care projects, family planning activities, and food programs, later grouped together under the label "the welfare approach."[4] The WID approach also became part of Dutch development policies. The first Dutch policy memorandum on women and development, which was issued in 1980, identified the following goals: to increase the influence and participation of women in the preparation and implementation of development policy, to promote greater economic independence for women, and to strengthen women's organizations in developing countries (AIV 2002, 10). In 1985, Dutch Women in Development specialists were assigned to Dutch embassies in a number of countries and became responsible for setting up women's projects and integrating women's issues into already existing projects.

In 1986, a team of Dutch development experts visited Yemen in order to assess possibilities for support to women and development activities (DGIS 1987). Based on discussions with Yemeni women and men in and outside the government, and Dutch and other foreign development workers, the following priority areas for development aid were identified: education, health education, agricultural extension, attention to intrahousehold dynamics, the introduction of money-saving and income-earning activities and labor-saving devices, and strengthening Yemeni policy making with regard to women. One of the concrete outcomes of this mission was the appointment of a specialist on Women in Development to the Dutch embassy in Yemen.[5] The proposed strategy was first to focus on decreasing rural women's workload, so that women would have more time and energy to become interested in extension services, health education, and income-generating activities. Another recommendation was that Yemeni women in policy-making positions be trained in Women in

---

4. Moser (1989) has categorized the various approaches toward women and development since the 1950s and distinguishes the welfare approach, the equity approach, the anti-poverty approach, the efficiency approach, and the empowerment approach.

5. As a preparation for the arrival of a so-called sector specialist on women and development, a temporary specialist was appointed who filled this post in 1987–88. In 1989, the first official sector specialist arrived.

Development theories and research methodologies. Support to the Yemeni Women's Association was one of the development projects initiated in the mid-1980s.

Following the third World Conference on Women in Nairobi in 1985, "autonomy" became a key concept in Dutch development policies. Autonomy refers to women's economic, political, physical, and cultural rights of self-determination. The autonomy concept was from the very beginning contested and even led to questions in the Lower House of the Dutch House of Representatives. The applicability of the autonomy concept to women in Islamic countries was particularly questioned. The result was that a special study was carried out to find out whether and how this policy could work in Muslim countries (Jansen et al. 1993). A number of development projects in Yemen were included in this study. One of the main outcomes of the study was that "there is considerable scope in Muslim countries to improve women's access to and control over economic, physical, political and cultural resources, but that how this should be done depends largely on the specific context" (127). Although the autonomy approach was promoted by DGIS, the approach had very little impact on development projects, at least in Yemen.

The realization that women cannot be treated as a homogeneous category but that there are many differences among women depending on social, political, and economic contexts, even when they share, for example, the same religion, lies at the basis of the Gender and Development (GAD) approach. In the GAD approach women are seen as agents of change rather than as passive recipients of development assistance (Rathgeber 1990, 495). Mainstreaming gender (i.e., integrating gender perspectives in mainstream policies) became one of the priorities of the GAD approach, as the WID approach had led to little change in development policies. In Yemen, for example, only 15 percent of the Dutch-financed development projects conformed to the WID criteria of Dutch development aid (Jansen et al. 1993, 112). Following international discussions on gender and development, the GAD approach was integrated into Dutch development aid and also gained importance in Yemen.

A shift occurred from the building of infrastructure, support to hospital activities, the delivery of equipment and medicines, and support to vertical programs to primary health care, resulting from the international WHO conference on primary health care in 1978. As mentioned in chapter 2, the primary health-care approach emphasized the importance of equity, prevention, community involvement, appropriate technology, and an intersectoral approach. In 1986, the primary health-care approach was officially laid down in a policy paper on Dutch development aid for health care (DGIS 1989, 4). The document emphasized that special attention had to be paid to the health needs of women. In Yemen, Dutch-funded primary health-care projects were established in Rada' and Dhamar in the early 1980s. Providing mother and child health services in rural areas was the main focus of attention, and training and supervision of female health cadres was one of the priorities. In addition, health education activities were added to water and sanitation projects. In 1987, the Hodeida Urban Primary Health Care Project, the first urban primary health-care project in Yemen, was established.

The limited impact of primary health-care projects worldwide gradually led to the awareness that prevention could only succeed when it was complemented by good curative care. In addition, the organization and financing of health care became important issues. Establishing district health systems (instead of isolated primary health-care projects), the introduction of cost-recovery schemes, and a restructuring of the public health-care sector became the main priorities of health-care development in the 1990s. These new priorities coincided with a shift from project aid to program aid. The main aim of the program approach was to improve the sustainability of development activities. Support to government programs instead of separate projects was seen as a way to guarantee sustainability.

The International Conference on Population and Development held in Cairo in 1994 also had major consequences for Dutch development policies on women and health care. Reproductive rights became a key concept and was rapidly integrated into Dutch development policies. While population activities had previously concentrated on family planning services and mother and child health care, the reproductive health approach is a holistic approach taking all members of society into account. Moreover, the reproductive health approach promotes women's access to education, legal rights, and ways to alleviate their poverty. Its ultimate aim is to empower people to make their own decisions. Reproductive rights, the training of women as health workers, cost-recovery, and community participation, as well as a district health approach, are all part of the health sector reform program in Yemen (Ministry of Public Health 1999). Dutch-funded health-care projects in Yemen included the above-mentioned concepts and approaches in their activities. The Netherlands government supported the formulation of the health sector reform program and funded at least two government programs.[6]

Since 1998, following recommendations of the World Bank, Dutch development policies have taken a sectorwide approach, which means that governmental sectors are financially and technically supported in order to encourage "ownership" and guarantee sustainability. Within the sectorwide approach, the GAVIM[7] approach was introduced to ensure that good governance, poverty reduction, women and development, institutional development, and the environment would be taken into account in all policies (AIV 2002, 12). In 1998, Dutch development aid was concentrated in nineteen countries that had per capita GNPs lower than US$825, a track record of the government's social and economic policies, and that were supposed to be characterized by "good governance."[8] Yemen was selected as one of the nineteen

6. The Yemen Drug Action Program (YEMDAP) and the Training of Community Midwives Program are both examples of Dutch support to government health-care programs.

7. GAVIM is a Dutch acronym for Good Governance, Poverty Reduction, Women, Institutional Development, and Environment.

8. Good governance means, among other things, that the government is open about the way in which it spends the national budget; that there is little or no corruption; and that there are a democratic system, the right to organize, a free press, and no violation of human rights.

target countries, although heated debates followed about how good its governance was. From 1999, three main government sectors were to be supported: water and sanitation, health care, and agriculture. In 2000, education was added as a fourth sector. Environment, gender, and good governance are special points of attention.

The Hodeida Urban Primary Health Care Project lasted more than fifteen years, from 1984 until 1999. Because of the relatively long duration of the project, an analysis of the project history can give insight into the actual impact of policy shifts in Dutch development discourses. To what extent were project activities adapted to these policy shifts? How were the different approaches with regard to women and development integrated into the project? And how did the training and employment of Yemeni women as *murshidat* fit into the different approaches toward women and development?

A Health-Care Component, 1984–1987

The Hodeida Urban Primary Health Care Project officially started in 1987 but in effect project activities had already been initiated in 1984, as part of the Hodeida Waste Disposal and Health Improvement Project. Hodeida was considered one of the poorest cities in Yemen, with a growing belt of squatter areas[9] owing to increased migration from the villages in the Tihama. With the growth of the import sector, Hodeida soon developed as North Yemen's main port. Because of the growing importance of the city, the government paid a great deal of attention to developing the city's infrastructure. Water and sewerage systems were installed, main roads were paved, and schools were built. People from various other Yemeni towns, such as Taiz and Aden, settled in the city. The increased job opportunities and the improved facilities also attracted rural migrants, mainly from the Tihama region, where deprivation in the villages pushed many to leave for Hodeida or for Saudi Arabia. Large squatter areas came into

9. Squatter settlements can be defined as slums where most inhabitants do not have legal title to land (Rossi-Espagnet 1984, 48).

being on the outskirts of town. In 1983, Hodeida had about 180,000 inhabitants of whom approximately 45,000 were living in squatter areas (DGIS 1983, annex 1, 2).

While development projects worldwide had first concentrated on rural areas as a way to resist urbanization, in the mid-1980s the attention began to shift to urban areas and their perceived needs. It became clear that urbanization was continuing, despite the development activities that were directed at rural areas. Squatter settlements were one of the results of rapid urbanization. The poor living conditions in squatter settlements, ranging from dirty drinking water to insecure housing conditions, and from lack of job opportunities to the unavailability of health facilities, were believed to contribute to high rates of infant and child mortality.

Waste disposal was seen as a big problem in Hodeida. Large heaps of garbage were found all over the city forming an immediate threat to the population's health, in particular because of the heat and humidity that characterize the climate of the Tihama. The development of a waste-disposal project with a health-care component was seen as a first step toward the establishment of an integrated urban development project. The specific aims of the project were "to improve the environmental health in the city and to improve the general health condition of the squatters in the periphery of the city" (DGIS 1983, annex 1, 2). The two parts of the project would be implemented separately but under the same umbrella. The waste-disposal component of the project would be implemented in cooperation with the Ministry of Municipalities and Housing. Its activities would consist of building a workshop and a landfill site, distributing rubbish containers and compactor trucks, setting up health education activities about waste collection, and supporting the health inspection service of the municipality. Waste-disposal services would cover the entire city. The health-care component of the project would be implemented in cooperation with the Ministry of Health. Its activities would consist of establishing a primary health-care system based at a health center in one of the squatter areas, training male primary health-care workers, and introducing a health information system.

The squatter area of Ghulail was chosen as the pilot area because it was one of the poorest squatter areas of Hodeida. The area was situated at the southeastern edge of the city and mainly inhabited by rural migrants. Its estimated population in 1984 was 14,000 (Hodeida Waste Disposal and Health Improvement Project 1984, 8). The second area that was to be included in a later phase of the project would be al-Mughtaribin, in the north of the city. The entire project was intended to run for three years, from the beginning of 1984 until the end of 1986.[10] The project team that was to implement the project activities would consist of an expatriate project manager, an expatriate public health expert, and an expatriate social scientist, who would all work closely with "counterparts" of the Yemeni ministries involved.

In 1984 Cees van Oordt, the Dutch project manager, and Mohamed Ibrahim, a Tunisian public health expert, arrived in Hodeida. As there was no official counterpart assigned to the project by the Ministry of Health, the director-general of the Hodeida Health Office, Dr. 'Abdullah Ahmed, was closely involved in establishing the project. He had a major impact on developments in the project, in particular with regard to the training of health-care workers. The initial idea had been to train four male primary health-care workers, who would be assisted by female volunteers. Cees van Oordt formulated these initial ideas as follows:

> They would be men, classical primary health-care workers, supported by women, who would be some kind of extension workers. The women would be volunteers, coming from the areas, and willing to do this against a small allowance but not fully employed. They would do home visits in the area, because the male primary health-care workers could not pay home visits to families in case there were no men present.[11]

10. The Dutch contribution to the project for the period 1984–87 was 10.5 million guilders. The Yemeni contribution to the project was almost 8 million Yemeni riyals (in 1985, US$1 equaled YR4).

11. Interview with C. J. Royer, June 21, 1999. The translation from the Dutch is mine.

But after negotiations with 'Abdullah Ahmed it was decided to train women as primary health-care workers instead of men (Hodeida Health Improvement and Waste Disposal Project 1984, 8). This was a very interesting shift, and a telling example of the differences between Dutch and Yemeni notions of Yemeni women's public roles. Dutch policy makers had automatically assumed that professional health-care workers had to be male, based on their understanding of gender segregation and the subsequent idea that women were unable to take up paid work in a public setting. But in 'Abdullah Ahmed's view, gender segregation precisely offered possibilities to train women as primary health-care workers because they would be better able to reach women in the squatter areas, and he advised the project manager to make MCH services the main focus of the project. In the plan of operations, the following reasoning behind this choice was included: "As the key to hygienic conditions in the home is the housewife or mother, this part of the project is almost entirely women-oriented. Consequently a MCH clinic will be included" (8). As a health-care component aimed at improving the health-care situation in the squatter areas, the activities were limited to mother and child health care. It was decided that the women had to have finished six years of primary education, be over eighteen years old, and preferably have children so that they would be able to gain the trust of mothers and pass on health messages regarding mother and child health care. It was emphasized that the women had to live in the project area itself, conforming to standard ideas of community health workers. In addition, they had to come from reputable families in order to guarantee their respectability.

In 1985, Thera de Haas, a Dutch public health nurse, and Veronica Thijssen, a Dutch midwife joined the health component. Their main task was to establish MCH services in the Ghulail health center. They were not responsible for the selection and training of the first group of female primary health-care workers but were expected to contribute to their training and supervise them during their work in the health center. At around the same time, Joyce Bakker, a Dutch medical anthropologist, arrived in Hodeida. She became responsible for small-scale research efforts and for developing health education programs for both the waste disposal and the health-care component of the project.

Recruiting students and organizing a training course for female primary health-care workers was the task of the project's public health expert. In the plan of operations, which was drafted in December 1984, a job description for female primary health-care workers was added as an annex. The job requirements for this position were that "the candidate should be healthy, have finished the ninth grade, be chosen by the community and willing to work for her community" (DGIS 1983, annex 2, 3). An additional requirement mentioned in another annex to the report was that the women had to be between eighteen and thirty-five years old. The main duties of the female primary health-care workers would be health education and the promotion of environmental health. Because of the emphasis on health education, the female health-care workers were to be called *murshidat*.[12] The *murshidat* would receive nine months of training in preventive health services, environmental health, health education, and mother and child health care. They would primarily work in the field, giving health education to women at home, while the Dutch nurse and the Dutch midwife together with Yemeni auxiliary staff would run the MCH clinic. Local birth attendants (LBAs) were mentioned in the plan of operations as possible assistants in the clinics. The basic services to be offered in the clinic would consist of a vaccination program,[13] care for children under five, pre- and postnatal care, family planning advice (counseling), and distribution of contraceptives.

12. The term *murshid/a* is derived from the Arabic root *ra-sha-da*, which in its fourth form means "to guide," "to lead," or "to instruct." Morris (1991, 181) mentions that the religious connotation of the word (a *murshid/a* can also be a spiritual guide) increased the status of the young women trained as health educators. Just as in Morris's project, the *murshidat* in Hodeida were also often called *banat* (girls), even though some of them were married.

13. Children under one year of age receive vaccinations against diphtheria, whooping cough, tetanus, and polio (DPT+P), against tuberculosis (BCG), and against measles. Pregnant women receive a tetanus vaccination to protect their babies against tetanus.

On the basis of the estimated number of households in Ghulail, the required number of female primary health-care workers was put at ten.[14] Eight *murshidat* would work in the field and do home visits, and two *murshidat* would provide health education at the health center. The *murshidat* would work in teams of two and start in an area of around four hundred houses, to be expanded later. With regard to the background of the *murshidat*, the plan of operations mentions that the women should come from the project area itself, Ghulail. While one of the requirements was that the *murshidat* had to be selected by the community, no recruitment methods were mentioned. The only sentence referring to their recruitment is: "It is assumed that the Yemeni Women's Association/Hodeida can assist in the recruitment of students" (Hodeida Health Improvement and Waste Disposal Project 1984, 9). I will elaborate later on the recruitment and selection of the first group of *murshidat*. Here it is sufficient to mention that the first group was not selected by the community nor came from within Ghulail. Nine young women were selected by the Yemeni Women's Association and started their training in October 1985. They all came from old neighborhoods in the city of Hodeida.

From the very beginning the project management decided that the *murshidat* had to become state employed in order to safeguard the continuation of their work after the end of Dutch funding. However, there was not much consultation with the Ministry of Public Health in Sana'a, and the training of *murshidat* started without the official approval of the ministry. The curriculum used by the project as well as the job description of the *murshidat* had been discussed and approved by 'Abdullah Ahmed but not by administrators from the Ministry of Public Health in Sana'a. At the end of the training course, the consequences of this negligence became evident when the Ministry of Public Health refused to issue official certificates and employ the first group of *murshidat*.

14. The total population of Ghulail was estimated at 14,000. The average number of persons per house was estimated at 5 and the number of houses at 2,800. Ten primary health-care workers would be able to cover the area (Hodeida Health Improvement and Waste Disposal Project 1984: annex 4).

Soon after the start of the training course, a female Yemeni supervisor for the *murshidat* was recruited. Fatima Salem was a nurse-midwife in her early twenties who had worked for years as head of the maternity ward in Hodeida's main hospital. She became one of the key members of the project team. In addition to the theoretical part of the training course, which consisted of lectures by a broad range of teachers from the Health Manpower Institute in Hodeida and people working in health care, the *murshidat* also received practical training in the health center. They became acquainted with the MCH services offered in the center, and they learned how to do home visits and got to know Ghulail and its inhabitants.

In October 1986, the first group of *murshidat* graduated and started their work in the Ghulail health center. A month later, the first three years of the Hodeida Health Improvement and Waste Disposal Project were evaluated. The main conclusion was that the project had to be split into an environmental health project and an urban primary health-care project. On April 1, 1987, the Hodeida Urban Primary Health Care Project became a reality. Dutch funding for the project was extended for another five years, and a second health center in the area of al-Mughtaribin was to be included.

A Separate Project, 1987–1993

Another result of the evaluation was that Fred Mulder was asked to become the external adviser of the health-care project. Mulder had worked as a medical doctor in Peru in the early seventies and had long-term experience with primary health-care programs in Latin America. Since his return to the Netherlands, he had been working as an independent consultant to health-care projects all over the world. He was very committed to community health-care programs and believed in grassroots development. Fred Mulder was the first person with extensive knowledge and experience in primary health care to visit the project.[15] Although not permanently present in Hodeida, he became

15. Cees van Oordt was a medical doctor who had mainly worked in curative care, and Thera de Haas was a public-health nurse who had extensive experience in

a key figure in the project. The contracts of the team leader and the public-health nurse were extended, a new midwife was recruited, but the anthropologist was not replaced. To satisfy the need for anthropological research, it was agreed to attract short-term consultants with experience in applied research, preferably anthropologists.

The first phase of the project had mainly consisted of preparing the infrastructural needs for a health-care project. Cees van Oordt had been very good at discussing and negotiating with the director-general of the Hodeida Health Office and had convinced him of the importance of preventive health services. A health center had been obtained, repaired, and equipped; MCH services were being offered in Ghulail; and women were being trained as health education workers. During the second phase of the project, the team had to concentrate on establishing a primary health-care system. The project adapted the basic principles of urban primary health care: dividing squatter areas into blocks, training one or more community health workers per block, giving preference to those blocks that are most deprived of services, basing the work of community health workers on home visits, setting up an information system that allows workers to identify at-risk groups, and providing extra care to the chronically ill (Hodeida Urban Primary Health Care Project 1987, 8). The essential elements of the project in Hodeida had to be MCH services: training and employing female primary health-care workers, establishing a home-visiting system and a risk approach,[16] setting up a health information system, involving traditional birth attendants,

---

mother and child health care but not in primary health care. The Tunisian public health expert had left the project in an early stage.

16. A risk approach means that people with a relatively high health risk receive extra attention from the health staff. In HUPHC the following criteria indicated whether a family, a pregnant woman, or child was at risk: at the level of a family a single parent, no tap in the house, five child deaths or more, or a handicapped or chronically ill member constituted a high risk; among pregnant women pregnancy under sixteen or over thirty-five years of age, four or more previous abortions, or weight of less than thirty-four kilos constituted a high risk; among children low birth weight, no breast feeding, or no growth over the previous two months constituted high risk.

The logo of the Hodeida Urban Primary Health Care Project.

cooperating with social organizations outside the health sector, and conducting small-scale research (13). While expatriate involvement was still deemed necessary in implementing the project activities, the expatriate team members were gradually to hand over their duties and skills to the Yemeni staff. The *murshidat*, for example, gained a greater role in the provision of MCH services in the health center.

The extension of the activities to the squatter area of al-Mughtaribin was one of the main activities during the second phase. Yet of the nine *murshida* trained during the first course, only six had remained; three had left almost immediately after the end of the course because they got married. These six *murshidat* spent most of their time in the health center. Their numbers were too small to start a systematic home-visiting program, and the activities that depended on home visits, such as the identification of families at risk and regular health education in the area, could not yet get off the ground. A second training course for *murshidat* was necessary, and the opening of the health center was postponed till new *murshidat* had been trained.

In the summer of 1987 a rapid appraisal[17] was carried out in the area of al-Mughtaribin to gather baseline data. Young women from Ghulail and al-Mughtaribin were recruited as interviewers, and some of them were also interested in becoming *murshidat*. In September 1988 a second training course for *murshidat* was organized. Twenty young women started the course and eleven of them graduated a year later. The second training course was more in line with the Ministry of Public Health's ideas about the training of *murshidat*. Although there was still no national curriculum in existence, the ministry had more explicit ideas about the job descriptions of *murshidat*.

In 1989, the first official phase of the Hodeida Urban Primary Health Care Project was evaluated. The main conclusion was that despite the fact that the MCH services as offered in Ghulail had a high coverage rate, a well-developed primary health-care system was lacking (Koninklijk Instituut voor de Tropen 1989, 109). The home visits were not carried out systematically, and the risk approach had not yet been implemented. Moreover, there was little integration into the Health Office, little cooperation with other sectors, and no community participation. Implementing these recommendations became the responsibility of Peter Witsen, the new Dutch team leader. He was a young medical doctor with a strong interest in public health. While Cees van Oordt had spent most of his time preparing an infrastructure for preventive health services, Witsen was to focus on establishing an urban primary health-care system. Hamid Hassan, a nephew of 'Abdullah Ahmed, was appointed as codirector of HUPHC. Hamid had just returned from Russia, where he had studied medicine. His main task was to maintain contacts with the Health Office.

17. A rapid appraisal is a typical research tool used in development work. Instead of long-term fieldwork by one person, several people carry out the research, using a variety of research methods such as questionnaires, group discussions, and observations. The purpose of the rapid appraisal is to provide a broad overview of a situation or a problem, and to recommend directions or actions for improvement (Hébert 1987).

In 1989, the health center in al-Mughtaribin opened, and the primary health-care system as developed in Ghulail was introduced. The area was mapped, divided into sections, subsections, and blocks, and each house was given a number. The *murshidat* spent 50 percent of their time on home visits, visiting mothers at home and educating them about hygiene, nutrition, child care, and so on. They carried out regular home visits to all families in the area,[18] and "special home visits" to families at risk. The other 50 percent of their time, the *murshidat* worked in the health center, weighing and vaccinating children under five and giving health education to mothers. Mapping and dividing the area in subsections and blocks was also necessary for the so-called Health Information System (HEMIS). Through this system basic data about the inhabitants, and in particular about their health situation, could be gathered and the impact of project activities on the health situation in the area could be evaluated from time to time. The *murshidat* were divided between the two health centers; Thera de Haas became the main supervisor of Ghulail and Fatima Salem of al-Mughtaribin.

An impact study carried out by an external research team in 1990 revealed that the health center in Ghulail was well-known and that people were content with the services offered but also interested in more curative care, laboratory services, and the provision of essential drugs (Abdulghani et al. 1990, 5). In addition, the project was found to cover 80 to 90 percent of the MCH needs in Ghulail and al-Mughtaribin, and 40 to 50 percent of the MCH needs of the entire population of the city. In the meantime other donor organizations had also started to take an interest in urban primary health-care activities and had set up training courses for *murshidat*. This interest increased after the Gulf crisis in August 1990. With the return of thousands of migrants from Saudi Arabia and the Gulf States, the population of Hodeida had grown by approximately 50 percent, from 200,000 in

---

18. During routine visits the *murshidat* advise mothers on health, nutrition, family planning, hygiene, and childcare. They weigh young children and give oral rehydration salts (ORS) in case of diarrhea. They inform mothers about the services available in the health center and try to build a personal and trusting relationship.

1990 to at least 300,000 in 1991 (Lucet 1995, 28). New squatter settlements appeared on the outskirts of town, stretching into the semi-desert plains of the Tihama, with its extremely high temperatures and occasional sandstorms. The situation in the new squatter areas was very bad, with poor housing, lack of water and sanitation facilities, limited health-care services, and a big waste problem.

HUPHC was immediately affected by the Gulf crisis. First, the population of Ghulail and al-Mughtaribin suddenly increased and changed. Every empty piece of land was occupied, returnee families moved into the area, while other families moved out in order to benefit from the availability of land in the new squatter areas. Second, the mass influx of people and the sudden development of new squatter areas led to an increase in health needs in the city and the available health system was unable to respond adequately to these needs. A third effect of the Gulf crisis was that the expatriate staff was evacuated in January 1991. The position Yemen took in the crisis was interpreted as support for Iraq, and Western governments were afraid that their nationals would be at risk. Almost all expatriates left the country and only returned three months later.

The immediate consequence for HUPHC was that the Yemeni staff had to run the project itself. While Peter Witsen and Thera de Haas had been involved in almost every aspect of the project, now the Yemeni staff had to solve problems, make decisions, and implement those decisions. The project became financially as well as technically more independent, and a strong sense of "ownership" was the result. One of the best examples was the appointment of one of the *murshidat* as head of clinic. Prior to 1990, Thera managed the Ghulail health center, while Fatima Salem was in charge of al-Mughtaribin health center. When Thera left, Muna, one of the *murshidat* who had trained during the first course, took over the responsibility for the work in Ghulail. She had worked for years alongside Thera and knew exactly how to run the clinic. And although Hamid Hassan had not been convinced of the capabilities of the *murshidat* prior to 1990, he had to admit that they were very capable of running the health centers. When the expatriates returned in April 1991, Muna was officially appointed head of the clinic in Ghulail, while Riham, another *murshida* trained during the first course, became the official head of the clinic in al-Mughtaribin.

In the aftermath of the war, many local and foreign donor organizations became interested in providing assistance to the returnees. Two British NGOs had become involved in health-care activities in the squatter areas and had started training *murshidat*. USAID, the American bilateral organization for development cooperation, was also interested in training *murshidat*. Within a short period of time several training courses for *murshidat* were running. There was little cooperation among the different health-care projects present in Hodeida; every organization was setting up its own primary health-care system and organizing its own training courses for *murshidat*. Although all projects shared the basic elements of primary health care, with the emphasis on MCH services through home visits and health education implemented by *murshidat*, a coherent system was lacking. In May 1993, it was decided that the primary health-care system developed in Ghulail and al-Mughtaribin would function as a model for the establishment of a citywide urban primary health-care system and that there would be close collaboration among all donors and local contributors (Hodeida Health Office 1993, 12). All government health centers in Hodeida were to become part of this urban primary health-care program. The program would cover three main health centers offering curative and preventive health services and ten subcenters offering preventive services. Ghulail would become one of the main health centers together with the newly built health center in the squatter area of al-Salakhana. Establishing a primary health-care system in which curative care and preventive care complemented each other was born from the increasing worldwide awareness that working solely on preventive health care did not suffice.

A Citywide Program, 1993–2000

In August 1993, the Hodeida Urban Primary Health Care Program started. The program became an integrated part of the Hodeida Health Office, with its own office space and personnel. Integration

*Four supervisors of the project. Their white head
scarves indicate that they work in health care.*

into the Health Office was central to working toward "sustainability," the buzzword in development discourses in the 1990s. The urban
primary health-care approach had to become a fully integrated part
of the Health Office. The director-general of the Health Office was
the one responsible for running the health centers in Hodeida, and
thus in charge of the citywide program. In August 1993, at the start of
the citywide program, 'Abdelhalim Ramzi became director-general.
Under his auspices an Urban Primary Health Care Department was
created. Hamid Hassan became director of this department, and Peter
Witsen became his adviser.

Because of the extension of the urban primary health-care approach to the other government health centers, the staff and personnel working in the health centers had to be redistributed. Six *murshidat* and a midwife would staff each subcenter. The *murshidat* trained in Ghulail and al-Mughtaribin were divided among the other centers in order to guide *murshidat* trained by other donor organizations. Moreover, in almost every health center, a *murshida* was appointed as head of clinic. In those centers where male nurses and doctors had been directors, the female head of clinic became responsible for MCH services, while the male director became responsible for curative services. A team of ten female supervisors was formed, with Thera and Fatima as heads. A number of experts working for a British NGO joined the program.[19] Richard Simons, a British team leader with extensive experience in development projects in Palestine and Yemen, replaced Witsen as team leader.

In September 1994, the planned activities of the citywide program got off the ground. Almost every health center was to be repaired, extended, and equipped according to a list of standard requirements. All the areas of the city were to be mapped, the health information system was to become citywide, and the project was to become fully integrated into the Health Office. A community participation and cost-recovery program was to be established to guarantee "sustainability." Curative services were to be integrated with preventive health services, and the project would extend its services to men in the three main health centers. An essential-drugs program was to be established, guaranteeing the availability of essential drugs for minor diseases both in the main centers and in the subcenters.[20]

Integration into the Hodeida Health Office was a slow and difficult process. 'Abdelhalim Ramzi replaced Hamid Hassan with a

19. Four expatriate midwives became responsible for training and supervision, and a female demographer was to assist the Statistics Department of the Hodeida Health Office.

20. Fifteen essential drugs would be available in the subcenters, to cure minor diseases, and thirty essential drugs in the main center.

young medical doctor who had just started working in one of the health centers. The main reason for Hamid's dismissal as director of the Urban Primary Health Care Program was his continuous challenge to the director-general's authority. The fact that Hamid had obtained the most expensive and biggest car paid for by HUPHC was the last straw.[21] The dismissal of Hamid Hassan ushered in a new period in the history of the project. While Peter Witsen and Hamid Hassan had functioned as father figures to the female staff in the health centers, Richard Simons and Yusuf al-Qadri were not able to build the same kind of trust. However, Simons and al-Qadri worked well together and developed good relations with the male managers in the Health Office and in the Ministry of Public Health in Sana'a. At the local level of the Hodeida Health Office, the Urban Primary Health Care Program continued to be regarded as a foreign project with a lot of money, and the differences with other departments in the Health Office remained. The building of a separate wing for the program at the Health Office in 1996, fully furnished with desks, chairs, carpet, and curtains and equipped with photocopy machines and computers, while the other departments hardly possessed a chair to sit on, accentuated these differences. Health Office employees often envied the people working for the Urban Primary Health Care Program and requested additional money when they were asked to cooperate with the program.

Another main activity in this third phase was the establishment of cost-recovery and community participation systems. Cost-recovery, in the form of small user fees and a revolving drug fund, was intended to guarantee the sustainability of primary health-care activities in the future. The community itself would have a voice in the management of the funds recovered. Local health committees would represent the community and manage the health center income, which

21. Dresch (2000, 177) also mentions the importance of a specific type of car as a symbol of the age in Yemen. A big four-wheel-drive Toyota, popularly known as Layla 'Alawi after the famous Egyptian film star, symbolized status and modernity and was therefore very popular among businessmen, bureaucrats, and tribesmen alike.

they could use for items that were not paid by the Yemeni Ministry of Public Health. A revolving drug fund was also part of the cost-recovery system, but its management was not in the hands of the local health committees.

Another major change took place with regard to the training of female health-care workers. In 1993, there were forty *murshidat* working in the city, and this number had to increase to seventy-five to one hundred to cover MCH services in the whole city. At least three new training courses for twenty *murshidat* each were planned, but only two courses took place, in 1993 and 1996, because of the Ministry of Health's new policy to train community midwives instead of *murshidat*, a policy that was fully supported by foreign donor organizations and partially financed by the Dutch government. As mentioned in the previous chapter, community midwives have nine years of basic education, and their professional training is mainly focused on midwifery, not on health education. From 1996 onward, *murshidat* training courses were only allowed to take place in remote and isolated areas where the level of education among young women was not high enough to train community midwives. In Hodeida, the training of *murshidat* therefore came to a halt. The last group of urban *murshidat* who were trained graduated in 1997. Since 1997, several community midwife courses have taken place, almost all directed at rural areas. In order to give *murshidat* the chance to upgrade their qualifications to community midwife, three upgrading courses were organized in Hodeida. Only *murshidat* who had finished nine years of basic education were allowed to participate in these courses. HUPHC financially assisted those *murshidat* who were willing to finish intermediate school but could not afford the school fees. A large number of other training courses were organized and funded, but most of these courses were not directed at the *murshidat* but at the (male) program staff.

In September 1999, Dutch assistance to HUPHC came to an end. The activities were supposed to be fully integrated into the Hodeida Health Office, and Yemeni employees of the Ministry of Public Health were in charge. The government budget and the cost-recovery system were supposed to finance the activities. In June 1999, a closing conference was organized to celebrate the achievements of fifteen years of urban primary health care in Hodeida. The Minister of Public Health, the governor of Hodeida, and former project members and people from other health-care projects and organizations attended the conference. Remarkable was the fact that the *murshidat* were not invited, which for me was a clear sign of their changed position in the last phase of the project.

Conclusions

The different phases of the Hodeida Urban Primary Health Care Project are in a way congruent with the changing development discourses of the Dutch Ministry of Foreign Affairs, yet there are also interesting differences. The first phase of the project was on one hand an example of a technically oriented idea of development, embodied in the waste disposal component, and on the other hand socially inspired notions of development, embodied in the health-care component. The combination of waste disposal and health care was artificial and was the consequence of the negligence of urban development activities in DGIS. In the second phase of the project, urban development had become more acceptable within Dutch development discourses, and urban primary health-care projects saw the light. The emphasis in this phase was on developing an urban primary health-care system with a special focus on mother and child health care. There was increasing attention to women living in the squatter areas, which was embodied in the organization of literacy and sewing classes for poor women. In the third phase the buzzwords were sustainability, cost-recovery and community participation, essential drugs, and gender and reproductive rights. Curative services were included in the project activities, and men made their entry, as patients but also as staff in the health centers.

With regard to the differences, the women and development policies as developed by DGIS had very little impact on project activities. First, the Hodeida Urban Primary Health Care Project was designed as a health-care project, and not as a women's project. The goal of the project was to improve the health status of people living in the squatter areas in Hodeida, and the training and employment of *murshidat* was one of the main ways to achieve this goal. Second, the idea of training women health-care workers instead of men came from a Yemeni health administrator and not from the Dutch project staff. The fact that the training and employment of women fitted well into Dutch development discourses, particularly in the early 1990s when Women and Development became an official "spearhead" of Dutch development policies, was more an additional advantage than a planned goal.

The course of the project was more affected by individual people working in the project and by events that took place in the local, national, and international context than by policy shifts. With regard to the importance of individuals, the shifts in personnel resulted in changes in project practices. In fifteen years' time, the project had three expatriate team leaders, four expatriate midwives, four expatriate anthropologists, and two Yemeni directors. The only two people who stayed throughout the entire project period were the Dutch public-health nurse and her Yemeni counterpart. They gave continuity and inspired many people, just as the external adviser to the project did. The team leaders all had different approaches to management. In addition, the different relationships they had with Yemeni health administrators in power positions affected the course of the project. The opinions of the project managers and the managers of the Hodeida Health Office on development projects with foreign finance differed, resulting in long negotiations and decisions that were not always in accordance with Dutch development policies.

The project was a clear example of the idea that social change can be effected by outside interventions. High expectations of what could be achieved were present throughout the project period. Yet many of the project activities were a result of particular events at the local, national, and international level. The training and employment of young unmarried women as *murshidat* was one example of an unplanned outcome resulting from local developments. Another example is the fact that the extension of project activities to all government health centers in the city, and subsequently the appointment of *murshidat* as heads of clinic, was not planned but a result of the Gulf crisis. The extent to which social change was effected by the project was thus relatively limited; although the project influenced certain processes of social change, the extent to which the project was influenced by outside events was greater.

PART THREE

Shifting Boundaries

5

Longing for Education

Women from the City

Hawa

HODEIDA, MAY 1997. I am preparing for the first interview of this study. Hawa, one of the *murshidat* of the first group trained in 1985–86, has agreed to talk with me about her training and employment. I have known Hawa since my very first days in Hodeida. She is head of the MCH section of one of the main health centers in Hodeida, so we have worked closely together, and I have often visited her at home. I had heard about the problems Hawa had in the first years of the project when her relatives did not approve of her working. But since I have known her, these problems have not reoccurred, and she seems to perform her work without obstacles. Once I asked her how her husband reacts to her activities, as she is a busy head of clinic, working mornings and afternoons and sometimes even in the evenings as a birth attendant, and she replied that as long as he gets his food on time he does not complain: "You should never neglect your husband. Continue to give him the attention he has always received, so that you don't give him a chance to complain." In my view that is easier said than done.

I get into my car and drive from Hay al-Tijari via al-Hamdi Street, my favorite street, with its small local shops and restaurants, past the park to the end of Sana'a Street. Near the edge of Hodeida, where the road enters the flat Tihama plain, I turn right and put my car into four-wheel drive to cross the sand in front of Hawa's house. One of Hawa's sons opens the door, and Hajar and Huda, Hawa's two youngest daughters, come running toward me and welcome me with kisses. Hand in hand we walk to the house at the end of the compound where Hawa is waiting for me. "Welcome, Marina, welcome," she says, and she guides me to the guest room, one of the two rooms of the house. The house is made of bare concrete blocks and also has a kitchen and a bathroom. It occupies only a small part of the large compound where most of the daily activities take place. But today we stay inside. The interview is a special occasion, and I am received as a guest. Hawa is known for her hospitality and her cooking and will never skip an opportunity to invite people over. I wonder how she manages to be a head of clinic, mother of five children, wife, birth attendant, and a good friend and sister. One thing I know is that she takes life seriously and that she is a good organizer, in her professional as well as in her personal life. In that way she very much resembles Thera, who has been a close friend of Hawa's since her training in 1985. Both Thera and Hawa are key figures in the project, committed, practically oriented, hospitable, and always willing to help. And what's more, both Hawa and Thera love to talk about the project, and in particular about the first years when the project was still in its infancy, with no systematic plans and only a small number of *murshidat*. They are proud of what has been achieved in the past ten years, and that is also why Hawa agreed so wholeheartedly to being interviewed. Hawa likes sharing her ideas and experiences with others, and my research interests her very much. She feels very committed to the project and finds it important that the experiences of the *murshidat* are written down. After finishing our first cup of tea, we are ready to start. Hawa's daughters are sent outside, and I turn on the tape recorder and begin by asking Hawa where and when she was born. Within a couple of minutes the interview has lost its formality, and Hawa clearly takes pleasure in telling her story.

The focus in this part of my research is on the backgrounds and social positions of the first group of *murshidat* trained in 1985 and the ways in which they shifted boundaries by entering a new type of paid work for women. What were the family and educational backgrounds of the first *murshidat?* Why did they decide to enter a new type of work? How were they recruited, and how did that affect the selection? In what ways did the work of the first *murshidat* challenge existing gender ideologies? And how did the first *murshidat* negotiate their new positions?

Hawa was born in Hodeida in 1962, in the neighborhood of al-Mitraq.

> I have six sisters and three brothers. I am the only one of the girls who is working. The others are all married and do not work. My brothers are also married, and they have good jobs. Two studied in Russia and one studied at the police academy. As for the girls, in the past they did not let girls go to school a lot. The most important thing was that a girl knew how to read and write. I went to school before, but I did not finish primary school, I left school after the fourth grade.

There was a girls' school in Hodeida, but Hawa first went to Quran school: "All the members of our family studied Quran first. With regard to the girls, not one of them studied as much as I did. Girls had to stay home. If a girl knew how to read and she knew the *umur al-din* [religious instructions] it was enough. Then she would know how to read and how to pray and what *amr Allah* [God's command] is. More studying was not necessary." But did her brothers go to school? "Yes, they finished secondary school. And my father himself paid for their studies abroad. We could afford it. We had a house here and we had a house in Taiz. We were well off."

Hawa's parents came from a village near al-Mahwit, a governorate in highland Yemen, and were maternal cousins; the mothers of Hawa's father and mother were sisters. Her parents migrated to Hodeida in the years of the Imamate when Hawa's father was a soldier in the army. After the revolution he opened a shop, and later he became a contractor. With the money he earned he built a number of houses and was able to live from the rent of the houses. Hawa continued, "I liked to study very much. I was one of the best at school. When my father decided to withdraw me from school, the school director went to see him and advised him to let me continue my studies. But my father said that four years was enough." I asked her whether she was angry when her father withdrew her from school but Hawa only replied, "He said that it was enough." Hawa was about twelve years old when she stopped going to school.

When Hawa was sixteen she married Ahmed, her maternal cousin. Ahmed had been working in Saudi Arabia since the early 1970s[1] and came home only briefly to get married. Hawa first lived with her parents, but when her first child was born and she was pregnant with the second, she and Ahmed moved to a separate apartment in Hodeida. Ahmed continued to work in Saudi Arabia.

> He used to go to Saudi Arabia where he worked as a laborer for six months at a time and then came back for some time. When he was away my sister Bilqis stayed with me, and sometimes one of the neighbors, because I was alone and the children were still small. There was a lot of time in which I did not know what to do. I was just sitting at home. First I thought I wanted to learn how to sew or something like that. I had a neighbor next door to me and she knew how to sew. I sat and watched how she did it, and I learned it from her. I borrowed money and I bought a sewing machine myself. I started to sew for my own family. I made trousers, clothes for the girls and for my sisters. They even gave me money when I sewed something.
>
> After a while one of my older sisters said to me, "We have to study." She knew how to read the Quran but she wanted to learn more. And I thought "Yes, why don't I go back to school when I have time?" So together we registered for literacy classes[2] at the

1. In chapter 9 I elaborate on the migration of Yemenis to Saudi Arabia and the Gulf States.

2. Literacy classes are organized for men and women over fifteen years of age, in both rural and urban centers. People who did not have the chance to attend basic education can obtain a primary school certificate via literacy classes. The curriculum is similar to the primary school curriculum, with two primary school grades taught in one year and teaching hours are only two hours per day. The result is that a primary school certificate can be obtained in three years instead of in six.

Yemeni Women's Association.[3] In the beginning we did not attend classes, but we prepared ourselves at home for the exams. We did the exams for the fourth and the fifth grades in that way. For the sixth grade we went to the Association and attended the whole course. Sometimes I took the children with me in the afternoon, or I left them at home. They fell asleep after lunch, and I left them like that from four till six o'clock.[4] When they did not want to sleep I took them with me.

And her husband, did he agree? Hawa answered, "When Ahmed phoned from Saudi Arabia I asked him if it was all right for me to go back to school again, and he said 'Okay.' I could not have done it if he had been present!" I asked her if he would not have allowed her to go to school, but Hawa emphasized that that was not the case; rather the work at home would have been more. "Because he was not present I could go to school, and I obtained the diploma of the sixth grade." And what did her family say about her schooling? "They didn't say anything. Because I was married, if Ahmed agreed, it was okay."

After obtaining her primary-school certificate, Hawa registered at the Teachers Institute[5] in order to continue her studies and become a teacher. But at the time of her registration Abla Nadia,[6] the director of the Teachers Institute, took her aside.

3. The Yemeni Women's Association was North Yemen's main women's organization. It was officially established in 1965 but already existed informally at the time of the Imamate. The YWA mainly organizes literacy classes, sewing classes, handicraft classes, and typing classes for urban women. After unification in 1990, the Northern Yemeni Women's Association and the Southern General Union of Yemeni Women amalgamated into the Yemeni Women's Organization (Badran 1998, 505). For an early account of the activities of the Yemeni Women's Association in Sana'a see Makhlouf (1979, 56–59).

4. Mothers in Yemen commonly leave their children at home, in the company of their father, a relative, or even without anyone to take care of them.

5. The Teachers Institute prepared students with a primary school certificate to become teachers in five years.

6. *Abla* is originally a Turkish word for older sister. In Yemen it is used as a term of respect for women, in particular for teachers.

She said to me, "Look, what do you think, Hawa, would you like to attend a health education course?" I said, "But I have just registered for five more years to become a teacher." You know what she said? She said, "You could first attend this course and benefit from it, then you will know a lot about health care. And then you come back and you can attend the teachers training as well." I thought about it, and I agreed with it. I could benefit from the health education course, it was only for one year, and after that I could go back to school for another five years. And so I decided to attend the course. But before I decided to register for the course, I discussed it with Ahmed. He was at home at that time, and I told him about the health education course, and he approved of it. But I also had to talk to my father because otherwise my family would find out later and my father would say "Oh, she didn't tell us, she does everything on her own." You know what I told my family? I said, "I will only study but I will not work afterwards," because I knew that they were going to say "no" if I had said that I was going to work. I convinced them by saying that I would learn about health care and if someone in the family was ill I could give her an injection, if someone had to give birth I could assist. At least someone would have some background knowledge. And that is why they agreed. So that is how I came to study health education, and after I finished the course I started to work in the health center.

I asked Hawa if she had ever thought about working in health care before and she replied, "In health care, no. Before I hadn't thought about health care. I had only thought about the Teachers Institute because when I finished the sixth grade I thought, 'What will I do?' I knew that my family would not allow me to work in health care. They don't want that. In the past, it was not good for a girl to work in health care." Why was health-care work not good? "I will tell you why, because the girl would stay in the hospital, she had to sleep there while there were men who were going in and out. People would say that she sits together with male nurses and with the doctors. And the patients sometimes walk around, they can sit inside and outside the rooms." I asked Hawa what these ideas were based on, and she said,

People see it happening. For example, if someone takes a sick person to the hospital, this person will sleep at the hospital. My sister was

hospitalized, and her husband would bring her supper,[7] and he sometimes saw male and female nurses putting on a music tape and listening to it together. The people say "If my daughter becomes a nurse,
she will be like them." That is why they had never liked it. Only very
few people allowed it, only families that were not so strict.

Because of these negative ideas about women's work in health care,
Hawa had to hide her job from her family.

My brother was studying in Russia,[8] and when he came back and
heard about it he said, "What are you doing? Are you working as a
sibhiyya [health worker]?" I lied to him and said, "No, I don't work."
After that when my brother came to visit he would say to me, "Are
you working?" And I would answer, "No, I don't work." I would stay
home from work for as long as he was in Hodeida, and only when he
had left I would go to work again.

But while her brother was against her work, Hawa's husband approved
of it.

He knows me and trusts me. But problems arose when there were
training courses in other places or a trip somewhere; then I was not
allowed to go. Ahmed is a humble man but if someone talks to him
then. . . . One time I told him that we would go to a training course
in Dhamar. He agreed and so I went. But when I came back there
had been problems with my family. In my absence my family had
approached my husband saying, "How can you let her go alone to
Dhamar? Are you not a man?" And my husband had answered, "But
she wanted to go." To which my family replied, "If you agree that
she can go, then you have to accompany her. You can rent a house in
Dhamar and join her. You cannot let her go alone!" After that Ahmed
did not allow me to work in the afternoons anymore. He said, "*Khalas*,
that's it, you will not work in the afternoons anymore. Your family

7. In both public and private hospitals in Yemen, family members have to provide food for their hospitalized relatives.
8. Studying in the former USSR and Eastern European countries was common
for people from North and South Yemen.

does not allow it. They are angry and they are saying 'If you can't earn a living for her, then let her come to us and we will take care of her.'" So for a long time I did not work in the afternoons.

Hawa emphasized that, especially during the first years of her employment, the money she earned was not the main reason for her to work. "The most important thing was that I worked, or that I studied, that I obtained a certificate. I wasn't thinking about money before. And then when I obtained a salary, it was great." What did she do with the money? "Nothing, I spent it on the household together with the money Ahmed sent from Saudi Arabia. I bought gold, a ring. We had a *hakba* [savings club], me and the other girls, we used to put part of our salaries in this savings club and every month one of us could buy something expensive for herself." After a number of years Ahmed returned to Yemen permanently.[9] He found employment as an office worker in the army but because of problems with his eyesight he had to leave his job. He became a self-employed worker, writing letters for illiterate people in front of government buildings.[10] In the following years Hawa's income became gradually more important to maintain the household.

> Look, in the beginning it was different, we did not have to pay rent because the apartment we were living in was my sister's property. I could use my salary to buy gold or something else, or when I visited people, for example when I visited someone who had given birth.[11] But at a certain moment we were obliged to pay rent

9. With the decrease in oil prices in the second half of the 1980s, a number of Yemeni migrants working in Saudi Arabia and the Gulf States returned home (see Carapico and Myntti 1991, 25; ESCWA Secretariat 1993/94, 110–11).

10. Because of the high illiteracy rates in Yemen, literate people (men) offer their services to illiterate people, in particular in front of government offices, where letters or forms have to be handed in.

11. It is a Yemeni custom to give money to the mother of a newborn baby. For a detailed description of the special visits paid to mothers and their newborn babies see Dorsky (1986, 158–64).

and that is why we moved to this piece of land, which we already owned. Now I try to save money to build the house. We use the money Ahmed earns for daily expenditures, and I use my income to construct our house.

Hawa had worked a couple of years as a *murshida* when the project staff proposed that two *murshidat* of the first group would become heads of two health centers in town, while the others would be upgraded to midwife.

I said that I would like to become a midwife because I knew that if I chose to become a head of clinic Ahmed would not approve of it. I also discussed it with him and he said, "I don't want you to be head of clinic, a head of clinic has to receive men, she has to go to the Health Office, she has to talk to men. People want to meet the head of clinic, they want papers from her, I don't want that. It is better if you study midwifery, then you will always be with women." I agreed and informed the project team. The idea was that I would study midwifery at the Health Manpower Institute in Hodeida. But there they said that I could only attend the three-year course in midwifery. I was not allowed to skip the first year even though I had already attended a one-year course in health education.

In addition, the *murshidat* who wanted to study midwifery needed an intermediate-school certificate, implying another three years of basic education. Hawa didn't give in, and she obtained her intermediate certificate, finishing all exams for three grades in one year. Yet it did not help. The negotiations between the Health Manpower Institute and the project did not lead to a satisfying solution, and only in 1995 did Hawa get the chance to attend a three-year midwifery course in the city of Taiz, three hours away from Hodeida by car. But Ahmed did not agree; he found Taiz too far away, and he did not want his wife to spend three years away from home.

In the meantime Hawa had accepted the offer to become head of the mother and child health section of one of the main health centers in Hodeida. What did Ahmed think about that?

I spoke to him, I said, "Look, you said that all the heads of clinics receive men, but the other heads of clinics, like Muna and Riham, they don't receive any men." And that is true. They don't go to other places; they are always in the health center. All the work is in the center, and the project team brings them everything. I knew that. I said "You excluded me from the responsibility. I didn't study midwifery and I didn't become head of clinic although I was better than the others." I said, "Come and have a look at the center." I let him sit in the office, and I said "Look, they are all young women." I introduced all the *murshidat* to him in the office, instead of allowing him to go around the center. And after that I explained to him, "We have a curative section in the health center as well, it is not like the center before where only preventive mother and child care services were offered." In the curative section a doctor is working and there is a laboratory. But the curative and the preventive sections of the center are separate from each other. The doctor is responsible for the curative section and I am responsible for the preventive section.

In this way Hawa tried to convince Ahmed that the work she was doing was respectable because women and men were segregated in the health center, even though there were male staff as well.

I asked Hawa whether her father and her brother were still against her work, and she explained,

Look, it was not my father who was making problems, it was someone else in my family. The husband of my sister has a high position and he said, "How can she work like that?" Even my sister would sometimes say to me that it was not good and not necessary for me to work. And they influenced my father. Eventually I said to him, "Look, father, you are right that I can get money from you when I am in need of it, but I cannot continuously ask for money. And you know that Ahmed is not like you and like my brothers, you are different because you are well off. The whole family is well off. But Ahmed's circumstances are difficult and he has had bad luck. *Ma sha allah*,[12] when my brothers were still small, Ahmed was already in the army. And now my brothers all

12. *Ma sha allah* literally means "what God wants/intends" and is used to express surprise.

have high positions: one is in the general military staff, the other is an engineer, one is a finance officer, and Ahmed is still as he was before. Should I stay home and ask for money all the time? I am married and I have children, there is no need to make my life more difficult. I can divide my time between my family and my work, and nobody has to interfere in that." And then my father said, "Okay, I won't interfere anymore, and you can do everything you want to do and whatever you think is right." That happened about two years ago. Since then there haven't been anymore problems.

Although Ahmed sometimes complains that Hawa is working too much, she continues to succeed in keeping him happy. "I sometimes stay at home on Thursday afternoons and then we spend time together." And he knows that the family cannot do without her salary, which is being used to finish the construction of the house. Moreover, all the children are at school, and school expenditure is high. Hakma, Hawa's eldest daughter, has almost finished secondary school and wants to study medicine. "I really hope that my daughters will be able to study, and that they do not have to face the same problems I had. As for marriage, we will try to find the right person for Hakma, someone she likes. We have already engaged her to her cousin, according to our family customs, but she won't get married quickly. If she decides that she doesn't like the man, we'll put an end to the engagement."

At the time of the interview, in 1997, Hawa had joined an upgrading course for *murshidat* to become community midwives. After completing this course she was appointed head of MCH services in al-Tahrir, the oldest health center in the city. In 1998, Ahmed stopped working completely as he was nearly blind. From that moment on, Hawa became the sole provider. She receives a government salary for her work as head of MCH services in the health center in the mornings, and she earns an additional income in the afternoons working at the registration counter of the same clinic.[13] When I visited Hawa and

13. Since 1995, a number of government health centers in Hodeida offer curative and laboratory services in the afternoons, financed by well-known merchants who are also members of Parliament.

her family in April 2002, Ahmed had become completely blind, and Hawa was still working as head of MCH services in al-Tahrir. They had another daughter in September 2000. Hawa told me that her relatives had accepted her professional life and even expressed their appreciation of the fact that she is employed and provides for her husband and children. Without her salary the family would have been lost. The engagement of her eldest daughter ended after a year and a half. Hakma did not get along with her cousin, who was not interested in studying or working, while she herself is a dedicated student. Hakma is now enrolled at the Faculty of Nursing in Hodeida. She would have preferred to go to Sana'a to pursue studies at the Faculty of Medicine and become a doctor, but Ahmed would not allow his daughter to study in Sana'a, even though the family has relatives there who could take care of her. He did not want Hakma to leave her parental home before she was married. Boundaries have shifted but gender ideologies have not changed completely.

"I Just Wanted to Learn"

Families, Fathers, and the Access to Education

Hawa was born in Hodeida but originally came from a tribal family (*qaba'il*) from the area of al-Mahwit, in the highlands west of Sana'a.[14] Her stories about schooling, her marriage, and the way her family reacted to her work as a *murshida* are examples of *qaba'il* notions concerning gender and labor. Tribeswomen (*qabiliyyat*) living in rural areas are responsible for a major part of the agricultural and livestock work in addition to their domestic tasks such as cleaning, cooking, washing, and child care. In the past (and still often today), they were denied any participation in public affairs because their modesty represented the honor of the tribe and therefore had to be protected. Women from the upper classes (the *sada* and *quda*) were sometimes educated at home,

---

14. For a detailed description of the life of *qabili* women in a village in the governorate of al-Mahwit, see Destremau (1990).

but tribeswomen had no access to education. The heavy workload of women in rural areas and the lack of separate girls' schools and female teachers affected women's access to education. In addition, gender ideologies in which girls' education was not deemed necessary, as a girl was supposed to marry and move out of the parental house, affected the education of tribeswomen. Although the ideology of the male breadwinner was also part of elite notions of gender and labor, education was an important status marker for the elite and contributed to the prestige of families (vom Bruck 1988, 398). Elite families were also the first to send their daughters to public schools at the end of the civil war in the 1960s. Access to education for all Yemenis, both men and women, was propagated as one of the main roads to development. According to vom Bruck, elite values such as learning and knowledge have nowadays gained general validity in Yemeni society, yet although school enrollment of girls has increased considerably since 1970, a large number of girls still do not have access to education.[15]

In the 1950s Hawa's family moved to Hodeida, where her father first joined the army but later set up his own business. Her family story is an example of upward mobility, and of the increasing importance of economic class over social status after the revolution of 1962 (Carapico 1996, 88). The overthrow of the Imamate brought an end to the power basis and privileges of the aristocracy. Social status was no longer a guarantee of economic success but was increasingly being replaced by the right educational certificates, the right political connections, and money (Carapico and Myntti 1991, 25). The result was that people with *qaba'il* and lower social backgrounds could gain

---

15. Between 1970 and 1994 the total number of children enrolled in primary school grew elevenfold, from less than 250,000 in 1970 to almost 2.75 million in 1994 (in view of the rapid population growth of 3.7 percent per year, this is 55 percent of the children six through fifteen years of age). Yet female enrollment has grown much more slowly than male enrollment. Only around 37 percent of girls in aged six through fifteen are enrolled in school. Enrollment in rural areas lags far behind enrollment in urban areas. According to the 1994 census, only 14 percent of six-year-old girls in rural areas were enrolled in school (UNICEF 1998, vol. 3, 3).

economic status, while people from *sada* and *quda* families sometimes lost economic power. Hawa's father became a rich merchant owning shops and houses in Sana'a, Taiz, and Hodeida, and he was even able to send his sons abroad to study. His daughters were allowed to attend Quran school, and some of them also went for a couple of years to primary school, but after that they had to stay at home. Whereas upper-class women in the cities increasingly went to school and sometimes took up paid work in the educational and administrative sector, the mobility of tribeswomen diminished in urban areas. With migration to the city, tribeswomen lost their agricultural tasks, and their responsibilities became restricted to domestic work and child care (see also Lackner 1995, 86).

Yet migration to the city could also have positive effects for tribeswomen as some of them benefited from the increased educational opportunities after the revolution. Hawa was born in 1962, the year of the revolution, and her longing for education can be attributed to the revolutionary slogans about the importance of education. She attended Quran school and four years of primary school, after which her father withdrew her from school. Hawa explained that four years of primary education was deemed sufficient for girls, as they were then able to read and understand religious instructions. Access to written texts, in particular religious texts, still meant an increase of status: being able to read and recite the Quran was an important sign of being a good Muslim. Because women were seen as the primary transmitters of cultural and religious values, women's education was to some extent allowed. With the increased schooling of children in urban areas, mothers had obtained the new task of assisting children with their homework.[16]

16. In a study about the impact of literacy classes on women in Hodeida it was found that the main reasons adult women wanted to become literate were: to be able to read the Quran and know how to pray; to be able to read books, letters, or anything else; and to assist children with their homework. Quranic study and Islamic education are also part of literacy classes in Yemen and most liked by women attending the classes (de Regt et al. 1996).

Hawa had attended four years of primary school, but there were other women in the first training course for *murshidat* who had not been allowed to go to school at all. Muna was also born in 1962, and she told me that her brothers went to school but the girls did not. "My father did not want us to go to school" is the only answer I received when I asked her why she did not go to school. Her sisters accepted her father's decision but Muna secretly went to school in the mornings when her father was away at work. She told me proudly that she was able to finish primary school without her father knowing. Riham's father had worked in Ethiopia and returned to Yemen at the end of the 1960s. The family first settled in al-Baidha, her father's parental town, where Riham was born in 1969. Six years later they moved to Hodeida, where her father took up work as a factory laborer and her mother started to sell small foodstuffs to make ends meet. Riham has two brothers and a sister. Both brothers finished secondary school; the older one became a mechanic and the younger one finished university. But her sister only finished three years of primary school, and Riham herself six years. "In our family girls normally go to school till the sixth grade and then they stay at home."

But in the first group of *murshidat* there were also women whose fathers were not against schooling and who did have the chance to continue their education. Two of them were Hawa's nieces, daughters of one of her older sisters, and therefore sharing the same family background. Hanan and Mariam are ten years younger than Hawa, born in the early 1970s, and both went to school in Hodeida. The fact that they were born after the revolution may be one of the main reasons for their easier access to education: girls' education, in particular in urban areas, was more common at the end of the 1970s, owing to the promotional activities of the government. Moreover, the mother of Hanan and Mariam, Hawa's sister, was a fervent adherent of women's education and attended literacy classes at the Yemeni Women's Association. Their father was also in favor of their schooling; he himself had not had the chance to go to school and regretted it. The two sisters attended three years of primary education in a regular school and then decided to continue their education at the Yemeni Women's

Association because it was closer to their house.[17] Two other participants in the first training course for *murshidat* were the sisters Najwa
and Nadhira, from an Adeni family who came to Hodeida at the end of
the 1960s. Their father had studied law and was a high official in one
of the ministries in the newly established socialist state; their mother
was illiterate. Their father was soon forced to leave South Yemen and
settled in Hodeida, where he opened a printing office. A product of
the socialist revolution, he had sent his children to school in Aden
and continued to do so in Hodeida. Najwa's father had outspoken
ideas about the future occupations of his children, and he encouraged Najwa to become a doctor. Despite his encouragement, Najwa
and Nadhira left school of their own free will after the third class of
intermediate school. When I asked her why she left school, Najwa
answered that she didn't like school anymore, an answer I was given
in many cases when I tried to find out why young women left school
of their own accord. In the eyes of these young women, a number of
years of intermediate school was enough. They were not interested
in continuing their education. Some of them stayed at home, while
others attended vocational training in nursing, midwifery, sewing,
hairdressing, and the like. Najwa registered at the Health Manpower
Institute and attended a nursing course for a couple of months but
then switched to the *murshidat* training course.

This group of *murshidat* shows the variety of opinions in Yemen on
women's education. Family background (in particular social and economic status), household composition, women's position in the household, age and generation, historical context, and personal preferences
all determine women's access to education. It is particularly important
to look at family and household strategies with regard to women's education and employment. In patrilineal systems, parents of lower-class
families often support their (eldest) sons to continue schooling, while

17. The fact that there was no school close to their house is an indication of the
limited number of schools available at the end of the 1970s, in particular for girls. In
1977, there were four primary schools in Hodeida and one secondary school. In 1985,
the total number of schools had increased to fifteen.

the education of girls is seen as less important. The rationale behind this practice in many cases is that daughters will leave their parental families when they marry, while sons are supposed to support their parental family financially after they get married. Sons therefore need better jobs, which requires education (see Salaff 1981). According to Ibrahim (1985, 260), "individuals employ strategies for maximizing their interests within the family context, and families in turn adopt collective strategies for confronting larger society." She therefore argues for a more comprehensive analysis of family strategies in relation to women's education (and employment), and a look at what she calls "adaptive family strategies." I am interested in the views of the young women who attended the first training course for *murshidat*. What did they think about education and employment? Which aspirations, hopes and expectations did they cherish about their future lives? And which strategies did they employ to realize their ambitions?

Education as the Road to Self-Development

Although Hawa liked going to school and was even one of the best pupils in her class, she accepted her father's decision and left primary school after four years. Only after she married and had two children did she start to think about studying again. She said that she was bored at home and wanted to fill her spare time. She first learned sewing, and then her sister, the one who was a fervent adherent of women's education, encouraged her to obtain her primary-school certificate at the Yemeni Women's Association. Hawa presented it as if she had not thought of it herself, but her desire to learn is a recurring theme in her life story. Other participants in the first course for *murshidat* shared this desire, like Muna, who secretly went to school when her father was not at home.

"I just wanted to learn" was an expression I often heard during the interviews with the first *murshidat*. It was also given as the main motivation for attending the *murshidat* training course. Education was promoted as a gateway to development. It would free Yemen from inequality, status differentials, poverty, and underdevelopment.

A murshida *with two of her children at the health center in Hodeida.*

Although the government made no great effort to develop girls' education, the revolutionary discourse about education as the gateway to development impressed many Yemeni women. In particular, girls and women in urban areas became interested in education, but also women in rural areas increasingly saw the need for schooling, if not for themselves then for their daughters (see Dorsky and Stevenson 1995, 316). In a survey carried out in 1978, many girls and young women of school age expressed their educational aspirations, hopes, and expectations for their futures (318). While they all expected to marry, they also expressed the wish to continue their education and have jobs as teachers or nurses. Yet when the same women were visited again in 1992, most of them had left school, married young, and had several children (322). They had not been able to fulfill their desire to study and many regretted the choices they had made or their families had made for them.

The ambitions and experiences of the first group of *murshidat* are interesting in this respect. These young women came from families in which education and paid work for women was in general negatively valued. Yet they all wanted to learn, and some even had the ambition to become teachers or nurses. After completing primary school, they all planned to continue their education. In the late 1960s and early 1970s, the government established various types of vocational training centers to train professional cadres. Technical institutes, teacher training colleges, and health institutes offered training courses to people with at least primary-school certificates. Four of the first *murshidat* had registered at the Teachers Institute, which was the only school offering intermediate education to girls. Two of the *murshidat* were too late for registration at the institute and had to wait a year until they could register again. Two others were sitting idle at home while they wanted to work in health care, and one had registered at the Health Manpower Institute. Some of the women wanted to become teachers, while others considered the Teachers Institute to be a next step in continuing their education. Hanan and Bilqis, for example, wanted to become doctors, and finishing the Teachers Institute would qualify them to attend the university. Teaching and medicine were some of the very few respectable possibilities open to women who wanted a profession. In addition, the ambition to become a teacher, a nurse, or even a doctor, must be understood in a context where there were limited examples of female employment outside the home. "Many young schoolgirls of the late seventies had vaguely formed high educational goals but no realistic idea of what would be involved to pursue them seriously" (Dorsky and Stevenson 1995, 317). The fact that these young women showed an interest in becoming nurses is remarkable in view of the negative status of nursing in Yemen. While teaching has a relatively high status, as it involves a certain level of education and guarantees gender segregation, nursing has a low status because of the implied contacts with bodies and bodily fluids as well as the contacts with unrelated men as patients and colleagues (see chapter 3). Yet both teaching and nursing are professions that are compatible with conventional attitudes regarding women's work, as they are seen as an extension of women's work at home. In addition, the interest of women in becoming nurses also shows that women do not automatically adopt negative views regarding respectable work but adhere to their own interests.

The majority of the *murshidat* (seven out of nine) did not want to study or work because they needed an income but because they wanted to develop themselves. Almost all the women who attended the first course for *murshidat* had taken the initiative to start or continue primary education and had fulfilled their desire for schooling, sometimes after a period of staying at home. Except for the two Adeni sisters, they had all decided to attend literacy classes at the Yemeni Women's Association in Hodeida, and in doing so succeeded in gaining a primary-school certificate. The fact that they took the initiative to join these classes shows their determination, and this determination is very important in explaining why they were also willing to join the *murshidat* training course. In a way a preselection had already taken place before they joined the *murshidat* course, a preselection of women who used their "agentive power" to improve their situations. While other women who had the same desire for schooling may have failed in their attempts to attend school, this group of young women had been able to pick up schooling again. And even though most of them did not intend to enter paid work, their participation in literacy classes turned out to be a crucial step in the development of their professional lives.

The fact that the first *murshidat* often emphasized that they "only wanted to learn," or that they wanted to develop themselves (*ashti atawwar nafsi*) is an example of the (Yemeni) notion that being educated is equal to being developed. In addition, it should be regarded as a strategy to attend school without challenging the dominant gender division of labor. By stressing that their only goal was to receive education, they intended to make clear that they did not have other plans beyond being educated, such as taking up paid labor, and that their schooling was acceptable because it did not challenge the ideologies of the male provider and of gender segregation. I will come back to this strategy later. In a way, the first *murshidat* can be compared to Yemeni upper-class women who enter paid employment for personal fulfillment or with social ideals in mind. Yet whereas upper-class women are often encouraged to gain an education and sometimes to enter paid employment, most of the first *murshidat* had to overcome many obstacles before their schooling and work was accepted.

Room to Maneuver

Hawa's story is a strong example of the ways in which some of the *murshidat* gradually shifted dominant gender boundaries in order to fulfill their desires and ambitions. They did not challenge these boundaries in a direct way but they cleverly created and made use of the available room to maneuver, accepting gender prescriptions to a certain extent but stretching them whenever possible. As a young girl, Hawa accepted being taken out of school, although she liked school very much. She married the son of her mother's sister. Ahmed was not rich, and he was not highly educated. He was a migrant worker spending most of his time in Saudi Arabia. For Yemeni women living in rural areas, male labor migration often had negative consequences, in particular because of their increased workload (see Adra 1983; Myntti 1984). But for women in urban areas, male labor migration could work out positively, as Hawa's story shows. Hawa clearly benefited from the fact that Ahmed was abroad by taking several initiatives to shape her own life. She made use of the available space for maneuvering to take up sewing and attend literacy classes, and later she even entered paid work. Hawa is convinced that she would not have been able to continue her schooling if Ahmed had been at home, not because he would not have allowed her to go back to school but because she would have had more household responsibilities.

As mentioned before, Hawa's statement that she "just wanted to learn" can be regarded as a strategy; in theory she endorsed the dominant gender ideology of the male breadwinner, emphasizing that she was only interested in studying and not in obtaining paid work, but in practice she took advantage of her participation in the training course for *murshidat* to enter paid employment. Hawa's statement in the introduction of this chapter is another example of the strategies she employed to shift gradually the boundaries of the dominant gender ideology. "You should never neglect your husband. Continue to give him the attention he has always received, so that you don't give him a chance to complain," she told me. As long as she was able to perform her tasks as spouse and mother, her husband would accept her work and not complain. Many other *murshidat* repeated this statement to me, showing the efforts they had to make to reconcile their paid work with their domestic tasks.

The fact that (male) relatives did not complain as long as the *murshidat* performed their domestic tasks is also related to another important Yemeni notion. The *murshidat* were able to create room to maneuver by making use of the notion that what people are not directly confronted with is acceptable, even though they may know what is going on. Hawa, and the other *murshidat*, made strategic use of this notion, as I will illustrate with a number of examples. First of all, Hawa's husband was abroad when she restarted her education. She asked his permission and he agreed by phone, but he did not see what it meant in practice. Muna also made use of this notion; she attended primary school in the mornings when her father, who was fiercely against his daughters' schooling, was not at home. As long as he did not see that she was going to school, there were no problems, and even her mother and her sisters quietly accepted what she was doing. Hawa's answer to her brother's question about whether she was working in health care is a third example. She denied that she was working as a *murshida*, but as soon as he left she continued her work. Her brother was not living in Hodeida, and as long as he did not see that she was working, there were no problems, although he may have known about it.

Some of Hawa's actions can be seen as consciously applied strategies, with a clear goal in mind from the outset, but other initiatives she took can better be regarded as part of a slow but steady process of which she herself could not know the final outcome. Hawa's own ambitions and aspirations also shifted gradually, with the gradual steps she took to shift the boundaries of the dominant gender ideology. After marrying and having two children, she started to think about possible ways to fill her free time. When she had learned sewing she decided to go to school again, and when she finished primary school she intended to continue studying at the Teachers Institute. Filling her free time was no longer her main motivation; she now intended to work as a teacher. Yet in her search for a possible future profession, she conformed to the dominant ideology on women's paid work, as endorsed by her family, and asserted that she did not attend the *murshidat* training course with the aim of working in health care. Health-care work was not seen as respectable in her family, and Hawa shared this opinion. Therefore teaching was the only option left. But although she joined the *murshidat* training course without the intention of becoming an employed *murshida*, she started to like the work so much that she again created room to maneuver and gradually shifted the boundaries of what was culturally acceptable. Although her family was opposed to education and paid employment for women, in particular in health care, Hawa ended up managing one of the largest health centers in the city, where male staff were also working. Hawa's story shows her ability to shift the terms of what was seen as respectable for women of her background, and in doing so she created new ways of living for herself and for others. Moreover, the fact that the *murshidat* profession was a new and unknown type of work in Yemen enabled the women to negotiate the boundaries of what was culturally acceptable, a topic I will elaborate on in the next chapter.

6

The First Phase of the Project,
1985–1988

HAWA WAS PART of the first group of nine *murshidat* trained in 1985–86. While the emphasis in the previous chapter was on the backgrounds of the women trained during the first course and the motivation and the strategies they used to attend the training course, this chapter focuses on the way in which the first *murshidat* were selected, the organization of the training course, their duties and the status of their work, and in particular the ways in which they shifted social boundaries by taking up a new type of paid work for women. My main argument throughout this chapter is that the selection, training, and employment of the first group of *murshidat* was not so much the result of well-planned projects as of the particular confluence of circumstances. The fact that the first *murshidat* gradually shifted social boundaries was also not intentional but the result of the ways in which they cleverly made use of the available opportunities, on the basis of which they also shifted their own aspirations and ambitions.

"We Didn't Know What a *Murshida* Was"

An Arbitrary Selection?

In chapter 4, I described the changing ideas in the project for the recruitment and selection of urban primary health-care workers. The initial idea had been to train male primary health-care workers to be assisted by female volunteers. But after discussions between the project management and the director-general, it was decided to train women rather than men. One of the requirements was that the women come from the project area itself, but no recruitment methods were mentioned except for the fact that the Yemeni Women's Association in Hodeida could assist. Abla Nadia, the director of the Yemeni Women's Association in Hodeida, was in contact with many women and could assist with finding women willing and able to become *murshidat*. In addition, the project managers assumed that her respectability would guarantee the respectability of the women. Cees van Oordt said, "We needed women of a reliable background, educated, of a respectable family because otherwise people would say 'Oh, you are the daughter of so and so, no, we cannot let you come into our house.' Everyone knows each other and one has to be careful."[1]

Abla Nadia, who is now director of a girls' school in Hodeida, vividly remembered the project's request for assistance in the recruitment of suitable women for the training course. When I asked her about the way in which the women were selected, she said, "I did not approach anyone in particular, I just went to all the classes and told the girls that there was an opportunity to be trained as *murshidat* for a Dutch project. I explained that the training course would take one year and that they would be employed afterwards. I encouraged everyone to go; I did not make a selection." Whereas Hawa had told me that she was individually approached, Abla Nadia denied this. According to her, Hawa was one of the few women who showed interest in the *murshidat* training course. Most women did not believe that they would be employed after attending the training course because they only had a primary-school certificate, and therefore they did not apply.

Hawa encouraged her younger sister, Bilqis, and her two nieces, Hanan and Mariam, to join the course, and she also persuaded her friend Amina to join. She had met Amina during the literacy classes

1. Interview with C. J. Royer, June 21, 1999. The translation from the Dutch is mine.

at the Women's Association, and they had become friends. Amina wanted to become a nurse, and after receiving her primary-school certificate she was going to register at the Health Manpower Institute. But on that same day, she met Hawa in the street. Hawa told her about the *murshidat* training course and convinced her to join the course. Hawa also knew Riham and Muna, the other two women who joined the course, through the Yemeni Women's Association. Even though they had not been in the same class, they were acquainted with each other. Riham had heard about the *murshidat* training course from a cousin who was in contact with Abla Nadia. Only Najwa and Nadhira, the two Adeni sisters, did not know the others and had not attended literacy classes at the Yemeni Women's Association. They heard about the *murshidat* training course from a male acquaintance.

These connections indicate Hawa's essential role in the formation of the first group of *murshidat;* at least three other women joined the course because she persuaded them. It was easier for her and for the other young women to attend a course knowing that friends or female relatives would also participate. In addition, enlarging the group made the women feel stronger entering the unknown terrain of the *murshidat* training course, as none of them knew exactly what a *murshida* was and what the course implied. The fact that most of the young women knew each other may have contributed to the coherence of the group, keeping the group together while they were being trained.

Although nine young women were interested in the training course, they did not meet the selection criteria as formulated in the plan of operations. The only criterion they met was that they had finished primary school. First, none of the women came from Ghulail. They all lived in the old neighborhoods of Hodeida, and they came from (lower) middle-class families, not the families that lived in Ghulail. And second, while the project staff had wanted to train women eighteen years and older, preferably who had children, only three of them met that criterion. Hawa, Muna, and Amina were in their early twenties and had children, but the other six were under eighteen and unmarried. In order to be admitted to the course they had said that they were eighteen years old, but they were in fact much younger. Hanan was the youngest of the group; she was only fourteen. The project management did not request birth certificates,[2] and ages were not checked. A primary-school certificate and a certificate of good behavior,[3] signed by the *'aqil* (government representative in the neighborhood), were the only two concrete documents requested. Fatima Salem, the supervisor of the course who was appointed after the selection had taken place, said, "The selection was arbitrary. They did not select the women well. They did not look at the criteria, no, everyone was happy as long as the women agreed, whoever they were. The main thing was that they knew how to read and write." Abla Nadia confirmed this statement when I asked her about the selection criteria. "Anyone who wanted to join the training course was welcome. There were no other selection criteria than that they knew how to read and write."

The fact that these nine candidates were admitted to the course despite not meeting the selection criteria shows that practical considerations were often more important than policies and project plans.[4] The project team was happy that there were women willing and able to attend the *murshidat* training course, and almost immediately they dropped three of the four selection criteria. The project was in need of women, and any woman willing to join the training course was received with open arms. In addition, Yemeni health administrators said that there were no suitable women present in Ghulail who could be trained as *murshidat* because the large majority of the women in the squatter area were illiterate. The Dutch project staff adopted this view and, as mentioned before, little was done to get to know the women in the area and check whether there were eligible women available. In 1986, the results of the baseline study

2. Registering newborn babies and obtaining birth certificates are only recently becoming common practices in Yemen.

3. A certificate of good behavior *(shahada husn sir wa suluk)* is an official document that states that a person does not have a police record. It is requested of every person seeking employment.

4. Justice (1986) comes to a similar conclusion in her book on a rural health-care project financed and coordinated by the World Health Organization in Nepal.

carried out in Ghulail confirmed the prevailing idea that there were very few literate women in Ghulail: of the 165 women interviewed, only one woman was literate (Buringa 1986, 26).

Explaining the Work

All the women who were interested in the training course were first asked to come and see Abla Nadia, who told them briefly about the Dutch project and the ideas behind the course. For some of the women, taking the initiative to get information about the course and finding out about the possibility of joining the course was a big step. Muna, for example, came from a conservative family in which women hardly ever left the neighborhood. "I didn't know many places in Hodeida, I didn't know the *suq* and the shops in the city center, and the first time I went to a party I was surprised to see such a completely different world." Muna was the one who secretly went to school, which shows that she had already taken steps to look beyond the boundaries of her family life in her childhood. Unfortunately, her primary-school certificate got lost, and after marrying and having two children, she decided to attend the literacy classes at the Yemeni Women's Association in order to obtain a new certificate. "When I married I moved to another area where people were less strict, and when I saw that many women were going to school I decided to join them. My husband encouraged me to go, and my sister took care of my children."

While working toward her new primary-school certificate Muna had acquired a taste for studying and wanted to go on to the Teachers Institute. But she was too late for registration and had to wait another year.[5] Muna was upset and did not know what to do until Abla Nadia

---

5. In the past thirty years the qualification necessary to enter training institutes has gradually become higher. While a primary-school certificate used to be sufficient in the 1980s, nowadays at least intermediate school (nine years of basic education) has to be completed before one can enter a college or an institute. Only people with secondary-school certificates can enter university. The demand to attend vocational training institutes, colleges, and universities has increased tremendously resulting in fierce competition.

asked her to come to her office. She told me how special it was for her to go by herself to an office: "The first time I went out of the house without someone accompanying me was when I went to register at the Teachers Institute, and the second time was when I went to see Abla Nadia about the *murshidat* training course. And then Abla Nadia referred me to the Health Office and I was really scared. I did not know what kind of office it was and what people did there. Really I had no idea." Muna told me this vividly, amazed at her own lack of knowledge at that time, when the Health Office is such an important part of her life nowadays, where she, as a head of clinic, goes to meetings to get money and hand in her bills, and to discuss problems with the department director. Other women, like Hawa, had traveled more in and outside Hodeida and were better acquainted with government offices and the like. Muna said, "If you look at Hawa, she comes from a well-known family and she had heard and seen a lot of things. She had visited the *suq* and the shops and she knew where the factory was. She had been to Taiz and to Sana'a. But I only knew the road to my father's village, that was the only other place I had been to outside Hodeida."

Taking the step to join the *murshidat* training course was a leap in the dark for all the nine women as none of them had much idea what being a *murshida* implied. Before being admitted to the course, they were asked to come to the Yemeni Women's Association to meet the project team and to be informed about the aims of the project, the course, and their future work. Cees van Oordt formulated the aim of the meeting as follows: "I had to tell them a story that was convincing about what they were supposed to be doing." It was the first time that *murshidat* were going to be trained in an urban setting. It was a pilot project, and therefore nobody knew exactly what the *murshidat* were going to do, least of all the young women. "We didn't know what a *murshida* was" was the expression almost all of them used. "We had never heard about *murshidat* before they told us about it." Muna thought that a *murshida* was the same as a nurse, and Hanan wanted to become a doctor. Bilqis hoped that she would learn how to give injections, how to apply wound dressings, and how to assist at deliveries. And Najwa said, "We wanted to attend a *murshidat* training course, but we wondered what they meant with *murshidat*. A *murshida* can be anything." Amina said, "They did not make clear what the field of work would be. They only spoke about health education. They said that we had to inform women about the importance of vaccinations for children." Although the young women were convinced that they could benefit from the course, and that they would be trained in health care, the exact contents of their future work remained mysterious to them. The fact that the main tasks of a *murshida* were in preventive health care was not important in their eyes; most of them considered the *murshidat* training course as a continuation of their educational trajectory, and a way to develop themselves.

Another reason for concern was the place of work. None of the young women had ever heard about the squatter area of Ghulail. They all told me the same story:

> The project managers spoke to us and said, "You will work as *murshidat*, you will do home visits in Ghulail," and we said, "Oh, no, we are not going outside the city. We will only work in Hodeida but outside Hodeida, no." They said, "But Ghulail is part of Hodeida!" It was the first time we had heard about Ghulail. I thought, "Where is that village? I don't know that village."

Some of them knew other parts of the city, like Hawa, who visited her family in other neighborhoods and who traveled to other cities, while young women like Muna hardly ever left their neighborhood. But none of them had heard of the squatter areas on the outskirts of town, let alone visited them.

These new ideas of becoming a *murshida* and working in an unknown place had to be discussed at home first. "The project team sat with us and asked us what we thought about this course. We said, 'Okay, but we first have to talk with our family.'" The project management requested official approval by the legal guardian (*wali al-amr*) of each young woman, usually her father or in his absence her eldest brother. According to Fatima, the guardians approved on the strict condition that the women would not work in the afternoon and would not work or have contact with men. The project staff agreed on these two points. The fact that the activities of the *murshidat* focused on

MCH services was used as the main argument supporting the condition that they would not be in touch with men, while the fact that it was a training course for women helped as well. Najwa said, "We liked it that we were all girls." She had earlier started training to be a nurse but did not like the fact that boys and girls were together in the same class and had stopped attending the course after two months. Now she had found a course for women only.

Halfway through the training course the *murshidat* were asked to participate as interviewers in the baseline survey, and in time home visits in the afternoon became a common part of their work. These activities were clearly in contradiction to the promises made to the women's male relatives and were therefore the most sensitive part of the work. Throughout the duration of the project, there were often problems with male relatives who did not allow their daughters, wives, or sisters to do home visits in the afternoon. But boundaries gradually shifted in this respect.

Attending the Course

When I asked the first *murshidat* to tell me about the training course, they almost always recalled the same experiences. The first experience that had impressed them was that they were picked up from home in a project car and were driven home afterwards. The fact that transportation was organized and paid for by the project was very important for the status of the *murshidat*. First, the availability of project transportation meant that the young women did not have to pay transportation costs. But what was more important was the fact that they did not have to take public transportation and harm their reputations because they had to move in public in order to go to work. The project car that stopped daily in front of their houses and honked, audible and visible for all the neighbors, had the opposite effect. It increased their status because being taken to and from work by a driver in a brand new four-wheel-drive car was usually restricted to women of the upper classes. Female employees of factories, banks, and government offices are also sometimes taken to and from work, but they go to work in buses and in the company of their male colleagues. While these women workers benefit from the transportation made available to them, it also affects their reputation, as they are daily in visible contact with unrelated men.

The first group of *murshidat* was clearly proud of being taken to and from work by a project car, and its importance is comparable to the modes of image making used by data processors in Barbados. For Barbadian women working in data processing, the ability to assume new styles of dress is very important to construct a modern identity. These new styles of dress give them a "professional" look and therefore separate them from other female factory workers, even though their salaries and labor circumstances are as bad as those of others (Freeman 2000). For the *murshidat*, the use of the project car gave their work a similar touch of modernity and the ability to create a new identity, separating them from working-class women. Yet the provision of project transportation also had negative aspects. The intimacy of the daily car rides and the frequent contacts between a male driver and the *murshidat* affected practices of gender segregation, which could harm the reputation of the *murshidat*. I will elaborate later on the problems with male drivers and on the measures taken to avoid these problems. However, these problems did not often occur at the beginning of the project, and the first group of *murshidat* emphasized the positive aspects of the availability of project transportation.

Another important fact most *murshidat* recalled was that the course was held on the top floor of the main hospital in Hodeida, where the Health Manpower Institute (HMI) was located at that time. Although the HMI was not responsible for the organization of the *murshidat* course, one of its classrooms was used for theory classes. There are a number of reasons the *murshidat* almost always mentioned that the training course took place on the top floor of the hospital. First of all, the HMI had a high status because it was the main training institute for health cadres. Second, the hospital was a well-known place, and despite the low status of nursing it must have impressed the *murshidat* that they were receiving their training in the hospital, which shows the ambiguous character of being trained in health care, a topic I will return to in the next section. And third, the HMI moved in 1987 to a new location on the outskirts of town and continued to be an important location where the *murshidat* often went for refresher courses. Because they knew that I was only acquainted with the new building of the HMI, they liked to recall the early years in which the HMI was still on the top floor of the hospital.

The training course was divided into a theoretical and a practical part. The theoretical part took place in the HMI, and sometimes in the health center at al-Tahrir, located in the city center close to the *suq*. The al-Tahrir health center was the only health center the *murshidat* had been to before they entered the training course, and it was their main point of reference for what their future work would entail. Those who had children had been to al-Tahrir for vaccinations and other preventive health care, while the unmarried women had sometimes accompanied their female relatives to al-Tahrir. It was a big and busy health center, with lots of rooms and personnel, and a waiting room full of people. People from all over the city and even from outside Hodeida came to al-Tahrir for basic health services. In the 1980s, USAID financed part of the running costs of the health center because it made use of it for the training of rural health cadres.[6]

The teachers in the *murshidat* training course were (male) doctors from the HMI, doctors working in the hospital and in the health center, and people from the Health Office. A number of midwives and female nurses were involved as well. The practical part of the course consisted of on-the-job training in the Ghulail health center by Thera de Haas and Veronica Thijsen, who were then in charge of MCH and midwifery services in the center. They taught the *murshidat* how to weigh children, how to give vaccinations, how to provide health education, and how to do home visits. But although the Dutch staff thought that it was logical to train women in preventive MCH services, it soon appeared that not everybody was content with the

6. The Tihama Primary Health Care Project was a big development project financed by USAID focusing on improving primary health-care services in the rural areas of Hodeida governorate.

training of *murshidat*. The Health Office staff felt threatened by the *murshidat* because they were taking over work the Health Office employees were supposed to do. The Yemeni Ministry of Public Health, and subsequently the Health Office in Hodeida, was organized in departments that were responsible for vaccinations, health education, nutrition, and MCH services. But in place of these vertical programs, with their separate staff, the project wanted the *murshidat* to work in an integrated way, transcending vertical lines. This stirred up ill feelings among some of the people working in the Health Office, in many cases educated young men who felt bypassed by a group of young women with "only" primary education. For them, the project's way of working meant a loss of control. The project's interpretation of primary health care, as horizontal and comprehensive, was incongruent with their notions of health-care development. The *murshidat* were the pawns in this conflict, representing Western development discourses on health care in a Yemeni environment.

The fact that the *murshidat* were taking over tasks that used to be carried out by other people was not the only reason for ill feelings. Being trained and employed by a project with foreign funding also gave rise to envy. Although the Health Office departments had few financial resources, the project had a lot of money, and during their training the *murshidat* received a uniform, stationery, and transportation. The association with modernity can also explain the fact that this added to their status and led to jealousy. The project was seen as a sign of modernity, being a Western-financed project and introducing a new model of health care. The presence of four Dutch team members driving around in four-wheel-drive cars and living in nice villas in Hodeida's commercial area contributed to this association with wealth and modernity. Some people were attracted to this form of modernity and valued foreign projects highly. They hoped that these projects would "develop" Yemen, while they were also interested in benefiting personally from these projects.

Both the association with development and modernity and the practical advantages of working in a foreign project may have contributed to the approval of the relatives of the *murshidat* for the training and employment of their wives and daughters. Najwa's mother, for example, was very much in favor of *al-hulandiyyin* (the Dutch) and continued to stress how important the work of foreigners was to developing Yemen.[7] But there were also people in Hodeida who despised foreigners and foreign projects, seeing foreigners as intruders trying to change local customs. Najwa recalled how people in Ghulail would ask the *murshidat* why they were working with foreigners, in a foreign project. "What is the Dutch project? Those people are foreigners; what are Yemenis doing with foreigners?"[8] She was the only one who spoke about the negative views on working with foreigners, however. In the stories of the other *murshidat* these views were never expressed, even though I asked about it. The fact that the *murshidat* did not want to hurt my feelings, as a foreign woman working in Yemen, may have played a role.

Stark (1985, 272) discusses the fact that expatriate health professionals are sometimes seen as spies who gather data that could be useful in propaganda and intelligence gathering. In particular the family-planning activities of foreign donor organizations are suspect because they interfere with people's ability to control their own lives. I have heard several stories about imams who spoke out in their sermons against the *murshidat* and advised people not to receive them in their houses, in particular because they gave family-planning advice. The fact that a foreign development project propagated family planning was suspect, but so was the fact that young and unmarried women were involved in these activities, because they would not be expected

7. The fact that Najwa's family came from Aden and had been acquainted with British influences is important in this respect.

8. The *murshidat* with whom I worked in Rada' told me that their names were often tarnished because they were working with foreigners. People accused them, for example, of dancing for foreigners at parties and serving alcohol to foreigners. These accusations must be seen in light of the expatriate culture many development workers cherish, with evening parties where alcohol is served. The local population is often aware of these parties and has its own perceptions of what is going on. Also, the social status of the female extension agents in Rada' was already low, as some of them came from the lower social classes, which also contributed to the fact that they were regarded as having "loose morals."

to have knowledge about sexual relationships. But for the *murshidat* that was never a reason to stop their activities. In some cases they became even more fervent in their health education activities.

Wearing White

Working in Health Care

"I knew that my family would not allow me to work in health care," said Hawa, and she explained that only women of families that were not strict would be allowed to do so. When I asked the *murshidat* why some people in Yemen thought that health care was not respectable work for women, almost all of them said that it was because of the contacts between female nurses and unrelated men in hospitals. A female nurse had to treat male patients, but what was even worse was that she would work together with male nurses as colleagues. According to Hawa, people saw with their own eyes that female nurses behaved improperly. They listened to music together with men, and the fact that they worked nights made the risks of indecent behavior even more probable. These contacts between women and men *(ikhtilat)* were fiercely condemned as they challenged the dominant ideology of gender segregation. Amina mentioned another possible reason for the low status of health-care work: nursing was not seen as clean. Nurses had to wash, clean, and dress sick people and were in contact with human fluids, such as blood, urine, and sweat. Various beliefs exist around these bodily fluids, linked to notions of purity and impurity. People who work with substances that are seen as impure in Yemen, for example barbers, butchers, and traditional healers performing healing practices that involve touching the body, such as bone setting and blood cupping, come from lower social-status groups.

In the first group of *murshidat* there were a number of women who joined the training course with the aim of taking up work in health care. Amina, for example, had a clear interest in working in health care. "I saw nursing as something big, or something sacred. I liked to help people, and I really wanted to be a nurse." After earning her primary-school certificate at the Yemeni Women's Association, she wanted to register for a three-year nursing course at the Health Manpower Institute. Yet Hawa persuaded her to join the *murshidat* training course instead. I asked Amina about the low status of health-care work, and she confirmed that there were people who had negative ideas about women working in health care. But that was no reason for her not to enter a health-care profession, and her relatives also did not prevent her from doing so. Amina's social background may have been the reason she was allowed to take up work in health care. She was born in Zabid, a small town south of Hodeida, and her father worked as a butcher, which is a low-status occupation. Nursing may have been more acceptable in these groups than in Hawa's highland *qabili* family.[9]

There were other reasons that women did not mind working in health care, or even had a strong desire for health-care work. Riham's family was clearly in decline, and when her father died she made the sacrifice of taking up paid work to allow her younger brother to continue his schooling. The *murshidat* training course was one of the few routes to gaining paid work in a relatively short period of time. Riham had wanted to become a teacher but abandoned her dream to provide for her family. For Najwa things were again different. She came from an Adeni family where ideas about nursing were less negative. The socialist regime that came to power in South Yemen in 1967 placed a lot of emphasis on the provision of basic welfare facilities such as education and health care and successfully encouraged women to be trained in nursing and other paramedic professions.

There was a shortage of female health cadres in North Yemen, which was particularly serious in view of the fact that most Yemeni women prefer to be treated by other women. The first group of *murshidat* were

9. Yet I never came across references made to Amina's lower status, and everyone always talked about her with a lot of respect. As Meneley (1996) shows in her study on social relations in Zabid, economic class has to a large extent replaced the old status hierarchies, and social status is continually being reformulated. In chapter 7, I will elaborate on social status in the Tihama.

made aware of this shortage during the training course, when teachers from the Health Manpower Institute approached the young women and asked them whether they would be willing to become nurses. Muna told me about the efforts of the HMI staff to convince the *murshidat* to train as nurses, a clear sign of the need for female nurses:

> We had been studying for about three months when the people from the HMI said, "Join us, we will give you another year of training and you will be a nurse." They encouraged us to join them because there were hardly any women trained at the HMI before, only one or two in each course, and sometimes there were no women at all. They thought, "Where did the Dutch get these young women?" But we said, "No, we don't want to. We have only five months training left and then we will finish." We thought that our course was the same as being trained as a nurse. They said "No, it is not like a nurse. Come to us and we give you one extra year and you will be a nurse."

The *murshidat* gradually noticed the difference between their training and the training of nurses, for example when they compared their study books with those of nursing students. But they did not feel the need to change. Muna said, "I considered a *murshida* to be like a nurse. I wore white and I went into the hospital." When I pointed out that the *murshidat* were not going to work in a hospital but in a health center, she made it clear that this did not make a difference to her. "I didn't know where I was going to work and I didn't mind. The hospital or the health center, it was all the same to me."[10]

For Muna "wearing white" had a positive connotation, as she had always wanted to work in health care. She sometimes accompanied her female relatives or neighbors to the hospital and liked to watch the nurses when she was sitting in the waiting room. "I looked at what the nurses were wearing, and how they walked and what they were doing, and I liked it." Hawa explained that people did not see the difference

10. The fact that Muna was going to work in a foreign development project may also have been of importance for her decision to accept her training as a *murshida* instead of being trained as a nurse, but she did not express that to me explicitly.

The weighing room in one of the health centers.

between *murshidat*, nurses, and doctors, as they were all wearing white clothes. "The people don't know what a *murshida* is and what a nurse is. They don't know. The main thing is that they see that you wear white." Hawa's statements point to an interesting ambiguity in the way people looked at nurses, and the way the *murshidat* looked at their own profession. Hawa argued that "wearing white" defined the status of the profession, and that people automatically assumed that the *murshidat* were nurses because they wore white. Interestingly, she seemed to imply that wearing white contributed to a respectable status, perhaps because people working in health care often performed curative services, which were highly valued. At other moments, most of the *murshidat* emphasized their differences from nurses in order to make their work more acceptable to the community. They stressed that they did not work in a hospital but in a health center. Working in a hospital implied contacts with unrelated men, as personnel and patients, and carrying out night duties. Both aspects were fiercely condemned because they undermined gender segregation. Health centers were less threatening, as the main services focus on mother and child health care and the clients are mainly women with children. Besides that, the official working hours in health centers were from 8:00 A.M. until 1:00 P.M.,[11] and *murshidat* do not have to work night shifts. A closer look at the work of *murshidat* reveals that the outside picture of their work as not challenging dominant gender ideologies does not correspond to their actual work; in reality *murshidat* were shifting more boundaries than had initially been expected.

Going on Home Visits

One of the most challenging parts of the work of the *murshidat* was the home visits they had to pay to families in Ghulail in order to spread health messages. Home visiting in the context of health-care work was a completely new phenomenon in Yemen, and the *murshidat* had to overcome a number of obstacles before they were comfortable with doing home visits. While Yemeni women have an extensive culture of paying afternoon visits to each other (see Makhlouf 1979; Dorsky 1986; Meneley 1996), these visits always take place within specific social circles and serve to strengthen social relations. Meneley (1996, 181) argues that women's gatherings are central to understanding the connections between consumption, sociability, and status in Yemen, as the ability to be hospitable is crucial for a family's reputation and standing. But the *murshidat* were not invited by the families they visited and therefore put both themselves and the receiving family in an awkward position. Moreover, women's social visiting was restricted to married women, and the mobility of young and unmarried women was limited to visiting neighboring families or walking to school. In addition, the *murshidat* ran the risk of encountering unrelated men in the homes they visited. Obliged to go on home visits as part of

11. On October 30, 1999, official working hours in government offices changed to 8:00 A.M. to 3:00 P.M., and Thursdays became a free day for government employees. Health centers continued to open from 8:00 A.M. to 1:00 P.M. and from 4:00 P.M. to 8:00 P.M. Health centers are also open on Thursday mornings.

their work, the *murshidat* had to overcome their own embarrassment at knocking on doors of unknown families and asking women to allow them to come in.

The home visits were also challenging because the *murshidat* were crossing geographic boundaries. As mentioned before, the *murshidat* did not come from Ghulail and were not even acquainted with the area before they started the *murshidat* training course. Entering a squatter area and visiting the homes of people was for them a totally new experience, and they often recalled what Ghulail looked like in the mid-1980s. "There was nothing, there were no paved roads, and our car could sometimes not even enter the area and then we had to walk." Sandy streets, bordered by fences of straw and corrugated iron separating people's compounds, were the only roads in Ghulail. The people in the squatter area lived in large compounds where they had built one or two huts of straw or wood, depending on their financial situation. Those who were a little bit better off had built wooden dwellings (so-called *sanadiq*),[12] and replaced the fence of corrugated iron by a concrete block wall to guarantee security. The huts and the rooms of concrete blocks were mainly used for storing personal belongings; daily activities took place in the compound, where a number of typical Tihama couches and beds[13] could be found. A corner of the compound was separated by a piece of corrugated iron for use as a kitchen, and cooking was usually done on kerosene or sometimes on bottled-gas stoves. The bathroom consisted of another fenced-off part of the compound where a toilet was made by digging a hole and inserting a pipe in it so that the waste would flow some distance into the ground. Most people had a well in their compound and used this water for cleaning. Water for cooking and for drinking was obtained from the nearest public tap or was purchased in jerricans from delivery trucks. Kerosene lamps were used for lighting, and car batteries were rigged up for watching television, in the absence

12. The word *sandaqa* (pl. *sanadiq*) is derived from the word *sunduq*, meaning crate or box.

13. A typical Tihama couch (*qa'da*) or bed (*sarir*) consists of a wooden frame and a seat strung with rope made from palm leaves.

of electricity. As there was no regular rubbish collection in the squatter areas, mounds of refuse accumulated in which goats and dogs scavenged for something edible.

The area was sandy and often dirty, and the extreme temperatures in the Tihama made home visiting in Ghulail a difficult task for the *murshidat*, who lived in relatively better-off parts of the city. In addition to the physical difficulties of home visiting—going out in the heat, getting dusty, dirty, and sweaty—this activity did not contribute to the "modern" status of the work, another reason home visiting was not liked. Moreover, physical and tiring work is associated with low-status groups, and therefore looked down on. In view of these obstacles, and in view of the fact that home visiting was a new phenomenon, the project staff had to develop an approach that would make the *murshidat* accustomed to home visiting. The idea was that the *murshidat* would spend 50 percent of their time in the health center and 50 percent of their time in the area, visiting and educating mothers at home. The baseline study of Ghulail offered an opportunity to make the *murshidat* acquainted with the area and its inhabitants. According to Buringa (1988a), the *murshidat* needed a lot of guidance and supervision during their first research and home-visiting activities. They had to learn not to be arrogant to the people living in the squatter area, how to work accurately, and how to ask questions in a structured way, which can all be seen as ways to discipline the women.[14]

The *murshidat* learned how to introduce themselves to unknown families and how to gather health related information via questionnaires. In the beginning home visits only took place after a mother had visited the health center. The *murshidat* would tell the mothers in advance that they would be visiting their homes, so that they were not complete strangers paying visits to unknown families. But gradually the home visits increased, and people in the area were visited without

14. Morris (1991, 201) also mentions that the *murshidat* in the primary health-care project he describes were at first arrogant toward the people in the villages, as they themselves came from a small town, but soon established excellent relationships with the local people.

prior notice. The area of Ghulail was divided into subsections and blocks of houses, and a team of two *murshidat* was made responsible for a certain part of the area, visiting each family with children under five. Each house was numbered, and Thera often told me about the many afternoons she had spent together with the *murshidat*, driving and walking through Ghulail, trying to map and divide the area into subsections and blocks.

Despite the fact that doing home visits was not at all an easy task, and the *murshidat* sometimes complained about the difficulties they encountered, few of them refused to go. Hawa explained why home visiting was not a big problem for her: "At first when we started to do the questionnaires the project staff helped us. They taught us how to do it, and I don't know why, but I understood immediately how to do it. It was easy, not difficult." I asked her if she was not embarrassed to enter the houses of strange people and to talk to the mothers, and Hawa answered,

> First of all, anything you do for the first time is difficult, but it was easy because it was far away from our neighborhood. It became difficult when they first asked us to work in our own areas, during Ramadan. They said, "During Ramadan you have to work although there is no work in the center."[15] We had to work in our own area and to check how many children were vaccinated. That was a problem for us; first because it is difficult to knock on the doors of people in Ramadan, and second because these are people you know.

Hawa touched upon an important point; it was easier for the first *murshidat* to carry out home visits because they did not know the people in the area of Ghulail. They came from very different parts of the city and had never visited Ghulail before. That made it easier for them to do home visits, and it also prevented problems with their families, who may have been opposed to their work in case neighbors and friends saw their sisters, daughters, or wives walking in the street knocking

15. During the fasting month of Ramadan, very few people visit the health center.

on doors.[16] Still, the home visits were always an issue when there were problems with relatives about the work of the *murshidat*. Hawa told me she was forced to stop working in the afternoons when her family discovered that she had been to a training course in another town. And Riham's brother did not allow his sister to work afternoons once he discovered that she was going on home visits. Working afternoons and doing home visits were the most sensitive aspects of the work of *murshidat*. In addition to the increased mobility of the young women, the reactions of the community to the home visits of *murshidat* will explain why.

The inhabitants of Ghulail did not accept the home visits of the *murshidat* easily. They were suspicious of the work of the *murshidat* and did not let them enter their houses in the beginning. This was, in the first place, because the work of *murshidat* was completely new in Yemen. People did not believe that walking in the streets and visiting families could be part of the work of the *murshidat*. Common remarks were: "Those girls are out in the streets so what are they doing?;" "They are knocking on doors but what do they want?;" "It must be (their) free time"; "They are playing around"; or "They are looking for something." Fatima Salem said, "People had very bad ideas about the *murshidat*. It was not easy. Some people closed doors in their faces. They would say, 'What do you want?' And if the *murshida* answered, 'I am an employee [*muwazzafa*],' they replied, 'If you are an employee then what are you doing in the street? An employee should be doing her job.'" The prevailing idea was that employees were people who worked in offices and did not go out in the street unless they were playing around. The fact that the *murshidat* also went on home visits in the afternoon increased the suspicion. As mentioned before, governmental working hours used to be from 8:00 A.M. to 1:00 P.M., and government employees usually did not work in the afternoons. Many

16. This is similar to El-Messiri's description of domestic servants in Cairo, who prefer to work in areas far away from their local neighborhoods as domestic work is looked down on (1978, 527).

people therefore thought that the *murshidat* were trying to get into their houses to steal something, or trying to seduce men.

A second reason for suspicion was the fact that the majority of the inhabitants were rural migrants who had just moved into the city and were living illegally on a piece of land. They were afraid of government interference. In 1985–86, at the time of the first *murshidat* training course, an Urban Development Project financed by the World Bank was initiated with the aim of improving the infrastructure in Ghulail. The streets were to be paved, and water and sanitation facilities and electricity were to be installed. Although improving the living conditions in the squatter area was the aim of the Urban Development Project, people feared that urban planning of the area would mean that illegal inhabitants would be sent away.[17] The *murshidat* were suspected of being spies gathering information for the government, and some inhabitants were not willing to cooperate with them for fear of losing their land.[18]

A third reason home visits were not easily accepted is related to the fluid boundaries between public and private spaces. In an interesting article on the impact of an upgrading project on women and domesticity in the squatter areas of Amman, Shami (1997) shows that by restructuring space, the upgrading project also restructured notions of family, public and private domains, and women's domesticity. Despite the fact that several authors have challenged the prevailing idea that gender segregation is related to a public-private divide (see also Nelson 1974; Altorki 1986; Tucker 1985), development planners in Amman

17. The aim of the Urban Development Project was precisely to give people legal access to the land they were living on, rather than chasing illegal squatters away (for more information about the Urban Development Project see de Regt and Ghailan 2007).

18. Stark (1985) also confirms the fact that primary health-care workers are sometimes seen as spies who are gathering data for the government that will be used to control the community. Primary health-care workers can in this way be used as a kind of "medical police," which is similar to the role of the Egyptian *hakimat* as described by Fahmy (1998).

continued to define the dwelling space as domestic, private, and female and the space outside the dwelling as community, public, and male. Yet women's lives in Amman show that private is not "inside" and public "outside" the dwelling (Shami 1997, 87). Women move, for example, extensively between one another's dwellings and also make use of the space in front of their houses. Moreover, the same spaces become male or female spaces depending on the time of day, the people using the space, and the type of activity performed in it (87). With the upgrading of the squatter area, and more important, with the strict rules and regulations attached to upgrading the dwellings, spatial and social arrangements were disrupted (89). In addition, the areas were constantly being invaded by outsiders, such as the project engineers, surveyors, social workers, and visitors from the government and the World Bank, with the result that the entire area, including the dwellings, turned into a public space (91). This finding is very similar to what happened in Ghulail in the 1980s and explains the attitude of the people living in the squatter area toward the *murshidat*. While both Yemeni health managers and Dutch project members thought that the *murshidat* could easily enter the private space of women's homes because they were women themselves, the *murshidat* may have been seen as intruders because they represented "the public sphere."

Summing up, the *murshidat* had to overcome many obstacles before home visiting became an acceptable part of their work. First of all, they had to overcome their own embarrassment at visiting strangers at home. Second, they had to get used to poor living conditions and a poor infrastructure, making their task more difficult. Third, they had to build up confidence and trust in the area. The fact that the *murshidat* emphasized that they had overcome these difficulties and no longer had problems with home visiting can be interpreted as a form of self-development. As I have described, self-development through education was a very strong notion among the first group of *murshidat*, but the tasks they had to perform as *murshidat* also contributed to their self-development, and, in addition, to new forms of self-discipline.

In view of the obstacles related to home visiting, it is remarkable that the problems with relatives were not bigger. Whereas the work of nurses was condemned because of contacts with unrelated men and night duties, the work of *murshidat* was less strongly criticized by their (male) relatives. The ways in which the first *murshidat* gradually shifted the boundaries of dominant gender ideologies, the ways in which the project staff protected the *murshidat,* and the fact that the project was seen as a project of modernity were among the main reasons there were fewer problems. Women's government employment and the additional income that entered the family were other factors affecting the attitude of the relatives.

Being Employed

The home visits were one way in which the *murshidat* shifted gender boundaries. Obtaining government employment was another. Government employment had many advantages because it implied a tenured contract, a monthly salary, and employment rights such as sick leave and maternity leave. At the start of the training course for *murshidat,* the project management in cooperation with the governmental Health Office in Hodeida decided that the *murshidat* had to become government employees in order to safeguard sustainability. A government contract would prevent the employment and work of the *murshidat* coming to a halt after Dutch funding had finished. However, the project management did not discuss their plans in detail with the Ministry of Public Health in Sana'a and began to train *murshidat* without the ministry's official approval. The curriculum used by the project as well as the job descriptions of the *murshidat* had not been discussed and approved by the ministry. As a result, at the end of the course, the ministry did not immediately hand out official certificates to the *murshidat,* and they had to wait for their official employment.

During the course the *murshidat* received a monthly allowance from the project. After the course, the allowance changed into a salary paid by the project, awaiting the official government employment of the *murshidat.* Although both training allowance and salary were relatively high[19] the majority of the young women (seven out of nine)

19. In 1985–86, the training allowance was YR1,000 per month. An average salary was around YR2,500 (in 1985, US$1 equaled YR4).

said that they did not join the course because of the money. Muna said, "I was not in need of that money. And besides that, I had not thought that I would study and receive money. I did not know that a student could get money to study." And Hawa told me, "The most important thing was that I worked, or that I studied, and that I would get a certificate. I didn't think about the money. And then when I got it, it was great." It was the first time in their lives that they had earned money, and they enjoyed it very much. Depending on the situation, the *murshidat* used their income for a variety of things.[20] Some bought nice things for themselves, like clothes, especially the ones who did not take responsibility for contributing financially to the running of the household, while others began to share in the household expenditures. They set up a savings club *(hakba)*,[21] and for a period of time each of them contributed YR500 a month. With the money from the savings club some bought gold; others spent it on repair, maintenance, and extension of their houses.

The first group of *murshidat* was brought up with the idea that men were the main providers for the family, and they endorsed this ideology by saying that they did not intend to gain employment and earn a salary. They "just wanted to learn." But while earning an income had not been the initial intention of the *murshidat*, they gradually became used to a regular income, and some started to take on important financial responsibilities, as in the case of Hawa, which became increasingly accepted by their (male) relatives. But other *murshidat* were not allowed to continue their work. This was in particular the case with a number of women who married almost immediately after the end of

20. According to Islamic law, men are responsible for (financially) providing for their families, and women can spend the money they earn in any way they choose (see also Moors 1995, 247).

21. Savings clubs or informal savings associations are a well-known phenomenon in many countries of the world. Little is known about the importance of savings clubs in Yemen, but the situation is probably comparable to Egypt, where savings associations offer an alternative source for many of the economic needs in the community (Singerman 1995, 154–57; Hoodfar 1999, 219).

the training course and dropped out because their husbands did not approve of their paid work.

Dropping Out

Getting Married

Nine *murshidat* were trained during the first training course in 1985–86, but three of them left a couple of months after the end of the course because they got married. The initial idea of the project staff had been to train adult women with children, on the assumption that they would be able to gain the confidence of women in the area and pass on health messages about mother and child health care. However, as a result of the recruitment method, six young unmarried women joined the course. One of them was the youngest sister of Hawa, Bilqis, two were nieces of Hawa, there were the two Adeni sisters, and there was Riham. Out of these six young women, three married within a couple of months after the end of the course. They left the project and two of them stopped working altogether, while one moved to another town and continued to work there. Because Bilqis came from the same family as Hawa, it is interesting to compare her situation with Hawa's, in order to understand why Hawa was able to resist family traditions and continue her work while Bilqis was not and had to stop working.

Bilqis was sixteen years old and still attending the *murshidat* course when she married her cousin, who had studied abroad and who had a good job at the port. She wanted to get married and knew her cousin well, but she did not want to stop work. "Before we got married, when I was still attending the *murshidat* training course, I told him, 'When we get married, let me work' and he said, 'Okay, okay, okay.' But that was just between me and him, nobody else knew." Bilqis did not set any conditions in the marriage contract to safeguard her right to work.[22]

---

22. In Islamic marriage contracts it is possible to include particular conditions, such as the right for women to work (see Moors 1999, 160).

After the course I worked for about two months and then *khalas*, that was it. My husband and his father spoke with my eldest brother; they informed him that they wanted me to stop working. They told my brother, because they knew that I would not have listened to them. Really, I would not have listened. Then my oldest brother came to me and of course, I have to respect him. He said, "You can't continue your work." I said, "Why not?" He said, "That's it. When a girl gets married . . . " I was still young and I accepted what he said. I was not as old as Hawa. He told her the same thing but she did not pay attention to it. She did not listen to what he said. My brother said to me, "*Khalas*, that's it, I have already spoken to Hawa and she is going to leave the job too." After that Hawa came to me and she said, "Why are you leaving the job?" I said "If my husband does not agree, then that's it." I have stayed home from the day I married till now, twelve years. My husband does not want me to work nor to study nor to do anything else. Sometimes I talk to him, I say, "I want to work like my sister Hawa, and like my niece Hanan." He says, "No. What is the point? You will only tire yourself. Hawa and Hanan are always tired and have a difficult time." I say, "But I want to because I don't have children, I don't have anything. Let me go to work," but he says, "No. What do you want? Do you want a salary? Do you want money? I can give you money every month. I can give you the money you would earn in the center."

But Bilqis did not want to work because of the money; she wanted to develop herself. "I have a strong desire to work. In order to benefit, to learn how to give injections, how to give drips, to learn how a delivery goes. I want to get experience for myself." Bilqis is bored with staying at home, most of all because she has not had children.

Bilqis's story is a story of anger and frustration, and she looks with envy at her sister Hawa, who combines an important position in the health center with her role as a mother of five children.[23] Hawa is

---

23. In the first years of their training and employment, the three *murshidat* who had children left their children at home with relatives. In 1990, a nursery was opened in the Ghulail health center where women working in the health center could bring their children.

gradually shifting the boundaries of restrictive traditions, mainly by showing that she can work in health care and remain a respectable woman at the same time. In addition to Hawa's own strategies to continue her work, there are differences between her and Bilqis's starting positions. Hawa was already married and had two children when she joined the *murshidat* training course, and she did not change to a new position in which she had to negotiate her work again. Moreover, her husband was working abroad when she took the first step in shaping her own life and decided to pick up her education again. By the time he returned to Yemen, Hawa had been able to take more steps, which made it more difficult for him to reverse the situation. Bilqis, however, had joined the training course when she was not yet married and had to negotiate her work with her husband. Furthermore, the starting positions of Ahmed and Hassan, Bilqis's husband, were different. Ahmed was not highly educated and did not have a well-paid job, and Hawa's income gradually became of the utmost importance to support the family, whereas Hassan earned a good salary and was not in need of Bilqis's paid work. He did not want his wife to work and told her that he could give her money if that was what she wanted. Bilqis's desire to develop herself was not recognized by her husband.

Larger Ambitions

Another reason women dropped out after being trained as *murshidat* was related to limited opportunities to upgrade their qualifications and the lack of recognition for their work on the side of the Yemeni health establishment. Although the first *murshidat* course offered women the possibility to develop themselves and to obtain a profession, from the beginning the *murshidat* lacked recognition from (male) Yemeni health managers. First, their certificates were not immediately stamped and approved by the Yemeni Ministry of Public Health. While all the young women had the feeling that they had achieved an important position, and continued to be proud of the fact that they were the first to complete a *murshidat* training course, they were disappointed that this course was not officially approved. As mentioned before, the Dutch project management had not asked for official approval of the course before the course started. Moreover, the curriculum used in Hodeida did not correspond to the ideas of the Yemeni Ministry of Public Health in Sanaʻa. The *murshidat* had, for example, not learned how to assist at childbirth whereas pre- and postnatal care and delivery assistance were important parts of the job descriptions for *murshidat* developed after the first training course in Hodeida. The project management saw the *murshidat* in the first place as health educators and not as midwives. A few years later a short midwifery course was organized, and the first *murshidat* received official *murshidat* certificates. Another reason for the lack of recognition was that the position of *murshida* is one of the lowest positions in the Yemeni Ministry of Public Health. Their position is based on their level of education: six years basic education and one year training as a *murshida* is relatively little, and their salaries are therefore low.

In addition, the project curriculum focused nearly exclusively on preventive health care, another reason the *murshidat* lacked recognition. Although they all agreed that preventive health care is important, some of them had hoped to learn more curative skills. Bilqis said, "I wanted to learn how to give injections, how to give drips, I wanted to dress wounds" and others said similar things. None of them had a clear picture of what a *murshida* exactly was before they started the course. The only comparison they had was with a nurse. But even though they were "wearing white," they soon discovered that there were differences between the work of *murshidat* and that of nurses. Curative services are highly valued, and some *murshidat* had hoped to be able to carry out curative services as well. They did not like the fact that some people said, "They are only offering preventive services," and they wanted to improve their professional status by learning more about curative health care.

The project planned to upgrade the qualifications of the *murshidat* and to work toward career development, but not enough initiatives were taken to realize these intentions, and negotiations with institutes like the Health Manpower Institute did not lead anywhere. One of the women who suffered from the lack of possibilities to upgrade her qualifications was Amina. Amina joined the *murshidat* training course because Hawa had convinced her to do so, although she had planned to become a nurse. Amina had never attended primary school, and she was married when she was twelve years old to a man she did not like. "He was not educated. He was twenty years old but his mentality was of someone of seventy. We never agreed with each other and we were always quarreling." They had a daughter, but the problems continued. Amina wanted a divorce, but her father did not support her. Only after six years of struggle, and after Amina had become mentally depressed, did her father agree to a divorce. Amina left her husband and returned with her daughter to her parental house. In the same year that she divorced she returned to education. She had always wanted to go to school. "I wanted to know more things, and I wanted to learn how to read. My father did not agree at all to my going to school, but I did not listen to him. I went to school secretly, I had asked the opinion of my sister and my mother and they supported me. I went to literacy classes at the Yemeni Women's Association. After a while my father heard about it, but then he did not stand in my way anymore."

When I asked Amina why she wanted to study, she answered,

I did not go to school because I wanted to become a teacher or to become a *murshida* or something like that. I just wanted to learn how to read and write. But when I arrived at the sixth class, I got a longing or ambition to become something. Reading and writing was not enough for me anymore. I wanted to be something, and that thing had to be related to nursing. I saw nursing as something big, as something sacred. Honestly, I loved nursing. But when my mother suddenly died, my father said to me, "Don't leave the house, you are not going to school anymore. You have to stay home." My elder sister was married and had moved out of the house and I had to take care of my father. Fortunately my sister stood by me and talked him into changing his mind. After some time he said to her, "If she wants to go to school, let her go to school." My sister supported me and that is why I registered at the Health Manpower Institute.

On the day that Amina had registered for a nursing course she ran into Hawa, whom she knew from the literacy classes. Hawa told her about the project and convinced her to change to the *murshidat* training course. "I thought about it and then I said 'Okay, I will join that project and see whether I like the field of health care. If it is nice, then I can probably gradually rise to a higher position in health care."

But Amina was disappointed. Although she liked the *murshidat* training course and worked for about three years in the Ghulail health center, she was waiting for a chance to upgrade her qualifications.

> Every year they said, "There will be a course and you will be trained as a midwife." But every year they told us, "Later, later" and I thought, "Years are passing quickly and I am getting older and after a while I will not be able to attend a higher-level course." I was thinking all the time about a diploma, in nursing or in midwifery, in anything. I wanted to have a certificate that was better than the one of *murshida*. After three years a friend of mine said "You have to choose now. You can continue your work and forget about studying, or you can change to teaching, because this year is the last chance to register at the Teachers Institute. They are going to close the institute."[24] And so I changed from health care to teaching. I went to the Teachers Institute because I wanted to obtain a higher certificate.

Amina would have preferred to register at the Health Manpower Institute in order to become a midwife or a nurse because she liked health care, but the management of the Health Office did not want to continue paying her salary while she studied. "They did not encourage me to attend further education. They said 'If you want to study and continue to receive your government salary, you have to work afternoon shifts or evening shifts and night shifts in the hospital.' I knew that would be too difficult because I had a child, so I did not agree." A relative helped Amina get an afternoon job in a clinic instead of in the hospital, and so she was able to work and study at the same time. After she graduated from the Teachers Institute she requested a transfer

24. In 1990 the Teachers Institutes were closed. From then on, only people who finished secondary school could become teachers.

from the Ministry of Public Health to the Ministry of Education. She has been working as a teacher since 1991 and is very happy that she decided to change from health care to teaching.

Amina left the *murshidat* profession because she wanted to upgrade her qualifications and ensure her future position. She had attended the *murshidat* course as a tryout to see if she liked health care and as a first step to further education. Unfortunately, she did not get a chance to become a midwife or a nurse because the project staff did not come to an agreement with the Health Manpower Institute in time. While Hawa patiently waited for her chance to come, and eventually became head of clinic, Amina decided that she was not going to wait any longer. She was determined to improve her qualifications even if it meant that she had to give up working in health care.

Paving the Way for Others

Despite the high dropout rate, the lack of recognition from other health practitioners, and limited chances to upgrade their qualifications, the first group of *murshidat* became an example for other women interested in taking up paid work in health care. A number of factors contributed to the positive image of the *murshidat* profession. To start, the first group of *murshidat* was recruited via the literacy classes of the Yemeni Women's Association and consisted of young women coming from outside Ghulail, eager to learn and in most cases not in direct financial need of paid work. Although the project staff had not intentionally looked for women outside Ghulail, the backgrounds of the first *murshidat* affected the development of the *murshidat* profession in a positive way. Hawa mentioned that it was easier for her to go on home visits in an area where people did not know her because neighbors and relatives did not see her going into the streets and visiting unrelated families. The exact nature of her work remained unknown to them and gave her the necessary space to carry out her duties. Through her work in the health center and in the area, she was able to come into contact with inhabitants of Ghulail and make them acquainted with the work of the *murshidat*.

For the project management as well as for the *murshidat* themselves it was important to show that the work they were doing was
respectable, protecting their own status and paving the way for others.
The first group of *murshidat* had to be an example for other women,
functioning as pioneers and encouraging others to become *murshidat*
as well. In order to make the work of the *murshidat* acceptable to others, the project management followed a clear policy in protecting the
first group. First of all, the women were taken to and from work by a
project car, in the first instance driven by the Tunisian codirector of
the project but later by a Yemeni driver. As mentioned before, this was
initially seen as a sign of modernity, as only upper-class women had
their own private drivers, but the presence of a male driver in a project
car full of young women could also cause problems.

Another way in which the young women were protected had to
do with the home visits. It was a strict rule that *murshidat* were only
allowed to go on home visits in pairs. The *murshidat* themselves were
very much in favor of this rule, as it made the home visits less scary,
but it was also a means of controlling their behavior and showing that
the work they did was respectable. When they worked in pairs there
was less chance of them behaving in a way that would harm their reputation, such as developing relationships with men. The project staff
did everything to keep up the good names of the young women and to
protect their reputations, carefully trying to build up respect for this
new category of women involved in paid health-care activities. Fatima
was the supervisor of the first training course, and she was very strict
and did not allow any contact between the *murshidat* and boys or men
who had nothing to do with the work. Only relatives were, for example, allowed to make phone calls to the health center. And the *murshidat* themselves could only phone outside in emergency cases. These
restrictions prevented them from using their workplace as a means to
be in contact with boyfriends. Some of the younger *murshidat* liked
to flirt with males, and the teahouse in front of the health center happened to be a good target. They liked to stand in the doorway of the
health center talking and joking with the men in the teahouse. After a
number of incidents, the project management decided to build a wall

in front of the entrance to the health center. Only a few years ago was the wall broken down. The teahouse had moved to another place but, more important, the tearing down of the wall was a clear sign that gender relations have changed. The health center has become an integral part of the area, the fact that women are working there has been accepted, and the *murshidat* themselves are used to having contacts with unrelated men. Moreover, it shows the disciplinary aspects of the project: the women had learned to behave in a "proper" way.[25]

Despite the many obstacles the *murshidat* and the project management had to overcome, an increasing number of families in Ghulail became accustomed to the work the *murshidat* did, in the health center and in the area. Through the home visits, although they were not yet done in a systematic way, the first group of *murshidat* became acquainted with many families in Ghulail and met young women of their own age who showed interest in becoming *murshidat*. Some of them heard about the possibility of becoming *murshidat* and came to the center spontaneously to ask when a new training course was starting. While they were looking for paid work, their families and in particular their fathers were not always convinced they wanted their daughters to become *murshidat*. Fatima visited these families to try to convince them of the importance and respectability of the work of the *murshidat*. Coming from a well-known and respected family herself, she was seen as trustworthy, and she effectively convinced people to allow their daughters to register for the second training course. The next part of the book will focus on the second and third group of *murshidat*, women who had very different backgrounds from the first group.

Conclusions

Although the project's intention was to recruit adult women living in the squatter area as primary health-care workers, a group of young and

25. Najmabadi (1993) describes a similar process of disciplining women in her article on the transformation of women's writings in Iran at the end of the nineteenth and the beginning of the twentieth centuries.

mainly unmarried women from relatively well-off families living in the city formed the first group of *murshidat*. This selection was a result of the way in which the recruitment took place. By approaching the head of the Yemeni Women's Association, the project limited the selection to women of a particular background. The women who showed an interest in becoming *murshidat* were mainly from families not in need of additional income. Their (male) relatives often did not value education and paid employment of women. Yet despite these negative views, almost all of them took the initiative to start or continue primary education. They were born and brought up in the early years of the Yemen Arab Republic, a particular period in Yemen's history in which education was put forward as the way to development. They were clearly influenced by these revolutionary notions on the importance of education and saw schooling as an important way to self-development. The training course for *murshidat* was in their eyes another step in this process of self-development; it was a way to obtain new knowledge and skills. Becoming employed and earning an income was not their priority, and they emphasized that they "just wanted to learn."

The fact that the work of *murshidat* was new and unknown in Yemen gave the first group of women trained as *murshidat* plenty of possibilities for negotiating their right to training and work with their relatives. Some emphasized that they only wanted to acquire health-related knowledge so that they would be able to assist their relatives in case of illnesses and the like. They denied that they would take up paid work. Others stressed that they were only working with mothers and children, in contrast to nurses who worked with male patients and male colleagues. The challenging aspects of their work, such as the home visits they had to pay to unrelated families, were sometimes hidden from their relatives. The first group of *murshidat* gradually shifted the boundaries of dominant gender ideologies, paving the way for other women. On the individual level, they cleverly made use of the available room to maneuver, accepting gender prescriptions to a certain extent but stretching them whenever possible. According to the opportunities available, they also gradually shifted their own aspirations and ambitions.

On the social level they shifted boundaries by entering a new profession in health care, which contained elements that challenged the ideologies of the male breadwinner and of gender segregation. The attitudes of their male relatives changed accordingly, on one hand because their income became of increasing importance, on the other hand because of the various ways in which they were supported and protected by project members. In particular the use of certain status symbols, such as the provision of white uniforms and of project transportation, was in their view a sign of modernity and separated them from low-status professions. On a very practical level they were also shifting boundaries, or in a literal sense crossing borders. First, they crossed borders by coming from the city and taking up work in a health center in a squatter area. And second, they crossed borders by moving from inside the health center to outside into the public area, paying home visits to unrelated families. Home visits were therefore also the most challenging aspect of their work, and the most sensitive to negative reactions, from both the community and their male relatives. The gradual way in which the *murshidat* as well as the project team members shifted the boundaries of what was culturally acceptable led to an increasing acceptance of their work, and even resulted in young women in the squatter area expressing interest in becoming *murshidat*.

PART FOUR

New Positions and Identities

7

Looking for Employment

Women from the Squatter Areas

Iman

ON A MONDAY AFTERNOON in the middle of the summer I visit
Iman, one of the *murshidat* trained during the second training course
in 1988. I have tried to make an appointment for an interview for
weeks, but her busy schedule does not leave her much time. Now we
both have a day off, and I am looking forward to interviewing her.
Iman is head of a small health center in al-Sana'i, one of the new
squatter areas that had come into being after the Gulf crisis. While
Ghulail has changed since 1985 from a poor squatter area into a more
permanent residential area, with asphalted roads, electricity, water,
and sanitation facilities, al-Sana'i resembles the Ghulail of the mid-
1980s with its sandy streets bordered by fences made of corrugated
iron, bushes, or wooden boards. Large refuse heaps appear at regular intervals, and empty plastic bags can be found everywhere. How
many times have I driven through al-Sana'i on my way to the health
center? And how many times have I walked through its sandy alleys
and entered people's homes, looking for active community members
or interviewing people for research purposes? Iman often accompanied me on these trips, knowing the area and its inhabitants inside
out. Brought up in Ghulail, she moved to al-Sana'i after she married, and she has lived in the area since 1991. On an empty piece of

land, Iman and her husband have gradually constructed two wooden *sanadiq* (sing. *sandaqa*) and planted trees and plants, which give the compound a special touch. Iman shows me the sheep that she is keeping, and I also notice a number of dovecotes. After a tour around the house we settle down on the two Tihama beds in the compound. "Please, make yourself comfortable," says Iman while she puts some extra cushions behind my back, "My husband is not at home this afternoon, he went to visit my family in Ghulail, so we have the whole afternoon to ourselves." A neighbor comes over to meet me, and we drink tea, smoke the water pipe, and chat a little. The bubbling sound of the water pipe accompanies the interview.

In this chapter I focus on the second and third group of *murshidat*, trained between 1988 and 1990. On the basis of two life stories, I first discuss the backgrounds and motivation of the women. The main aim of the chapter is to show that different categories of women became *murshidat*. While most of the first *murshidat* were young women living in the city, interested in continuing their education and not in need of money, the *murshidat* of the second and third courses came mainly from poor families living in the squatter areas of Ghulail and al-Mughtaribin itself. They were younger than the first group of *murshidat* and had benefited from the increased educational opportunities in Hodeida. Yet most of them felt obliged to leave school to provide for their families as *murshidat*. Apart from exceptions, they can be divided into two broad categories. The first category consists of daughters of rural migrants coming from low-status groups. They were born and brought up in Hodeida and had lived a considerable part of their lives in the squatter area of Ghulail. The second category consists of daughters of returned migrants from East Africa. Their fathers had migrated at the time of the Imamate but returned to Yemen in the 1970s. The children of these returned migrants were often of mixed parentage because their mothers were African. Iman is from the first category, and her story gives details about her background and an insight into what motivated her to become a *murshida*.

I started by asking Iman when and where she was born, and she answered, "I was born in Hodeida, in the area of al-Mitraq, in 1971.

I am twenty-six years old now and I have lived my whole life in Hodeida." Did her parents originally come from Hodeida? Iman said,

> No, my mother came from al-Zuhra, a village north of Hodeida. She told me that she was still a young girl when she came to Hodeida with her uncle. Her mother had died and her father had married someone else. They sent her to Hodeida to work in the house of a high-ranking person and she grew up here and she married my father. As for my father, he is from Zabid but he was brought up here because his mother moved to Hodeida. His father had died shortly after he was born. His mother moved to Hodeida with him and stayed there. My father was brought up here and he worked as a water carrier. He sold water. In the past there was no piped water, there were no sanitation facilities, there was nothing. But in the neighborhood of al-Sadiqiyya there was a big water tank and my father sold water to the houses.

Does she know how her parents got to know each other? Iman answered, "I haven't asked them directly, but what I have heard is that my father got to know my mother because she used to sell bread next to the water tank where he got water to sell to the people. My mother was selling bread to earn some money for herself. It wasn't *'ayb* (shameful) in those days. That is how they met and they married." Iman's mother moved to her husband's house, but as soon as the first child was born the family moved to another place. "Every time my mother gave birth they moved to another place. They did not have a permanent house, but they rented houses. They were always moving from one place to another." In the first years of the marriage, Iman's father continued to work as a water carrier, but when the family moved to Ghulail, he became a soldier. "My father worked as a soldier in the military camp until he retired. He left the army and he stopped working, but he still has land in Zabid and every year he receives money from the land." Surprised to hear that her father had retired, I asked Iman how old he was, and she said, "He is in his seventies now. He is old. My mother is in her fifties," and she added, "We are, *ma sha Allah*, eight children in total; six girls and two boys.

My youngest sister is twelve years old." Iman has one older sister; her other siblings are younger than she.

> We have lived in al-Mitraq, in al-Duhmiyya, in al-Shahariyya,[1] next to the health center, and then we finally moved to Ghulail. We found a house, I mean land. People used to occupy land in those days. My father and my mother occupied a piece of land, and they built a house and it is our house now. It was in the year that 'Ali 'Abdullah Saleh became president.[2] When the president came to power there was no-body living in Ghulail and then people started to occupy land. The land was from the government and the people called it a rural area. Ghulail was first a rural area. The people who are now living in al-Rabasa were living there. They had camels and they had cows, and people in Hodeida didn't know about that place. When they heard that people were occupying land free of charge people moved out of Hodeida. Those who used to rent before came to live here. Like us—we were always living in rented houses but when we heard about the *bast* [the occupation of land] my parents went to Ghulail to occupy a piece of land. The owner of the last house we were living in always wanted to have the house himself and we couldn't find a place to stay. My mother said, "*Khalas*, that's it, I will squat like the others do."

I asked Iman why her mother made this decision and not her father, and she answered, "My father was not at home most of the time. He worked for some time in Saudi Arabia and when he returned he spent a lot of time in Zabid. My mother was the one in charge of the household." She continued,

> We took a big piece of land and we put a piece of wood in every corner and connected them with a rope so that we knew that that

1. All the areas Iman mentions are old neighborhoods in Hodeida.

2. 'Ali 'Abdullah Saleh came to power in 1978. Whereas most of the land in Yemen is in private hands, the land around Hodeida had previously been owned by the Imam and was expropriated after the revolution (Wenner 1991, 82). As most of the plots were not registered, they could therefore easily be occupied when the government allowed it (see also de Regt and Ghailan 2007).

A squatter area on the outskirts of Hodeida.

place was ours. We were still small and in the beginning there were no *sanadiq*; I didn't even know what a *sandaqa* was. There were huts as they use in the countryside, from branches and bushes, and we made huts like that to live in. Later on we built *sanadiq*. Those who didn't have anything made huts, and those who had money made *sanadiq*. There was no water, the streets were not yet asphalted, and when we wanted to go somewhere we had to walk a long way to get to a tarmac road in order to take a bus or taxi. In the beginning we didn't know what Ghulail was. The people used to call the area al-Khabt.[3] They didn't call it Ghulail. When the area started to grow and the people had lived there for a while, they heard that there was a health center in the area called Ghulail and so they called the whole area Ghulail.

I remember from the early years in Ghulail that the urban planners were always coming and we were still young, we didn't wear veils yet. We didn't have anything except for a blanket that my

3. *Al-khabt* literally means "the desert" or "the badlands" (F. Stone 1985, 13).

mother gave us and we sat on it and at night we got an extra blanket to sleep on. And every hour of the day the planners were coming to our house. They wanted to move us out. The planning of the area [*al-takhtit*] started because a lot of people came to occupy land, from Hodeida and from the countryside. Two or three months after we had occupied our land, the planning started, and they came immediately to our house because we were living on a spot where they had planned a school. They moved us out but they gave us another piece of land somewhere else, in a place they had not yet planned. It is government land but we did not buy it, we just lived there like everyone else did. They say that they are going to plan it but until now nothing has happened. We built a house there, first a *sandaqa* and later, bit by bit, a toilet and a kitchen from concrete blocks. We get our electricity by connecting to the neighbors' supply. And recently we also got a water connection.

I asked Iman whether she went to school, and she said, "I went to school when we moved to Ghulail. I was already quite big. I was nine years old." Her older sister did not go to school, though. "My father had always rejected education. He didn't let my oldest sister go to school. He also didn't want me to go to school but my mother decided to let me go." Together with other women in the neighborhood she decided that she wanted her children to be educated and not to be like herself, illiterate and uneducated. Iman continued, "Now all my sisters are educated. All those who came after me went to school." Was her mother so strong, or is there another explanation for this change? "Honestly speaking, it is my mother who rules the house. She is the one who decides." Had it always been like that? Iman replied,

> No, it wasn't like that before but when my father stopped working as a water carrier, from the day that we moved to Ghulail, my mother got the decision-making power. My father went to Sana'a to work as a soldier, and he was not at home most of the time. And when he was at home he didn't involve himself much, even when there were problems with the boys or something. Even nowadays, my mother solves the problems; my father doesn't do anything. So my mother rules the house now, like a man.

Iman was around fifteen years old, and attending the sixth class of primary school, when she heard about the *murshidat* training course in the area of al-Mughtaribin. Together with some friends who were also living in Ghulail, she had often inquired about the possibility of becoming a *murshida*. "We were always going to the health center in Ghulail to ask for work and then they asked us to participate first in a survey, a field survey, in al-Mughtaribin. The al-Mughtaribin center had not yet opened and they wanted to know which services the area needed. We decided to work taking the survey." The survey took place during the school holidays in the summer months. "We had to fill in questionnaires, in all the areas around al-Mughtaribin. It took a month or so, and we earned money." After the survey was completed, they went back to school. "We stopped working because the *murshidat* course was not yet starting, I don't know exactly why the course was delayed, and so we did the first class of intermediate school, my friend Nur and I. We attended the whole year and we also did the exams. When we were supposed to register for the second class of intermediate school the *murshidat* training course started. That was in September 1988."

I asked Iman what her ambitions were when she was at school, and she answered,

> When I was at school I had a desire to study and to become a teacher. I really loved the idea of teaching. I was the head of my class and I was always one of the best. I even assisted the teacher. I wanted to go to the Teachers Institute; there used to be a five-year program to become a teacher. But when we went there, after finishing primary school, they said that they didn't have courses for teachers anymore. You needed a secondary-school certificate to become a teacher. It was a problem for me. I really wanted to become a teacher, and I had hoped to finish the teacher's training quickly because my family was in need of money.

Iman explained that the Teachers Institute was close to their house and that it would have been very easy to attend classes as she would not have needed to pay for transportation and could have had lunch at home. Moreover, the Teachers Institute also financially supported students with excellent marks in their primary-school exams. She was desperately thinking of a solution when she heard about the *murshidat* training course and decided to join. "My family didn't have any income when I entered the course, so the money I received during the course was for my family." Was her father not working at that time? "No, my father wasn't working. He was in Sana'a to register for his pension and he didn't send us money to live on, nothing at all. First my mother, when she didn't see a solution, decided to work for us because she didn't have money, she didn't have anything. She started to work as a servant in a house, and thank God, I could continue my schooling till the first class of intermediate school, and then I started to work on the survey."

What did her father think about her participation in the survey, and her training and employment as a *murshida?* "My father was against it in the beginning, but when my mother spoke to him and said that it would bring in money, he had to agree. But in the beginning he did not want me to work in health care." I asked Iman whether her father was explicitly against her work in health care or against her taking up paid work in general.

> He refused to let me work in health care, I don't know why. He said, "I don't want my daughter to go out in the morning." My father is a bit old-fashioned. He doesn't like it when women go out a lot. Later he agreed because my mother pressed him. She said to him, "Because you are not bringing in money she has found employment. The money is hers. And she does respectable work [*'amal sharaf*], so there is no problem. Why don't you work yourself?" That is why my father eventually agreed.

But would her father have agreed if she had become a teacher? "If I had become a teacher it would have been different. When you study and finish your schooling it obliges you to work with your education, with your certificate." And she added that the fact that the Teachers Institute was close by also influenced her father's opinion. He saw that the girls who studied there were employed as teachers in girls' schools.

For Iman the financial benefit was the main reason for joining the *murshidat* training course. "Some of the women who participated in the survey decided to continue their schooling instead of becoming *murshidat*, but I joined the training course because my family was in need." Did she know anything about the work of *murshidat* before entering the course?

> Honestly, I have to say that I didn't know what a *murshida* was in the beginning. I just didn't want to continue at school because there was no course for teachers anymore. I went to the Ghulail health center and I saw the girls, but the center was not as developed as it is now. The girls were always going into our area and they gave health education, Muna and Riham and the rest. I heard that a *murshida* gives vaccinations and so on, but in the beginning I didn't know what it meant. In fact I didn't want to become a *murshida*. But because of the needs of my family I was forced to enter that type of work because there was nothing else.

Were there really no other possibilities for work? "There was no other work available, and this gave me the chance to increase our family income. The only income we had was mine. If it had been in my mother's hands she would not have let me become a *murshida*. She would have let me finish my studies. But it was not in her hands. And I entered the course and, thank God, I love the work."

So Iman took on the responsibility of providing for the family while her sisters got married. "When I was in the sixth class of primary school my oldest sister got married. She had been working and living in a house in al-Shahariyya for a long time but my father asked her to come home, and he arranged the engagement. My younger sister married soon afterwards." Her father also had plans to arrange an engagement for Iman, but she did everything to change his mind.

> When I was attending the *murshidat* training course my father wanted me to get married but I said to him, "Why should I get married when I am still studying?" I refused. And my mother supported me. She said, "She works, she isn't sitting at home without work like

others do, so why should she get married? It is better that she has work." Thank God, he let me continue my work. But if my mother had not supported me I would have gotten married, really, because two men had come to propose to my sister and me, and my father had already approved. My aunt and my grandmother also supported me. They said to him, "She has now entered health care and she has work. Why will you marry her now? Let her work for a while till her time comes."

In September 1989, Iman completed her training as a *murshida* and started to work at the Ghulail health center, close to her family.

I finished the course and started to work and was able to put all my brothers and sister through school. I paid for them. I paid everything, all the school requirements such as exercise books. Things were cheap at that time. I still buy everything for the girls. My brothers stopped going to school and they only work now and then. They don't have a regular income. My father gets a monthly income from the produce of his land in the village, but he buys *qat* from it. My father chews daily and all his money goes on *qat*. He goes to Zabid to collect the money and stays away for a month, or a month and a half, and comes back without money. My mother always says to him, "Why do you spend all the money? You could at least give me some of the money to provide for the family." But he doesn't listen to her.

In November 1991, Iman married Khalid, who is originally from a village in the Tihama. Iman said,

His parents died and his grandmother brought him up. There was no work in the village and he came to Hodeida to look for work. My brother-in-law knew him and found work for him in the municipality, as an agricultural worker. He stayed at my sister's house and that is how we got to know each other. We liked each other, and he proposed and we got engaged. We had an engagement party and I started saving money for the *mahr* [the dowry]. I saved the money for him, and I bought the clothes, the gold, I bought it all, but from his own money, not from my money. Because he receives a salary but he chews *qat* so I asked him to give me his whole salary.[4] I gave him some money every week to buy *qat* and the rest of the money I saved. We were engaged for about two years. Then he sold his father's land in the village and he completed the *mahr* fully. We had a big wedding party in my sister's house. We both shared in the costs of the party. He paid half of it out of money from the land and I paid half of it from the money of the *mahr*. And his friends helped him. Someone gave sugar, someone gave rice, someone gave wheat, and someone gave Vimto.[5] They helped and we completed the rest and we held the party. The party continued for four days.

I asked Iman whether they moved in with her family and she answered,

Of course; we did not have a house yet. We were thinking of renting a house but then my husband heard that there was *bast*, that people were occupying land in the area of al-Shuhada.[6] My husband went to look for land and he found someone who wanted to sell his plot. He bought the land from him for YR2,000, with a *sandaqa* on it. The other *sandaqa* we made ourselves. There were no neighbors yet, and the plot was big. The area was not yet developed and occupied like it is now. The people still had big pieces of land. The *sandaqa* was ready, the well was ready and, thank God, the bathroom. The house was fenced but there was no water tank yet. We still had to buy a lot of things, but I said to my husband, "We will do it bit by bit." We have been living here since we got married, but I haven't gotten

4. Shami (1997, 94) also mentions that many men in the squatter areas of Amman turn over their entire salaries to their wives or their mothers. "This money is an indication of a woman's authority in the household and the measure of her control over it. It also means that it is up to her to make the money last the month and to provide for the food, the necessities and the emergencies."

5. Vimto is a cold drink made of red syrup, offered to guests at home and on special occasions.

6. Al-Shuhada (lit. "the martyrs") is an area on the outskirts of Hodeida, close to a cemetery where Egyptian soldiers who died during the civil war in the 1960s are buried.

pregnant yet. I was examined but there is nothing wrong with me. So it is still in the hands of God.

Iman's husband works for the municipality.

My husband is not educated. He doesn't know how to read and write but it is not a problem between us. I don't look down on him and I don't talk to him in words that he doesn't understand. We talk normally to each other, we understand each other, and we don't get angry. He does not say, "You are more educated than me," nor do I say, "He is not educated, I don't want him." He knew that I was working and when we made up the wedding contract, my family and my father personally insisted that I should continue my employment. And he agreed, and we have put it down in the marriage contract. And he knew from the beginning that I was giving money to my family, I spoke to him about it before I married him. He doesn't object. On the contrary, he even helps. When my mother wants money or if I don't have enough, when I don't have money for the 'Id,[7] he gives them money. He doesn't have a family himself. He only has one brother. We bought a motorbike[8] for his brother, and we arranged his engagement and bought him a piece of land and built a *sandaqa* on it. We joined savings clubs and, to be honest, we bought a television and we connected water to the house and we bought gold for his brother. Some people think that I have a lot of money because my husband and I are on our own, because we don't have children, and so we can save a lot of money. But they don't know that we take care of his brother and my family.

In August 1993, Iman was appointed head of clinic in a newly established health center in the area of al-Sana'i. In 1996, she received financial assistance from the project to finish intermediate school. During my visit in April 2002, I heard that Iman had been replaced as

7. The 'Id is a religious feast. The two most important religious feasts are 'Id *al-Fitr* (the feast of the breaking of the fast) at the end of Ramadhan, and 'Id *al-Adha* (the feast of immolation) at the end of the yearly pilgrimage to Mecca.

8. Motorbikes are used as taxis and therefore a profitable investment.

head of the health center in al-Sanaʻi and was attending an upgrading course to become a community midwife. I found her in the Health Manpower Institute, and we agreed to meet in her parental house in Ghulail the next day. Her brother was getting married, and she was going to take two weeks off. I discussed her life story with her, in the presence of all her sisters and many women neighbors who were all busy with preparations for the wedding. Iman told me about the changes in her life. She told me that she had finished intermediate school and the first class of secondary school but only decided to attend the upgrading course to community midwife in 2002. She is still living with her husband in al-Sanaʻi and has no children yet. She is still financially supporting her family as she was five years ago. All her sisters and brothers have stopped going to school. Four of her sisters and one of her brothers have married. Her married brother works now and then; the other brother has become a soldier and also provides for the family. Her father is still absent most of the time.

"We Were in Need of Work"

Social Status in the Tihama

Although social stratification has received ample attention in ethnographic studies on the Yemeni highlands (see Gerholm 1977; Stevenson 1985; Dresch 1993), relatively little has been written on social stratification and status differentials in the Tihama.[9] This lack is unfortunate as the Tihama has a very distinct history, and the mutual migration flow from and to overseas areas have put an important stamp on its population, affecting patterns of social stratification. Most important are the age-long contacts with the African continent, which have led to the presence of a large group of dark-skinned people with clear African features. Their skin color ranges from light brown to black, and

9. Most anthropological studies on Yemen focus on the tribal highlands, as Walters (1987, 68) also mentions. Recent exceptions are the work of Meneley (1996) and Dahlgren (2004).

even children of the same parents can have very different skin colors. Despite the wide range of skin colors, non-Tihama residents often categorize all Tihamis (inhabitants of the Tihama) as black (*aswad*) (Walters 2001, 77), and very dark-skinned people as *akhdam*, which is the lowest social-status group in Yemen based on their assumed African ancestry. There are status differentials in the Tihama independent of skin color, and only a small part of the Tihama population belongs to the *akhdam*. Yet in addition to the system of social stratification, Yemen also has a regional hierarchy; people coming from the highlands have the highest status, followed by people from the central lowlands (the Hujjariyya), while people from the Tihama are located at the bottom of this ladder.

Walters (1987; 1998; 2001) is one of the few anthropologists who have looked into issues of race and ethnicity in Yemen, based on, among other things, fieldwork in the Tihama. She concludes that although skin color definitely has an aesthetic value in Yemen, and lighter skins are preferred over darker skins, social status in Yemen does not correspond to skin color (Walters 2001, 77). Social classes are first and foremost based on the ability to trace "an honorable lineage which others acknowledge" (76). *Akhdam* are unable to trace such a lineage and therefore are treated as social outcasts and excluded from regular social life. They live outside villages and towns and earn an income by street sweeping, collecting refuse, and other activities that are very much looked down on. But many Tihamis, even though they may have darker skin than people in the highlands, are able to trace their lineage and do not belong to the lowest social status groups. Among them are *'abid* (former slaves whose African descent is known) and also people of other social status groups.

In her study on women, social status, and identity in the Tihama town of Zabid, Meneley (1996, 12) argues that status differentials are very important but do not correspond exactly with the social status groups as described for the Yemeni highlands. The majority of the Zabidis refer to themselves as *al-nas* (which literally means "the people"). Within this group, families are distinguished on the basis of their wealth and influence. Both *sada* and non-*sada* families can be part of the elite; social status in Zabid is thus not something that is inherited but obtained through a complex set of social rules and practices, which mainly revolve around the importance of hospitality. In Meneley's view, Yemeni systems of social stratification are not as immutable as indigenous descriptions sometimes suggest; social mobility from one category to the next is possible, upward as well as downward (Walters 1998, 13; see also Messick 1993, 159). In the past thirty years, social status is increasingly being replaced by economic status; people from low-status backgrounds have been able to improve their positions through education and employment.

This elaboration on social status in the Tihama is necessary to understand the background of Iman's family. Iman was born in Hodeida, but her parents came from rural families in the Tihama. Her mother came from al-Zuhra, a small town in the northern Tihama, while her father originally came from a village near Zabid. From the occupations her parents performed, some conclusions about Iman's social background can be drawn. First of all, the fact that her mother first worked as a domestic servant in the house of a high-ranking person and later started to sell bread indicates that she came from a low-status group. Domestic labor in other people's homes was considered shameful.[10] In many parts of Yemen, market activities also had a low status and were performed only by people of low social status. It is interesting to note that Iman explicitly says that selling bread was not *'ayb* (shameful) in those days, which can be regarded as a denial of her mother's low status. Moreover, she seems to imply that activities that were not shameful in the past have become shameful nowadays. Before becoming a soldier, Iman's father worked as a water carrier, which also had a low status. Moreover, after the revolution many people of low social status were employed in the army. From the work Iman's parents performed it is therefore likely that Iman is from a low-status family, but it is not clear whether she belongs to the *'abid* or the *akhdam*.

---

10. According to Meneley (1996, 14), domestic labor in Zabid was only performed by *akhdam*. In contrast, an interviewee in Destremeau (2001, 3) mentions that in Sana'a people did not allow *akhdam* to work in their houses.

Many other women in the second and third group of *murshidat* had similar family backgrounds, being born in Hodeida although their parents originally came from villages in the Tihama and had performed low-status work. Based on her research among *murshidat* in the Tihami town of 'Abs, Walters (2001, 87) argues that "the *murshidat* . . . play a pivotal role in challenging Yemen's social divisions, especially Yemen's cultural, racial, and gender hierarchies."[11] In her eyes, the *murshidat* can be seen as agents of change, altering the health situation and the living conditions of the lower social classes and bringing about changes in their own lives at the same time. Walters bases her argument on the fact that women of low social status groups, especially those from *'abid* and *akhdam* backgrounds, have been trained and employed as *murshidat* and on the fact that health-care services are now extended to people of low social status. Such people, in particular those who are presumed to have African origins, were previously excluded from health-care services and nowadays, thanks to the work of the *murshidat*, are included in home visits and accepted in the health centers.

The training and employment of *murshidat* has shifted racial boundaries to a certain extent, but issues of race are still very common in Yemen. Whenever I tried to talk about social status, people would immediately deny that they were of low social status themselves (see Walters 1987, 43; vom Bruck 1996, 147). Yet in my encounters with women from higher social classes I realized that the people living in the squatter areas were considered to be of low social status. These women were often astonished when I told them that I regularly went to al-Sana'i or to other squatter areas on the outskirts of Hodeida, and visited people at home. My close relationships with friends and colleagues living in the squatter areas was for them very odd. The contradiction of a high-status woman enjoying the company of low-status women challenged social boundaries of status and identity and must

11. This is also the main argument of the documentary Walters made, entitled "Murshidat: Female Primary Health Care Workers Transforming Society in Yemen" (1999).

also have affected the image of the project (see Walters 1987, 30). The notions of development we, as Dutch development workers, promoted were inspired by ideas of racial equality, equity, and human rights, in particular for the poor and subordinated classes. Yet these notions were to a large extent incongruent with the notions of certain groups of people in Yemen, and in particular of higher social classes in control of health-care policies.

Responsible Daughters, Broken Dreams

Whereas the majority of the first *murshidat* joined the training course because they aspired to continue their education, many young women in the second group interrupted their schooling in order to become *murshidat.* Instead of continuing their education, they felt forced to take up paid work and to provide for their families. Iman, for example, had dreamed of becoming a teacher, but because her family was in need of money she decided to withdraw from school and become a *murshida,* even though she did not like the idea of working in health care. Iman is not the only one who took on the responsibility of providing for her family. From the life stories of the *murshidat* it becomes clear that many daughters feel responsible for their immediate and extended families, and in particular for their younger siblings, and that is the reason they take up paid work. In contrast to what is often thought, many of these young women are not forced by their parents to go out to work, but they themselves take the initiative to start working. Iman told me how her father in the first instance was against her participation in the *murshidat* training course. "He was against it in the beginning because I came home late and he didn't like that. He doesn't like it when girls are outside a lot." It was Iman's mother who supported her decision to enter the course, and who convinced her father. She did this by referring to her husband's neglect in providing for the family: "Because you are not bringing in money she has found employment. The money is hers. And she works with her honor so there is no problem. Why don't you work yourself?" The fact that Iman's mother supported the initiative of her daughter is related to the fact that her mother is the one who has to make ends meet and who lacks money to feed her children.

Amal, another *murshida* and a close friend of Iman's, also lives in Ghulail, and her story has remarkable similarities with that of Iman. Amal's parents come from the rural area of Jabal Rayma, in the mountains east of the Tihama, and are of a low social status.[12] They moved to Hodeida and, after having lived for some time in the city center, occupied a large plot of land in Ghulail. Amal's father used to be a soldier and was based in the military camp but, just like Iman's father, decided to retire when Amal was still at school. Amal said, "He wasn't very old, but he didn't want to work anymore." In order to register for his pension, her father had to go to Sana'a but every time he went to Sana'a he stayed away for a long time and came back without having completed the procedures, making up all kind of excuses. In the first years after he stopped working he was able to earn some money by selling parts of the land he had occupied, but it became gradually more and more difficult to make a living. Amal felt obliged to take up paid work: "I entered health care because of the circumstances [*al-zuruf*], because when my father stopped working there was no one to provide for the family. I needed to sacrifice myself because I was the oldest and my brothers and sisters had to go to school." When I asked her whose idea it was that she start the course she emphasized that it was her own idea. "Sometimes there was no work for my father, there was no one who wanted to buy or sell anything,[13] then we had a hard time. The family grew and we had to go to school, we needed exercise books and we needed clothes for school, and so on, and there were the daily

12. The fact that Amal is from a low-status family became clear to me when she once told me about the *zar* (trance dance) meetings she and her mother sometimes attended. According to Meneley (1996, 15), in Zabid only the *akhdam* and the *'abid* participate in the *zar*. Other *murshidat* were surprised when they heard that I was interested in attending a *zar* meeting as they looked down on it and saw it as an un-Islamic practice.

13. Many men in the squatter areas work as brokers *(dallal)*, mediating between buyers and sellers, in particular with regard to land.

household expenses. It was hard." Her older brother didn't take up paid work. "Honestly speaking, my brother doesn't want to work. He went to join the army, he stayed there for two days or a week and then he came back and said that he didn't like it." Amal became a *murshida* although she wanted to become a teacher. "I wanted to finish my studies and teach or something. I wasn't planning to take up paid work so quickly. But when I heard that there was work and when I looked at our situation, I decided that I could not continue my education."

The stories of Iman and Amal show the complexities of household relations, and the differences in opinion that may exist between individual members of households. In chapter 5, I quoted Ibrahim, who made a case for looking at "adaptive family strategies," in particular with regard to women's education and employment. In Ibrahim's view, important decisions in families are to a large extent collectively reached, albeit after negotiation (1985, 259). To do justice to the individual strategies and choices of household members and to capture the complexities of decision-making processes in households, concepts such as negotiation, bargaining, competition, and benefits have been introduced. Although some researchers have criticized the use of these somewhat "economic" terms, as they may homogenize certain highly contextual and varied behaviors (see Wolf 1992, 22), they have been very important to show the agency of individual household members. This applies in particular to the agency of working women, who were previously presented as victims of household survival strategies on the assumption that male household members were the main decision-makers. Complex family dynamics determine women's entrance into the labor market, and women often play important roles in decisions about the acquisition and spending of household income (see Dwyer and Bruce 1988; Singerman 1995; Hoodfar 1999). Their own employment is thus not necessarily something that is imposed upon them. Iman and Amal presented their decisions to become *murshidat* as individual decisions, but this decision was clearly inspired by the circumstances of their families. While their parents did not force them to quit school and take up paid work, they felt obliged to do so. By presenting their decisions as individual ones, they could better accept the consequences of the decisions, such as the fact that they left school without really wishing to.

In many studies on women's employment the particular positions of daughters come to the fore (see for example Salaff 1981; Ong 1987; Wolf 1992; Moors 1995; Rosenfeld 2002). In chapter 5, I said that girls' education is often not prioritized in patrilineal families because sons are expected to provide for their paternal family, whereas daughters are expected to leave the household after marrying. In poor families in need of income, eldest daughters often withdraw from school to take up paid work in order to contribute to the household income. In doing so they may finance the education of their brothers and their younger sisters. Iman financed the schooling of her younger siblings. Her brothers, however, were not able to find better jobs after they finished their education, and Iman continued to support her family even after marrying and setting up her own household. In the interview, Iman emphasized that her role is rather exceptional, and that people around her do not know that she is still supporting her family, probably because it is shameful to acknowledge that a married daughter is supporting her parents (see Moors 1995, 247). Yet other *murshidat* confirmed to me that there are many women who, after marrying, continue to support their parental family, and that their financial support may often be more stable and regular than the financial support sons give.

Many of the young women who took up paid work as *murshidat* were eldest daughters. Their fathers were sometimes against their training and employment, which can be explained by the important notion of the male breadwinner in Yemeni society. The employment of their daughters would be an expression of their incompetence to provide for their families. Yet the inability or unwillingness of certain men to offer a solution to the financial problems of the family forced them to allow their wives and daughters to take up paid work, albeit after negotiations. And even the brothers of some of the *murshidat*, who had been able to continue their education thanks to their sisters, were unable or unwilling to find paid work and provide for their families. I sometimes heard people in Hodeida say that it was more difficult for

A young woman participating in a training course.

men to find paid work than for women, in particular after the return of thousands of migrant workers from Saudi Arabia in the early 1990s. It is interesting to note the relative ease with which many Yemeni men stay at home without work and accept that their female relatives do paid work in a society where the status of men is linked to providing for their families.[14]

While fathers may often be ambivalent about their daughters' employment, which might threaten their position as provider, mothers have different interests. Their responsibility for cooking, feeding,

14. One of the heads of clinic told me that she often saw the husbands of certain *murshidat* in the Health Office, collecting the salaries of their wives before payday. She was amazed that these men dared to show so openly that they are in need of their wives' salaries.

and clothing their children means they are confronted on a daily basis with the lack of money. For mothers it is therefore of crucial importance that someone in the family earn an income, and many women without male providers decide to take up paid work themselves, if the situation allows it. They prefer to seek employment instead of sending their children out to work. In her study on Algerian "women without men," Jansen concludes that widows and other women without male providers in many cases take up paid work to enable their daughters to continue their studies. Education makes it easier for their daughters to find employment and build a career so that they will be able to support their mothers in old age (1987, 240). Moreover, in doing so, daughters can become socially mobile and improve their social status (248). Moors (1995, 189) comes to a similar conclusion in her study on Palestinian women and property but also mentions that some daughters pay the price of their mothers' employment. Depending on the type and length of work, older daughters sometimes have to take over their mothers' household responsibilities and are taken out of school at a young age. Iman emphasized that her mother would have preferred her to continue her schooling rather than start the *murshidat* training course. When Iman's father failed to provide for his family, her mother started working as a cleaner. Only at a later stage, when the financial problems of the family increased and her mother could not combine her work anymore with the care for her children, did she encourage Iman to seek employment. Yet while the young women who sacrificed themselves to become *murshidat* were certainly disappointed about the fact that they could not continue their schooling and fulfill their dreams, they themselves also seized the opportunity to be trained as *murshidat*. Being trained and employed as *murshidat* had certain advantages, as the next section will show.

The Benefits of Paid Work

Iman and Amal decided to sacrifice their ambitions for the sake of their families and take up paid work as *murshidat* instead of continuing their schooling. But to what extent was this really a sacrifice?

What were the advantages for them of taking up paid work? And how did they benefit from their employment? It is likely that these young women also saw some benefits in their training and employment as *murshidat*, which made a sacrifice worthwhile. In her study on working daughters in Hong Kong, Salaff convincingly shows that there is no unequivocal answer to the question of whether women's paid employment, and in particular the employment of daughters, sustains or tears down patriarchal family hierarchies. On one hand, young unmarried women of low-class families often stop going to school to take up paid work, whereas their male siblings continue their education, as they are supposed to provide for their families in the future. Women's labor is thus in a way exploited in order to sustain dominant gender ideologies. On the other hand, paid employment may give women a greater degree of self-determination, resulting in more control over marriage decisions, over leisure activities, over the use of their own money, and an increased contribution to family decision-making (Salaff 1981, 270). The particular ways in which gender hierarchies are sustained or challenged differ according to social, cultural, and economic contexts.

The women who joined the second *murshidat* training course definitely saw advantages in being trained and employed as *murshidat*. Iman had visited the health center in Ghulail several times and had met the first *murshidat*. She decided that she would not mind becoming one of them, even though she would have preferred to become a teacher. The fact that the work of *murshidat* was a new phenomenon in the area was in various respects beneficial for the development of the profession. The first group of *murshidat* had been able to negotiate their training and employment, cleverly making use of the fact that their work was new and unknown and selectively presenting aspects of the work to their relatives and neighbors. The young women who lived in Ghulail and who were interested in becoming *murshidat* did not have this possibility; their families were already acquainted with the work of the *murshidat*, through the activities in the health center and through the home visits of the first group. Yet the fact that the nature of the work was known was in the case of the second group a positive aspect of being trained and employed as a *murshida*. The new identities created by the first group were of crucial importance in making the profession attractive. Their white uniforms, the project transportation, the monthly salaries, and the contacts with foreigners all contributed to the image of a modern profession, making their training and employment as *murshidat* attractive to themselves as well as to their relatives. The modern image of the profession turned low-class daughters into professional service workers and, similar to the female data processors in Freeman's study (2000) who cherished their new identities as "pink-collar" workers, the *murshidat* greatly valued their new position and identity.

The positions of the *murshidat* changed in many other ways as well. As a result of their employment, their status in their families and in their communities altered. They were suddenly earning a salary and, with this salary, gained increasing decision-making power in their families. Iman became the main provider for her family, and so she was able to resist her father's pressure to get married and eventually selected her own spouse. "My mother said to him: 'She has her work, she isn't sitting at home like others without work, so why should she get married?'" But Iman added that she would not have been able to resist if her mother had not supported her. Her mother thus had a greater say in decisions regarding the marriage of her daughters than Iman had, even though Iman had an important role as provider. Iman was able to marry someone she chose herself, an acquaintance of her brother's who grew up in a village near Zabid. Iman's father agreed to the marriage but insisted that she should continue her work and support her parents. So before getting married, Iman discussed her employment and the financial responsibilities she carried for her family with her husband-to-be. He reacted positively, and she was able to continue the financial support to her family after setting up her own household. In that way she continued to take responsibility and be the main breadwinner for her parents and her siblings. They were able to go to school, and it is clear that she is proud of that.

Like many other *murshidat*, Iman "married down": her husband is less educated than she, he is illiterate, and he works as an unskilled laborer in the municipality.[15] Marrying down has advantages and disadvantages. With regard to class, marrying down is disadvantageous because it implies a decrease of social and economic status (see Moors 1995, 88), but with regard to gender relations, marrying down is often advantageous because it may give women more leverage over their husbands. The husbands of the *murshidat* who married down had low-skilled jobs with low salaries, and they were therefore often willing to accept the paid labor of their wives, so the *murshidat* were able to continue their work. While working-class and lower-middle-class women with paid work often aspire to get married and leave their jobs (see Pollert 1981, 100; Macleod 1991; 55), the *murshidat* valued their work highly and wanted to continue after marrying. In addition to the independent income they earned, they desired to continue their paid work because of the new positions and identities they had acquired as *murshidat*. They had become professional health-care workers, well respected in the project, recognized in the community and with important responsibilities. None of them wanted to give up this position to get married, and their choice of a husband of a lower social status who would accept their paid work is in that sense understandable. On the other hand, their own status as working women may also have affected the choice of marriage partners. Men who are better off prefer to marry a woman who has not compromised her social position by taking up paid work, in particular work of a relatively low status.

Noha, one of the *murshidat* trained during the third training course, told me that when she was thirteen years old she had married a man who was illiterate. She had three children but was able to obtain her primary-school certificate at the Yemeni Women's Association. She had wanted to become a teacher, but when she heard about the *murshidat* training course from a neighbor, she decided to join the course. Her husband first encouraged her to study and to work in the health center but gradually started to cause problems and tried to prevent her working. His relatives insisted that he should not allow his

15. Unskilled laborers working for the municipality are in many cases of low-status backgrounds, belonging to the *'abid* or the *akhdam*.

wife to be away from home so much. At a certain point he forbade her to join a training course in Aden, but Noha did not listen to him and went anyway (it helped that her father supported her). When she came back, her husband forced her to choose between him and her work. Noha chose her work; she told me that she did not love him anyway and that her work was much more important to her. The fact that she had an independent salary even enabled her to take the full (financial) responsibility for her three children.

Earning an income was not only important to support one's family but also of major importance for the positions and identities of the *murshidat*. Daughters from poor families previously had no choice but to take up unskilled work as cleaners, factory workers, or money counters in banks, work that was in general looked down on. The *murshidat* profession offered women from low-status backgrounds the opportunity to take up work that required at least basic education and offered an additional one-year training course, which helped to increase the status of the work. As mentioned before, they suddenly turned into government employees, earning a monthly salary, working for a foreign development project, and with an important task in their community. The new identities they gained through their training and employment as *murshidat* were of crucial importance to them. The fact that all *murshidat* with whom I spoke expressed how much they loved their work must also be understood in this context. As I will show in chapter 8, their new identities as professional workers were protected and promoted by the project team, while the *murshidat* themselves started to make use of their new positions to form a power block in the project. But first I will turn to another group of women who entered the *murshidat* profession, again introducing new identities in an already diverse group.

Badriyya

I met Badriyya during the poverty analysis survey carried out in Hodeida in 1993; she was an interviewer for the survey and stood out as an intelligent and outspoken young woman. I liked her and was intrigued by her independent behavior. She was tall and light-skinned with clear African features, and she wore colorful *balati*[16] and headscarves. Badriyya was one of the few *murshidat* who did not wear a face veil. Yet one day when I was waiting for her on one of the benches at the Ghulail health center to do some work, I didn't recognize her when she entered and greeted me. She was wearing a black *balto* and a black face veil; only her headscarf was still colored. When I expressed my surprise at this sudden metamorphosis, Badriyya laughed and explained that she had to dress that way because she had been admitted to the Faculty of Islamic Studies. All the women in the faculty dressed like that. "If you don't veil, the teachers don't pay attention to you" was her explanation. It was not her first choice to do Islamic studies. She had wanted to study economics, but her secondary-school grades were too low, so she decided to do Islamic Studies for a year.[17] Next year she would again do the final exams of secondary school and would, she hoped, be admitted to the Faculty of Economic and Commercial Sciences.

Badriyya stood out not only because of her way of dressing but also because of her perseverance in continuing her studies. She was intelligent, a quick learner, and very ambitious. When I told her about my plans to write a dissertation about the *murshidat*, she was very interested and asked me about the methodology of my research and the Ph.D. system in the Netherlands. She was very willing to be interviewed, and we agreed to meet in her parental house in al-Mughtaribin. At the time of the interview, Badriyya was engaged and still living with her parents in a house made of concrete blocks, which was their own property. We sat on mattresses on the floor of an empty room and

16. The *balto* (pl. *balati*)is a long overcoat, which is combined with a headscarf *(hijab)* and a face veil *(niqab)*. While the *sharshaf* was seen as a sign of modernity in the 1960s and 1970s, since the early 1990s modern (educated) women almost always wear a *balto* (for details on Yemeni women's clothing see Mundy 1983; Carapico 2001; and Moors 2003).

17. While studies such as medicine and economics require high secondary-school marks, the requirements to study Islam are lower.

talked for hours. Because Badriyya was one of the few women of mixed parentage willing to talk with me about her background, and because she was able to continue her education and even finish university, I decided to present her story in this chapter. Yet her story is atypical because she did not enter the *murshidat* training course to provide for her family.

Badriyya started her story saying, "I was born in 1972, in the city of Kassala in Sudan. My father is Yemeni and my mother is Sudanese. My father migrated to Sudan because there were problems in his village. In that period many Yemenis went to Ethiopia, to Sudan, to Somalia. My father went to Sudan." I asked Badriyya where her father originally came from, and she said,

> He is from the Tihama, from Wadi Mawr. He was young when he migrated. He went with his father and his mother and his brothers and sisters. Even my grandfather and my grandmother left. There were people who had left before and there were people who left in that same period. Most people migrated because there was a famine in the country, but my family left because of problems in their village. They first went to Ethiopia but my grandfather was of the type that protects his traditions, like Yemenis here, and according to him everything was *haram* [forbidden according to Islam]. But in Ethiopia everything is allowed: men and women mix freely, people drink alcohol, there are casinos, etc. And he didn't like that. He wanted a Muslim country, like Yemen. So that is why he went to Sudan. He took his children and everything and left for Kassala in Sudan. It is very far away from Addis Ababa, where they used to live, and the trip was hard. Two of my uncles died on the way; a lot of people died.

The family arrived in Kassala, in the southeast of Sudan and decided to stay there.

I asked Badriyya what kind of work her grandfather did in Sudan, and she answered, "My grandfather used to have a farm in Yemen. He supervised the farm and the land. In Kassala he had a bakery and later he also had a butcher's shop. And he sold small things. My father went to school in Sudan, and later on he worked in his father's business. He supervised the bakery, and he supervised the butcher's shop." And her mother, what was her background? Had she gone to school?

My mother is not educated, because her father did not want women to be educated. Women had to stay at home, to cook, to clean, and then my mother was the oldest and he did not want her to go to school. He wanted her to stay at home. My father wanted to marry a Yemeni woman, and in Kassala there were a lot of Yemenis. But he did not like the Yemeni women and neither did he like the Ethiopian women. He wanted a protected girl [*bint muhafadha*], and he did not find anyone good enough except my mother, who was Sudanese. My father married her because he thought that he was going to stay in Sudan forever. He did not want to go back to Yemen. Even my grandfather said to them: "*Khalas*, that's it, you will stay here." They never thought about going back.

But when President al-Hamdi came to power, he said that he wanted all the Yemenis to come back. If it weren't for al-Hamdi, the people would not have returned, but al-Hamdi said, "You have to come back. It is necessary." And then he said that Yemen had changed, that everything was okay, that there were houses, that there was I don't know what. Because of what he said, my father and my uncles thought that Yemen had changed, that everything was available now. The people were talking about Yemen all the time. They said that Yemen was like a paradise, that there were grapes growing everywhere. My cousin who lived in Sudan put the idea of going back to Yemen in my father's mind. He said, "Yemen is good, in Yemen everything is available nowadays." And the Yemeni government even gave plane tickets free of charge to those who wanted to return. So my father decided to go back as well. But when we arrived in Yemen we were surprised. We had lived much, much better in Sudan. We had been well off. We had a big house and even had maids at home.

I asked Badriyya when her family returned to Yemen, and she answered, "We came back in 1977. I was five years old and my oldest brother was around seventeen. I have six brothers and two sisters and I am the youngest. We lived in Sana'a for a while. But we found it difficult; we were living in a very small apartment and moreover, Sana‘a is cold. In Sudan the weather is not like the weather in Sana‘a. People told my father that Hodeida is better because the weather resembles the weather in Kassala. So we decided to go to Hodeida." I asked Badriyya why her father had not immediately settled in the Tihama as he was originally from Wadi Mawr, an area in the Tihama, and she answered, "My father could not return to his village because the people had changed, he did not know them anymore because he was small when he left the village. And on top of that, my mother had insisted that she did not want to live in a village in Yemen." And she continued,

> My mother did not know Yemen at all and she only followed my father because of her children. People in Sudan said to her, "Why do you go? Stay here with your father and mother," but she had said, "No, I will follow my children anywhere they go."
>
> As for housing, we liked Sana‘a better than Hodeida. We had been living in a stone house in Sana‘a but here we did not have a house. When we first arrived in Hodeida we lived for a while in the area of al-Duhmiyya but my parents did not like it there. The people in the area were always quarreling and using bad language. Then my father heard that all those who had come from Ethiopia, Sudan, and Somalia were living in al-Mughtaribin. He went there and he saw that there were no nice houses there, all of them were broken and they were made out of boxes but he still decided to move to al-Mughtaribin. That is how we came to live here. You could live anywhere you wanted. And we built a house, and there were big cars coming from the port to give us water, clothes, food, vegetables, everything. Al-Hamdi organized everything for the returnees. Initially President al-Hamdi had said that he would give the houses in the neighborhood of al-‘Ummal[18] to the returnees. He had encouraged us to leave Sudan and he had said that houses would be available in Yemen. But the inhabitants of al-‘Ummal went outside to demonstrate, they said,

18. The area al-‘Ummal (lit. "the laborers") was built for dockworkers, close to the port.

"We are laborers and we were living here before they came. How can you give this place to those who came from Ethiopia?"

So the government went back on its decision and left the area of al-'Ummal to the laborers and they gave us the area of al-Mughtaribin. Al-Hamdi wanted to make al-Mughtaribin like the area of al-'Ummal. Engineers came down from Sana'a. We had not yet been here for a year when the engineers came. They planned the area and so on, but al-Hamdi died in the same year. They killed him in 1978, a year after we came back to Yemen.[19] After that there was nothing we could do but live like this.

Did her father find work after their return to Yemen? Badriyya said, "None of the returnees had work in the beginning. There was no work in the port because most of the people from al-'Ummal were working there. But then they heard that there was work in the wood company of al-Aswadi, and they were employed there as laborers. Because my father had managed the business of his father in Sudan, he was employed as the supervisor of the laborers. He did administrative work."

In Sudan, Badriyya had gone to kindergarten, and in Hodeida she went to primary school.

Although I was smart I didn't like school when I was young. I played a lot and I didn't like to listen. My father spoiled me; he gave me everything I wanted. My sister had to carry my schoolbag for me because I didn't want to go to school. I even failed the exams of the first year of primary school. Then I changed to another school, where there were some Sudanese teachers, and they said, "You are the daughter of my sister, you have to go to school." My mother also encouraged us to attend school; she said to us, "I did not go to school, so you have to go to school." But my father only encouraged the boys to go to school. For five years I went to the primary school next to the health center and for the sixth class I went to another school because the school in our area closed down. I did the sixth class in Madrasa al-Khawla and also the first two classes of intermediate school. When I started to

19. In reality, al-Hamdi was assassinated in October 1977.

like school I became active. I was a school monitor and I trained the pupils when the sports teacher was absent. And I was the head of the Red Crescent[20] at school. They gave courses in first aid and so on and I participated.

Badriyya's activities did not stop at school.

When I was in intermediate school I started to work for the Ministry of Information. We organized parties in schools, when there were occasions like the Twenty-sixth of September.[21] I was earning YR800 per month. I liked the work but my parents did not approve of it. They said that I was too young and that there was no need for me to work. Then I heard about the project. A school friend who was living in Ghulail said to me, "There is a project in Ghulail where they train girls, and then employ them. You should go there and work with them." She always said that to me and to other girls in school. I said, "No, I don't want to go there. I want to work at the Ministry of Information." That was in 1986. But we did go to Ghulail to get more information about the training course and the work, and we spoke with Fatima Salem. And then at a certain moment Fatima visited me and said, "You have to join us. We are in need of girls." And when my father did not let me work at the Ministry of Information, I decided to work on the survey with the project. My parents approved of the work because it was with girls. They met Fatima, she came to our house, and they did not have any objections.

Badriyya participated first in the rapid appraisal, which was carried out in the area of al-Mughtaribin. "We had to fill in questionnaires and we got paid weekly." I asked her what she did with the money she earned, and she said,

I went shopping with friends and bought things for myself, clothes. After the survey we went back to school. The survey was in 1987,

20. The Red Crescent is an organization similar to the Red Cross.
21. The Twenty-sixth of September is the national holiday of former North Yemen, the day that the Yemen Arab Republic was established.

and then in 1988, in the beginning of 1988, I was in the first class of intermediate school and the same friend said to me: "Look, the project for which we worked, they are organizing a course now." That is what she said to me. She told me that there had been a training course in Ghulail in 1986 and that they were now going to do the same in al-Mughtaribin. We talked to Fatima, and she registered us and said that the course would start in six months' time. So I went back to school. I was at that time in the second class of intermediate school. When the course started I stopped going to school.

I asked Badriyya why she decided to attend the *murshidat* training course and not continue her schooling, and she answered,

In 1988 the rules for government employment started to change and I said to myself, "Maybe when I finish secondary school I will not find employment, so I have to find government employment first and then I can finish my studies." At the beginning of the eighties you could get employed with a primary-school certificate, but bit by bit they were saying that it was not possible anymore to be employed with six years primary school only but that you needed a higher certificate. The situation became more complicated, not like it was before, that anyone could be government employed. I said, "If I graduate for example in 1990 there may not be employment for me. It is better that I get employed now." The main thing was that I would obtain government employment and then I would finish my studies.

The project gave us a training allowance in the beginning and continued to give us a salary for about a year after the course. I gave some money to my mother, and I gave some money to my father, and the rest was for me. From the beginning of the course my thoughts started to change. I started to take tomorrow into account. What do I want to do in the future? Even though I was working I continued my schooling. I stopped buying clothes and makeup and saved money for transportation. I was young so I didn't need these things. And I started to take care of myself during my studies; from the second class of intermediate school until now at university, there is no one who is paying for me. I pay for myself from the money that I earn. From the moment that we received money from the project I took care of myself. My father doesn't have to give me anything.

I stopped going to school for a year when I was attending the course, but after that I continued with the third class of intermediate school. I was working in the Ghulail health center and I took my school uniform with me to work. When it was time I said to the director of the project, "Maybe I will leave at 12:00 or 12:30" and I told the head teacher, "I work in the center so sometimes I will be late." She said to me, "You can come at 1:00 or 1:30, the place is open." I left the center and I went to school. I had lunch at school. I ate a sandwich because at that time everything was cheap. When there were difficult lessons I went to a private teacher after school. Sometimes I left the house at 7:30 in the morning and I came home at 7:30 in the evening. In this way I also finished secondary school.

Badriyya worked from 1989 till 1993 as a *murshida* in the al-Mughtaribin health center and then became deputy head of clinic in the al-'Ummal health center. In the meantime she continued her studies and had big ambitions.

I wanted to go to university in Sana'a, because there was no university in Hodeida, but it would cost me a lot and I needed a place to stay. I only studied at the Faculty of Islamic Studies for a month and then the director of the National Institute encouraged me to register at the Institute and study management sciences. I studied two years at the Institute and I planned to do the third year in Sana'a. Then they opened a private university here and I continued the other two years here. When I heard that there was a private university I started to save part of my salary. I was trying to economize on my expenses. It is enough to have one *balto* and one *hijab*, the rest of the money I saved. I put it in the bank until it had become a big amount and then I started to pay. They requested YR26,000 per year,[22] without books, without clothes, without the extra lectures and the transportation. It was a lot!

I am studying economics and political science at the university. The dean of the university said to me that it would be possible for

22. In 1998, US$1 equaled YR160.

me to do my master's free of charge but on condition that I teach at the university after I graduate. But I don't want to teach at the university after graduation. I want to implement what I studied because how long do I continue to study? What's the point of studying without using your knowledge? That doesn't make sense. I have to practice. When I have done my master's in business administration I can manage more than a head of clinic. I can plan activities. I can do more things. I can develop a lot of things, especially because I have worked from the start, from the beginning of the survey to the management of the program.

I asked Badriyya what her ambitions were with regard to her personal life. Does she want to get married?

My fiancé is studying medicine in Eastern Europe; he is doing his master's and his doctorate at the same time. I met him in the health center where he was doing his internship as a doctor. When we got to know each other he said that he did not want to stay in Yemen. He only wanted to work in Yemen for three years and then go abroad again. But after we met he said, "Okay, I will study abroad and later I will take you with me. We will get married and live there." I said to him, "No, I have to stay here. I have to serve my country. I have to work, at least ten or twenty years." And then we agreed that he would finish his doctorate there and think about it. We bought land and when we have enough money we will start to build our house bit by bit. We will not have a wedding the way people normally do. We will try to do it as simply as possible because I don't want a dowry [*mahr*] of YR200,000–300,000. My parents are not like those people that want a lot of money. When my fiancé came to them, he said to my father, "How much do you want?" And my father said, "I don't want anything. I want a man." They still have not agreed on the conditions. They said that after he comes back he is free to see what he wants to give. They also did not set a lot of conditions. Everything will be sorted out in the future.

In 1998, Badriyya graduated in economics and political science with a specialization in management science. She wanted to do a master's, but she did not have the money. Instead she obtained a position in the Training Department of the Hodeida Health Office, and I ran into her during my very first days in Hodeida in April 2002. She does not work anymore as a *murshida* but benefits from her experiences at the practical level of the health center to organize training courses and support the community participation program. She hopes to do her master's at the University of Sana'a in 2003, five years after she graduated. As to her engagement, she decided to end it because her fiancé was not willing to return to Yemen and insisted that she should come and live with him abroad. "I know what it means to be a *mughtarib*, an emigrant, and I don't want to move again to a new country" was her explanation. She left the land they had bought together to him, and she herself took the furniture and the other things they had bought.

"First Get Employed, Then Finish My Studies"

Being of Mixed Parentage

Badriyya started her story saying that she was born in Sudan, and that her mother is Sudanese. She is of mixed parentage, a *muwallada* (m. sing. *muwallad*), although she does not use that word herself.[23] In anthropological studies on Yemen, much attention has been paid to social stratification but very little has been written about the status of *muwalladin* (f. pl. *muwalladat*), despite their important role in Yemen's history and present day society. Ho is one of the very few contemporary scholars who have written about the *muwalladin* in Yemen, in particular about *muwalladin* in the Hadhramawt.[24] The large group of

23. With regard to the various usages of the term *muwalladin*, Ho (1997, 131) mentions that in Muslim Spain *muwalladin* were Spaniards who had embraced Islam. In other cases *muwallad* and *muwallada* refer to foreign slaves born and raised among Arabs. A third usage is to designate people of mixed parentage, the sense in which the term is used in Yemen.

24. In the introduction to her article on gender, class and ethnicity in Yemen, Seif (1995, 290) briefly mentions her own background as a *muwallada*, the hybrid

muwalladin is a result of the numerous contacts between Yemen and other parts of the world, through migration and trade relations. *Muwalladin* can have a variety of backgrounds. In North Yemen the age-long contacts with East Africa have resulted in a large group of people born from Yemeni fathers and African mothers, whereas the majority of *muwalladin* in South Yemen have mixed Asian parentage, owing to the migration of Yemenis to Southeast Asia (Ho 1997, 139).

Large out-migration from Yemen started halfway through the nineteenth century with the British colonization of Aden (1839) and the French colonization of Djibouti (1884). Both these colonial enclaves created work opportunities and attracted many Yemenis, from the surrounding areas but also from the interior (Swanson 1979, 51). But in particular, people living in the coastal areas, such as the Tihama, were easily tempted to make the crossing in periods of poverty and famine. The Tihama is one of Yemen's most fertile areas, situated next to the Red Sea but close enough to the mountains to benefit extensively from the full wadis during the rainy seasons, in particular since the introduction of spate irrigation (see Mundy 1985). But despite the fertility of the land, the population of the Tihama has recurrently been subjected to drought and famine, and entire villages were sometimes abandoned as a result of sand dune encroachment (see Ertürk 1994). As a result, many Tihamis migrated; Badriyya's father also migrated during a period of famine. Another reason mentioned by Stevenson (1993, 17) was that through migration people of low-status groups, such as the *'abid* and the *akhdam*, escaped the status ascribed to them in their home villages.

Yemeni migrants not only found work in the ports; working in Aden or Djibouti also functioned as a gateway to other countries, as numerous ships stopped at the ports to refuel and were often willing to take on Arab crewmen. British ships took the migrants to other British

---

status of *muwalladin*, and their discrimination, but she neglects the position of *muwalladin* completely in the remainder of her article. She limits her analysis to the *akhdam* and the *'abid*. In addition, Carapico and Wuerth (2000) discuss the case of a *muwallada* in their article on gender and citizenship in Yemen.

colonies in the Far East, such as India and Singapore, and to Britain itself, where there was a need for laborers in the growing coal industry. French boats functioned as means of transportation to French colonies, such as Vietnam and Madagascar, and in a lesser degree to France itself. Yemenis could easily find their way to other countries in Africa via Djibouti, in particular after the finalization of the railway to Addis Ababa in 1889. Yemeni communities can be found in Kenya, Tanzania, Uganda, Ethiopia, Sudan, and even Chad. Ethiopia was the main country to which Yemenis migrated since the end of the nineteenth century. According to Meyer (1986, 17), there were around 50,000 Yemenis in Ethiopia in 1970. Many Yemeni men were married to Ethiopian women and had set up families. In the 1970s, the increase in nationalism among Ethiopians and the changing of laws in favor of Ethiopian merchants over foreigners, coupled with the changing political climate in Yemen, resulted in large-scale return migration to Yemen. The peaks of this return migration were in 1972 and 1977. In 1972, the Eritrean Liberation Front (ELF) hijacked an Ethiopian plane that crashed, killing all the passengers. As Arab governments were known to support the ELF, there were massive demonstrations against the presence of Arab immigrants in Ethiopia. In 1977, the new socialist government in Ethiopia started to expropriate the property of foreigners; many Yemenis were victims of this new policy and decided to return to their homeland. In other East African countries, such as Sudan, Djibouti, and Somalia, nationalist governments also came to power and changed laws that had previously favored foreigners. Foreign migrants, including many Yemenis, lost the favorable positions they had held, and started to look for alternatives.

An additional reason for returning to Yemen was the new policy of President al-Hamdi. Al-Hamdi actively promoted the equality of Yemeni citizens and supported the rights of returning migrants to Yemen. He initiated housing and employment projects for people of low-status backgrounds, trying to improve their socioeconomic situation, and he made a strong call to Yemenis living overseas to come home. His main aim was to bring educated people to Yemen, and many *muwalladin* had benefited from the educational opportunities

offered abroad. Al-Hamdi promised returning migrants employment, free housing, and a better future.[25] These promises appealed to
many Yemeni emigrants whose stay abroad was already under threat
because of the changing political climate in their host countries, and
many of them decided to return home. However, some of them were
more interested in the opportunities offered by the oil business in the
Gulf and migrated there. Al-Hamdi used the promising economic
situation to start administrative reform and initiate major development plans in Yemen. Yet his progressive ideas were not received enthusiastically by everyone, and he was murdered in October 1977,
only two years after the start of his government. Little of what he had
promised got off the ground.

By sending home remittances, many emigrants had financially
supported the republican forces in their struggle against the Imamate,
but with their return to Yemen they became second- or even third-
class citizens. The returnees were blamed for many of Yemen's social,
economic, and political problems and had a low social status.[26] In the
constitution of the Yemen Arab Republic, equality of all citizens was
proclaimed and status differentials were officially abolished. Yet although every Yemeni now became a *muwatin* (citizen) regardless of
family background, those who were born abroad and who were of
mixed parentage obtained the status of *muwallad*, an official designation used by both government officials and common people. The
term *muwallad* gained a negative connotation leading to overt as well
as covert discrimination (see Ho 1997, 132).[27] One of the fundamental
divisions in Yemeni society is the division between those who consider
themselves pure Yemenis and those who are denied this attribute (vom

25. As Badriyya mentioned, the area of al-Mughtaribin (lit. "the emigrants") in
Hodeida was especially planned for returning migrants from Africa.

26. In the early years of their return to Yemen, migrants were sometimes jok-
ingly called "*mu'awana* Haile Selassi": "Haile Selassi's development aid" to Yemen.

27. Also the other status differentials, which had for centuries determined social
relations, were not easily put aside, and discrimination on the basis of family background and skin color continued to exist.

Bruck 1996, 148). The fact that *muwalladin* are not of pure Yemeni descent affects their social status. It is hard to generalize about the status of *muwalladin* because there are differentials within the group; the status of the *muwallad* is dependent on the father's family in Yemen. If the father came from a high-status family, the *muwallad* will have a higher status than one whose father came from a low-status family. In addition to the social status of the father, his regional background is also important: a *muwallad* whose father originated from the Tihama has a lower status than a *muwallad* whose father came from the highlands.

Because of the negative connotation and the consequent discrimination, few people of mixed descent call themselves *muwalladin*, and many try to hide their family background. Badriyya speaks openly about her background and the history of her family, but there were also *murshidat* who tried to hide the fact that they were born abroad and had African mothers. Two *murshidat* trained during the first training course were *muwalladat* as well, but they did not want me to know about it and told me their mothers were Yemeni. Two other *murshidat* I interviewed lied about their places of birth and the ethnic backgrounds of their mothers. Only later did I hear from other women, who were *muwalladat* themselves, that these *murshidat* were both born in Ethiopia and had Ethiopian mothers. This denial of one's family background is telling for the negative connotation attached to *muwalladin* status, and the subsequent fear of discrimination.

Badriyya also suffered from discrimination. Obtaining government employment was her main concern, but she had to wait a long time before she was officially employed. "Because we were *muwalladat sudaniyyat* it was very hard for us to get an identity card (ID)." An ID was needed to get government employment; it was hard to get one because *muwalladin* had to prove that they were of Yemeni descent. They needed letters from their fathers' relatives, the approval of these letters by the *shaykh* of the village or town where their father was born, and the approval of the regional court. With these letters they had to go to Sana'a to obtain an ID. It often happened that relatives of the returnees did not want to confirm the family relationship because they were afraid that they would have to share their property rights, such as family land, with their returned relatives. Consequently, returnees sometimes preferred not to go back to their home villages. After unification it became easier for *muwalladin* to obtain IDs, and they are less (openly) discriminated against than before. The three *muwalladat* trained during the second training course also obtained their official labor contracts after unification. Yet there is still discrimination, and very few *muwalladin* are, for example, able to obtain high positions in the government.[28]

Most people I spoke with said that the differences between *muwalladin* and *muwatinin* have become less, and *muwalladat* who have grown up in Yemen sometimes even deny that there is a difference. They stress that they are Yemenis and that there is no difference between them and *muwatinat*. Yet I observed that many *muwalladat* socialize with other *muwalladat*, and the emphasis they put on "not being different" must be understood as a strategy to diminish the chances of discrimination. This strategy is in line with the situation described by Carapico and Wuerth in their article on gender and citizenship in Yemen: while Arwa, a woman born of a Yemeni father and an Eritrean woman, who spent an important part of her life in her mother's homeland, obtained Yemeni citizenship in the 1970s, she suffered from social discrimination and preferred to interact mainly with the *muwalladin* community (2000, 270).

The Impact of Return Migration

The changes, differences, and ambiguities in the identities of returnees, and in particular of the *muwalladat*, are a telling example of the dynamics of migration and identity. From the many anthropological studies on migration, the multiple ways in which migrants negotiate their identities in a new environment come to the fore. Benmayor and Skotnes (1994, 8) argue against the tendency to see migration as a

28. The place of birth of a *muwallad* is sometimes added as an adjective, such as in *muwallad sudani* (having a Sudanese parent), *muwallad habashi* (having an Ethiopian/Eritrean parent), or *muwallad somali* (having a Somali parent).

single movement in space and a single moment in time. In their view migration is "a long-term . . . if not life-long process of negotiating identity, difference, and the right to fully exist and flourish in the new context." In a similar way they argue for the use of identity as a dynamic concept, constructed, multifaceted, negotiated, and situational.

> Migration has disrupted static conceptions of identity . . . and nation-states are being forced to confront their own myths of cultural unity or racialized purity. New generations born out of mixed ethnic/racial, and cross-cultural marriages resist conformity to an "assimilated" norm (whether that of the dominant society or of the home culture) and affirm instead a more consciously complex notion of who they are. (Benmayor and Skotnes 1994, 9)

What was the role of migration and ethnicity in the training and employment of women of mixed parentage as *murshidat?* Was their low status in society the reason that they entered this new profession? Or was it the migration process they had gone through that made them open to taking up paid work in a new profession? In the analysis of the stories of the *muwalladat,* a number of answers to these questions can be found.

The majority of Yemeni emigrants who returned from East African countries had lived for decades overseas. Young men and boys had left their home villages in Yemen at a young age to seek employment in the docks and later as traders. They had set up their own families, often by marrying local women. As long as they were doing well and were able to make a living, nothing had made them think of going back to Yemen. The changing political circumstances in the countries of their migration and in Yemen persuaded them to return to their homeland. Yet while many Yemeni emigrants originally came from rural areas, few of those born in the Tihama returned to their home villages. They preferred to stay in big cities like Hodeida. One of the reasons was that they had become accustomed to an urban way of life and could make better use of the skills they had acquired abroad, in the cities (Meyer 1989, 2). Also, they no longer had links with their home villages. Sa'diyya, one of the other *muwalladat* trained during the second course, told me that her father went back to his village in the Tihama to look for his brothers and sisters but only found one of them alive. "My father had two brothers and three sisters. He only found one of his sisters alive. The rest had died. My uncle had died two years before we came back when he went on the *hajj* [the pilgrimage to Mecca]. The rest died of diseases." A third reason that few returnees went back to their original villages was that their African wives did not want to live in a village. Like Badriyya's mother, they agreed to the move to Yemen on the condition that they would live in a town. Fear of being marginalized in the village may have been one of the reasons for that preference.

Unlike most of the returnees, Sa'diyya's father had wanted to stay in the village, but because he did not find any relatives, the family settled in Hodeida in the area of al-Mughtaribin, together with many other returnees. "We know everyone in the area from before. We are like one big family. There are people from Eritrea, from Massawa, that my mother and my father know." Sa'diyya's mother was Eritrean, and her parents had married in Eritrea but the family had moved to Sudan at the time of the civil war in Ethiopia. In Sudan none of the children had gone to school. "We were migrants and we did not have a residence permit, so we were not allowed to go to school in Sudan. But my father was also against schooling for girls. He was strict. He did not want girls to study. He said that girls only needed to learn to read the Quran." But back in Yemen her father gradually changed his ideas. After staying at home for about two years, Sa'diyya and her sister started going to literacy classes at the Yemeni Women's Association. Sa'diyya was at that time around fourteen and too old to go to a regular primary school. After obtaining her primary-school certificate, she registered for the *murshidat* training course and became a *murshida*, despite her father's initial ideas on women's education and employment.

While Badriyya's story about Sudan is a story filled with nostalgia, Sa'diyya emphasized that her family was not well accepted in Sudan because they were migrants. The fact that Sa'diyya's family arrived as refugees in Sudan, together with many refugees from Eritrea, is one of the main reasons for these different experiences. In the struggle for a decent living and as a response to a new, and sometimes hostile, environment, migrants can become very conservative and decide to hold on strictly to their own traditions, protecting themselves against outside influences. Yet the return to Yemen ushered in a new phase. While fathers in the first instance continued to be conservative in their attitudes toward women's education and employment, they gradually loosened the reins. The experiences they had gone through abroad, and their contacts with other societies, may have affected their changing attitude toward education and employment of women. Return migration may also lead to a more flexible attitude in which new ideas and experiences are more easily accepted, sometimes inspired by the realization that the society at home has changed as well.

Another important factor in the lives of the *murshidat* of mixed parentage was the role of their mothers. The story of Iman has already shown how important the support of her mother was. Mothers in poor families often saw the need for education and paid work for their daughters, first because they wanted a better future for their daughters and second because they were in need of money to run the household. In the case of young women of mixed parentage, the support of the mother was of a different nature. Their mothers were of African origin and were born and brought up in countries that were in many aspects very different from Yemen. Yemen was a totally new country for these women, and they had to get used to the different mentality of its people, and to the different social environment. Many people who were brought up in East African countries, such as Ethiopia, Eritrea and Sudan, continue to emphasize the different social environment of their countries of birth (see also Carapico and Würth 2000, 270). The majority of the examples given refer to gender relationships: gender segregation is less strict, women do not wear a veil (at least in the way Yemeni women veil), men and women can socialize easily, and education for women is more common.[29] In their eyes these examples

29. Interestingly, the idea that women's education is common in East Africa is not supported by the life stories of the women who were born in East African

show that they are much more modern than Yemenis, and they often look down on the Yemeni way of living, which they regard as "backward" (*mutakhalluf*).[30]

Ho mentions similar sentiments in his article on *muwalladin* in the Hadhramawt. A number of reformist authors in the mid–nineteenth century, of Hadhrami descent living in Indonesia, "saw the homeland as backward and culturally retarded, and believed that the light of modernism and reform would come from the East Indies" (Ho 1997, 139). But many other migrants worried about the moral upbringing of their children abroad and decided to send them home to study (141). *Muwalladin* who returned to Yemen in the second half of the twentieth century, forced by the changing political climate in the countries of migration, also encountered ambivalent attitudes concerning morality and modernity. As Ho formulates it, "Perhaps their cheerful disregard for time-honored local ways, coupled with familiarity with the paraphernalia of modern life, present a contradictory complex, which challenges local self-conceptions of the superiority of ancestry and home-land" (145). And this may also explain why, despite the many contacts between Yemen and the outside world, *muwalladin* are still discriminated against. The fact that they often have a relatively liberal attitude, and do not adapt to (traditional) norms and values, puts them in a special position that evokes discrimination.

In my encounters with women in Hodeida, I often heard discussions between *muwalladat* and *muwatinat* about how to interpret Islamic prescriptions such as veiling. *Muwalladat* were often less strict and had less

---

countries. Their mothers had not attended school. The emphasis *muwalladin* put on women's education must therefore be interpreted as a symbol of modernity. As mentioned before, education, and in particular women's education, is often used as measurement of development of a country.

30. Morris (1991, 158) mentions that two of the *murshidat* trained in the primary-health-care project in 'Abs each had a Yemeni father and an African (in this case Ethiopian) mother. Their parents were in favor of their education and employment even though the local population criticized them for letting their daughters go to school and take up paid work. The social status of the daughters was low, and Morris rightly asks whether they would be able to win the confidence of local mothers.

conservative interpretations of Islam, which they expressed by wearing *balati* and colorful headscarves and by not wearing face veils. Badriyya's way of dressing is an example of a more progressive interpretation. Yet social pressures at the university forced her to shift to what many Yemeni women saw as an Islamic way of dressing, in black and with a face veil. And there were other *muwalladat* who decided to wear a black *balto* and a black face veil. Most of them explained that they were forced to dress that way to avoid harassment from Yemeni men who saw unveiled women as easy prey for their advances, in particular after the influx of returnees from Saudia Arabia and the Gulf States in September 1990. Others wanted to hide their identities as *muwalladat*. Only a small number of *muwalladat* did so for religious reasons, believing that this was the proper way for Muslim women to dress.

The migration to Yemen offered the *muwalladat* ample opportunities to negotiate their identities through, for example, their way of dressing, their work, or their interpretations of Islam. Their position was hybrid, as they could draw on various registers of gender, labor, and development, combining "Yemeni" notions with other notions they had picked up abroad. One of the main claims they made was that they were more modern and "civilized" than people who had never left Yemen, a response that may have been evoked by the low status ascribed to them in Yemen. The *murshidat* training course gave them a chance to take up paid work in a profession that also had a kind of hybrid status—a new profession in health care but not in nursing, a profession for which a limited level of education was needed, a profession with an ambiguous status as it had a modern image but contained aspects challenging gender and social boundaries, linked to mother and child health care but crossing the boundaries of public and private in other ways. It therefore made sense that women of low status who were actively carving out their identities in a new society joined the *murshidat* training course. Their employment as *murshidat* enhanced their status as modern professional workers and gave them the opportunity to develop themselves.[31]

31. I also heard from various people that *muwalladat* had been the first to take up paid work in nursing in the 1970s and 1980s. Because of their ambiguous status they

The First Step in a Career

Badriyya succeeded very well in "developing herself." She was able to continue her schooling while working as a *murshida* and she managed to finish university. In her eyes her employment as a *murshida* was only a first step in a career. Although her story is quite exceptional, it gives insight into the strategies she used to achieve her ambitions and can shed light on the reasons other *murshidat* could not follow her example. First of all, Badriyya was ambitious and active from a young age. Although she said that she was not initially interested in school, as she was too playful and not serious, she became a very active student in later years and had outspoken ideas about her future. She wanted to work at the Ministry of Information, but her parents did not allow her to continue in that direction. They said that she was too young and that there was no need for her to work. But when she was approached to participate in the health center survey of the area, her parents approved and did not use those arguments anymore. An important reason was that Fatima Salem, the supervisor of the *murshidat*, visited Badriyya's parents and explained the work.

Badriyya liked the work on the survey but went back to school afterwards. When the *murshidat* training course started, she registered, but for a very important and specific reason that few of the other *murshidat* mentioned to me: the changing rules of government employment. Around 1988, the ways in which a person could obtain government employment started to change. In the 1970s a primary-school certificate had been enough to become a government employee, as the government was rapidly trying to build up a state apparatus, but in the second half of the 1980s fewer people were employed because of the deteriorating economic situation. Badriyya was cleverly looking ahead and planning her future. She saw the advantages of obtaining government employment before higher school certificates were being required. Government employment was very attractive because it

functioned as pioneers, entering certain categories of work that were not yet culturally acceptable for Yemeni women.

meant a tenured contract, a monthly salary, and the right to sick leave and maternity leave. Government employment used to be restricted to two categories of women: educated women who were employed as teachers in girls' schools and uneducated women who were employed as cleaners or as factory workers in government-owned factories. With the employment of *murshidat* as government employees, a new group of women entered civil service: young women who had finished primary school and who came from lower social classes. For them, obtaining government employment meant an increase in status, and they referred to themselves as *muwazzafat* (employees), a term that had a positive connotation.

Whereas Iman was in need of paid work to provide for her family and only entered the civil service by coincidence, Badriyya strategically planned to become a government employee before it was too late. She did not really need the money in the early days of her employment and used it for clothes and other personal necessities. But gradually her salary became essential to finance her studies. She proudly said that she financed her studies herself and that no one helped her. In the second course for *murshidat* there was another young woman who was as ambitious as Badriyya and who succeeded in finishing secondary school while working as a *murshida*. But Halima could not afford to go to a private university. She had a lot of younger siblings and lacked support from her family. She went to the National Institute instead, where she did a two-year diploma course in business administration. She planned to finish her degree, which would take another two years, and followed a community midwife course in the meantime. The differences between Badriyya and Halima show the importance of one's starting position for the development of a career. Being the youngest one in her family, Badriyya did not have household responsibilities and could spend all her income on study.

Only a few *murshidat* were able to combine schooling and work to the extent Badriyya and Halima did. While most of them aspired to continue their studies, they encountered various obstacles on the way. The main obstacle was that those who had finished primary school and wanted to continue with intermediate school could not do so because intermediate school classes were taught in the mornings, when they were working in the health center. In Yemen, one can study at home and sit school exams without attending classes, but that requires a lot of discipline and assistance from someone who can explain the material. Badriyya said that she took private lessons when she needed assistance, but not everyone can afford to pay a private teacher, and it was difficult for the young women who were providing for their families.[32] The women who had household responsibilities at home encountered another problem: for them it was very hard to make time for study. Badriyya mentioned that there were times when she was not at home during the entire day. Her family situation allowed her to do this; she was the youngest in the family and her parents gave her the necessary freedom to go her own way. But many women were obliged to stay at home and help their mothers or take care of their siblings. For those *murshidat* who were married and had children, it was even more difficult to find time to study. But even some of them managed to continue their studies, like Hawa from the first group of *murshidat* who obtained her intermediate-school certificate while she was working and taking care of her five children.

The importance of government employment for women of low-status families, and the intentions of many of the *murshidat* to continue their studies and gradually upgrade their qualifications, were things the project management was not aware of. There was a clear difference between the aspirations of the women trained and the intentions of the project staff. In the eyes of the Dutch development workers, the work of the *murshidat* was of vital importance for the development of Yemen's health-care sector. Yet in the eyes of many

---

32. Singerman (1995, 160–62) discusses the importance of private lessons in the Egyptian educational system. The situation in Egypt is to a large extent comparable to the situation in Yemen, where overcrowded classrooms, underpaid teachers, and poorly equipped schools also affect the quality of teaching. In addition, private lessons are essential for those who prepare themselves at home for schools exams, as do many of the *murshidat* who combine their work with studying.

of the *murshidat*, their training and employment was only a first step in a career. They were often far more ambitious for themselves than the project members expected. These different notions of development sometimes led to disappointment and frustration for the *murshidat*, who had aspired to continue their education and obtain work with a higher social status.

8

The Project at Its Peak,
1988–1993

IMAN AND BADRIYYA were both part of the second group of *mur-shidat* trained in 1988–89. In the previous chapter I discussed their backgrounds and motivations for becoming health workers. I paid particular attention to the social status of young women living in the squatter areas in Hodeida, most of them being daughters of rural migrants or of returned migrants from Africa. Their social status was often low, and their training and employment as health workers can be viewed as a form of upward mobility. In this chapter I will further elaborate on the way in which the women trained and employed in the Hodeida Urban Primary Health Care Project acquired new positions and identities. While the first group of *murshidat* was confronted with negative attitudes about health-care work and women's employment, the second group benefited from the way in which the first group had shifted boundaries. The fact that their duties and positions in the project changed had a positive impact on their social status.

A New Group of *Murshidat*

The stories of Iman and Badriyya show that the women in the second group had different backgrounds and motivation than those in the first course had. Some came from Ghulail and others came from al-Mughtaribin. Some were looking for paid work while others only wanted government employment and planned to continue their studies while they were working. But there was one thing they all had in common: all the participants in the second group, with the exception of one, were young women who were unmarried and did not have children. Although the initial idea of the project management had been to train mothers from within the squatter areas as *murshidat*, assuming that they would be better able to build up relationships of trust with the mothers in the area, young and unmarried women were attracted to the work. This was remarkable because the experiences of training unmarried women as *murshidat* in the first group did not have encouraging results.

As mentioned before, three out of the six unmarried women got married immediately after the course and stopped working altogether. The three *murshidat* who were already married and had children before they started the course continued their work and even became heads of clinic in a later period. Their starting position was different from those of young, unmarried women. The women who were already married before starting the course had discussed their training and work as *murshidat* with their husbands and had been given the green light. But the women who married after the training course had to negotiate their right to work with their husbands and sometimes had to withdraw from work. Married women seemed to be a more reliable and less vulnerable category of workers, but it was hard to find married women willing to become *murshidat*, so the project team registered the names of all women, married or unmarried, interested in following the course. In Ghulail a number of young women came by themselves to the health center to ask for work. Others got to know about the project via friends and schoolmates, like Badriyya, who was informed by a friend at school. By January 1988, thirty-five candidates had registered for the course. This number increased in a couple of months to sixty. The number of interested young women was so large that the project management did not need to contact the Yemeni Women's Association for assistance with recruitment.

Although the marital status of the women was no longer a determining selection criterion, another important issue was discussed time and again. Was it better if the *murshidat* came from the area itself, or was it more effective if they came from outside the area they would work in? The first group of *murshidat* had come from outside the squatter area because there were no literate women living in the area. The experiences of the first group showed that there were a number of advantages in employing women from outside the squatter area. They were not known to the people and could therefore build up a certain image of being "knowledgeable" and respectable. In doing so, they had successfully gained the confidence of the families in the area and they had functioned as an example for young women in the area interested in becoming *murshidat.* In a relatively short period of time the educational level of women living in Ghulail had increased, and many young women were interested in attending the *murshidat* training course. But would unmarried women from Ghulail itself be able to build the same level of confidence with mothers in the area? They would probably know the area better, and the families living in the area, but would they be accepted as health educators? Would women in the area tell them their problems and ask their advice? Despite these questions, the fact that so many unmarried women showed an interest in becoming *murshidat* was for the project enough reason to drop the idea that *murshidat* had to be mature women with children. The ease with which the selection criteria were changed shows that practical considerations were more important than policies and project plans. The unintended consequences of this decision will appear later.

A selection procedure was set up for the second group, and each woman was invited for an interview. A selection committee consisting of Fatima Salem, Thera de Haas, and someone from the Health Manpower Institute in Hodeida interviewed the women in order to assess their backgrounds and motivation. After the interview had taken place, the women took a simple written test to check their educational level. In the first group there had been a number of women who had not yet finished primary school, and some had been very young. In the second group the minimum age was set at eighteen, and the rules were applied strictly. Amal, Iman's friend, was not accepted for the second course because she was only seventeen. She was accepted one year later when the third group of *murshidat* was recruited. The age rules were applied strictly because it was felt that age, and a certain level of maturity, were important in health care. The *murshidat* had to deal with mature women with children and had a responsible task in communicating and assisting these women. But age alone was not a guarantee of maturity, and therefore the interview had to show whether the candidate was serious and mature enough to take on the responsibility of being a *murshida*. Thus, because it was hard to find married women with children who could become *murshidat* extra attention was paid to the selection process. Motivated women in need of money or explicitly interested in working in health care, who were over eighteen and had a primary-school certificate, were selected.

The rapid-appraisal survey carried out in the area of al-Mughtaribin in the summer of 1987 functioned as a kind of preselection. Thirteen young women participated in taking this survey. Some of them had come regularly to the health center in Ghulail looking for work, while others found out about it from friends. The rapid appraisal was a tryout, for the women as well as for the project management. The young women became acquainted with the project and gained some experience in home visits, while the project management was able to find out how serious the women were. The survey took place during the summer holidays, and after the work was finished the women all went back to school because the training course was delayed, as the health center in al-Mughtaribin was not yet ready. When the official registration for the training course began, Fatima contacted the women to see if they were interested in participating, and they were invited to take the exam. All those that chose to join the course were accepted.

Three women joined the course as late applicants without going through the selection procedure. Samira was one of them. She was the only woman with children in the second group and had already been married twice. Her family was originally from a rural area near Taiz, but they had moved to Hodeida when Samira's father died. Her older brothers had found work and supported their mother and their younger brothers and sisters. When Samira was fifteen years old she was married to a much older man who had worked in Saudi Arabia. He was a kind man and relatively well off, but Samira resented the marriage so much that she continually ran away to her mother's house. A year later, after many problems, her husband finally accepted a divorce, and Samira returned to her family. Two years later she decided to marry a friend of her brother's who was working in Saudi Arabia and who occasionally came to Hodeida. But this marriage also failed because her husband did not want to take financial responsibility for Samira and their two children and often disappeared without leaving money behind. Her husband would only agree to a divorce if Samira would take care of herself and her children. Samira lived with her mother, whose only income was the salary of her deceased husband,[1] and the money her brothers sometimes gave her. "I became tired of the responsibility. And you know what happened then? I saw an Egyptian soap opera on television, and there was an Egyptian woman who had children and was divorced and she went to literacy classes. By God, she was the reason that I left the house. Really, the soap was useful."

Samira went to literacy classes although she had never been interested in education before. Her mother took care of her children, and she spent day and night studying. After a couple of years, she obtained her primary-school certificate at the Yemeni Women's Association and started to look for work. "I said, I will do any kind of work. In those days a certificate of the sixth class was acceptable. With a certificate of six years of primary education you could get employment anywhere, even at the bank." So she first applied to work as a money counter at the Central Bank of Yemen. She passed the selection exam but was overwhelmed by the noise and the crowds in the bank and hesitated in accepting the post. By the time she had decided to take it, someone else had already accepted the work, and Samira was left empty-handed. "I stayed home for some time and then I went to Doctor 'Abdullah Ahmed. Do you know him? He was director-general of the Health Office before. He is from the same area as my parents; they

1. In Yemen, salaries of deceased people are paid to the dependents of the deceased person, as a kind of allowance. This is one of the reasons government employment is attractive but also explains the high percentage of the government budget paid in salaries, and the difficulties in cutting down on these expenditures.

know each other. I went to his clinic[2] with my sister and I told him that I wanted to work in his clinic. He told me about the health-education course and he wrote a letter to Fatima Salem. I went to Ghulail and gave the letter to her."

Samira's story was so convincing that she was immediately accepted to the course. In fact she fulfilled all the selection criteria: she was a mature woman with children in need of income, and she had a primary-school certificate. She did not live in Ghulail or al-Mughtaribin but in the new squatter area of al-Salakhana, close to al-Mughtaribin. Although Samira was a late applicant, she was perfect for the course. There were also two sisters who joined the course after it had started who came from a well-to-do family in town. They were not in need of income and came through a recommendation. Unlike Samira, they never really explained how they had joined the course, but they were always seen as a bit different from the others. Thera de Haas later said that the project team had made a mistake in accepting the two young women because they came from a higher social class. This statement shows that there were also unwritten criteria regarding the social background of the *murshidat*. While the first group of *murshidat* had come from relatively well-off families, the second group mainly came from lower social classes. The project team was in favor of training women who came from backgrounds that were not too different from the people they had to serve. Twenty women were selected for the second course. The project management had purposely sought women from different areas of the city: there were four women from Ghulail, three women from al-Mughtaribin, and a number of women from other parts of the city.

Again Some Dropouts

According to the stories of the *murshidat*, twenty students showed up in class. But within a short period of time, nine of them had dropped

---

2. Health managers employed by the government almost always have private businesses as well.

out. Participants dropped out for various reasons. One was that the students were informed that they had to sign an agreement with the project to work for least five years after finishing the course. If they resigned earlier, they would have to pay back all the costs of the course. The Yemeni codirector of the project, Hamid Hassan, invented this rule because he was afraid that the same thing would happen as with the first group, where three of the nine women left almost immediately after the end of the course because they got married. But five years was a long time, and some women were not sure they would be able to continue working for such a long time. Some preferred to finish their general education instead. The Dutch team members that I interviewed said that they also thought that five years was a long time, but they left the decision about this new rule to the Yemeni codirector. In their view the five-year rule was not the reason participants left the course. The rule was just a big stick, meant to show that the women had to take the course seriously, and the rule was not to be applied strictly because none of the participants would have been able to pay back the costs. According to them, women who dropped out had second thoughts. They were not interested enough in becoming *murshidat* and preferred to continue their general education. One girl in the group was disabled, and after further discussion she withdrew from the course. Two other women, who were initially friends, became involved with a male nurse at the hospital and were dismissed from the course, another example of the disciplining of the *murshidat*.

With the arrival of eleven newly graduated *murshidat* in September 1989, the total number of *murshidat* was now seventeen. *Murshidat* of the first and the second groups were distributed between the Ghulail and al-Mughtaribin health centers. Muna, from the first group, became head of clinic in Ghulail, under the supervision of Thera de Haas, while Riham, also from the first group, became head of clinic in al-Mughtaribin, under the supervision of Fatima Salem. Some of the *murshidat* from the first course were transferred to al-Mughtaribin, while some of the women from the second course were placed in Ghulail. This mixture was based on the personalities and capabilities of the women. The place of residence was not used as a

criterion, despite all the earlier discussion. The opening of the new
health center in al-Mughtaribin had been postponed until the new
group of *murshidat* was available. They had done their practical training in al-Mughtaribin and had already started mapping the area. A
third training course for *murshidat* was planned to start shortly after
the second course had finished.

Changing Positions and Identities

Getting Used to Home Visits

Previously, I described the obstacles the *murshidat* had to overcome before families in the area accepted them. Despite the fact that the first
group of *murshidat* had functioned as pioneers and paved the way for
other *murshidat*, the second group had to deal with many of the same
obstacles, in particular in the area of al-Mughtaribin, where home visiting was not yet known. And although many of the new *murshidat*
were acquainted with the work of the first group, they said that they
were surprised when they heard that home visiting was an essential
part of their work. There was no systematic home visiting system yet
at the time of their training, and they were the ones who would establish such a system, which may have contributed to this incomplete
picture of their future work. Some said that they would not have registered for the course if they had known beforehand that they would
have to do home visits. Yet they moved on to do home visits, and there
were relatively few problems with their families.

People in Ghulail were often suspicious of the intentions of the
murshidat because of the presence of the urban development project,
and in the area of al-Mughtaribin people also did not receive the *murshidat* with open arms. Some women in the area refused home visits
because they did not have confidence in the health center; others were
not interested in the services of the *murshidat*. Badriyya told me that
they were sometimes scared to go on home visits. "We hated to go to
the houses. The people might argue with us. They might harass us because it was a new idea that girls enter the houses. That was the reason

Health workers going on home visits in a squatter area.

we were afraid. And most of all we were afraid that when we knocked on people's doors we would meet single men." The main problems were encountered during Ramadan, when most people sleep during the day and stay up at night. While the *murshidat* preferred to stop their home visits during Ramadan, the project management was of the opinion that they should continue their work as usual. In chapter 6, I described the difficulties women encountered doing home visits in their own neighborhoods during Ramadan. The second group of *murshidat* continued to have these difficulties when they worked in their own areas. The only difference from the first group was that the families in the neighborhood knew that they were working as *murshidat*, while the first group of *murshidat* had hidden the nature of their employment from their neighbors. The result was that the *murshidat* were often confronted with women who were in a bad temper or whose husbands were still at home. The *murshidat* as well as the mothers felt embarrassed, and the *murshidat* often decided to come back another time, after Ramadan.

Another important issue raised by the *murshidat* was that their home visits were sometimes of limited use to the mothers. Especially in case of repeated visits to families at risk, the health education messages delivered by the *murshidat* did not yield results. Poverty was often the main reason that the health situation of the families was bad, and the *murshidat* were unable to improve the living standard of the families they visited. "The mothers get fed up and they say, 'Why are you coming every day? What are you going to do for us? What are you going to give us?'" Some of the *murshidat* became frustrated at the limited effect of their visits,[3] and their complaints resulted in the establishment of a food program[4] for poor families and the start of sewing classes for women in need of income. In this way the *murshidat* were able to offer more than just health education messages. For Amira, one of the *murshidat* of the first group, the limited value of the home visits was an additional reason to leave her job and become a teacher. She said, "When you visit someone who is ill, and her financial situation is bad, she does not have anything and you cannot give her anything. That is very difficult. It affects you mentally."

The repeated visits did also have positive effects. The *murshidat* were able to build up close relationships with the mothers in the area. Faiza expressed it as follows: "When you visit them many times and you repeat and repeat your visit, you start to develop a kind of compassion for them and they start to love you as well. That is when the home visits become well liked." Other *murshidat* expressed the same feelings about the home visits. Despite the difficulties they encountered, they

3. Van der Geest et al. (1990, 1029) also note the frustration of primary health-care workers, which they attribute to the fact that governments offer primary health-care workers insufficient opportunities to perform preventive and informative tasks. Moreover, if curative services function badly, primary health-care workers lose their credibility because community members are not prepared to listen to health education messages without adequate curative care.

4. The food program was set up with the aim of improving the nutritional status of families at risk who had no money to buy healthy food. The project distributed a food basket, with vegetables and cereals, to poor families in the area. In the mid-1990s, the World Food Programme became responsible for the distribution of food.

loved their work and their contacts with women in the area. Some of them said that they had become friends with mothers in the area and visited each other outside work time. There were *murshidat* who told me that the women cried when they heard that the *murshidat* were being transferred to another health center, as they had gotten used to each other and had built up close relationships.

The home visits became gradually more accepted and appreciated by the community, and the *murshidat* started to like doing home visits. Even though they were not able to improve the living conditions of the people living in the squatter areas in general, they noticed that the health education messages did have an impact on the community. They all said that people's ideas had changed and that they were much more open to health education than before. One of the *murshidat* expressed it as follows:

> The door was closed before. They did not understand what we wanted, what we could do for the woman. But nowadays, when the woman sees the car, she comes out of her house and says, "Come! Why did you not come to weigh my child?" So she knows what our services mean for her child's health. And there are a lot of people now who know about family planning, when they don't want many children. That is because we, the *murshidat*, are here and we have made a great effort in these areas to achieve what we have achieved now.

Yet the home visits were also a way of disciplining the community. New health-care methods were introduced and imposed on the community. The second group of *murshidat*, who came from the squatter areas, gradually adopted these new methods and followed the instructions of the project. As mentioned before, similar to the process Shami (1997, 91) describes for the squatter areas in Amman, the domain formally acknowledged by the project as private had also become public because the household and the family were being targeted for "upgrading": "lectures, censuses, surveys, child-rearing classes, nutrition classes, income-generating projects and so on were directed at them" (91). In addition, Shami argues, "the individual body of each woman also became public, or at least public knowledge, through surveys of fertility and reproductive behavior and family planning interventions" (91). This invasion of privacy is part of the process of disciplining imposed by the state. A particularly striking example of the ways in which women's bodies are used for the consolidation of state power is given by Kanaaneh in her study of Palestinian women's encounters with reproductive health care. Through the creation of new reproductive discourses and practices, the Israeli state attempts to increase the distance between the Jewish and the Palestinian population, emphasizing the modernity of Israelis and the "backwardness" of Palestinians, by referencing Palestinians' high fertility and the threat it forms for the Israeli state (Kanaaneh 2002, 252). Ali's study of governmental family planning activities in Egypt (2002) also shows the importance of reproductive health care for the state.

Although less obvious, the Hodeida Urban Primary Health Care Project is another example of state discipline through reproductive health activities, in this case supported by a foreign development organization. Individual policy makers and development workers, Yemeni and non-Yemeni, will argue that these health-care activities were carried out with "good intentions" (see also Porter, Allen, and Thompson 1991), but a close analysis shows the strong relationship with the larger project of modernity. The fact that the *murshidat* were accepted as health promoters in their communities was related to this association with modernity. Coming from low-status backgrounds, their training and employment as modern health-care workers was, in the eyes of the community, a step toward development and modernity. The challenging aspects of their work, such as the home visits they paid to unrelated families, were accepted because they were linked to this perceived modernity. Moreover, the status of the *murshidat* profession in the community also improved because of the new tasks they undertook and the clear way in which they were protected and promoted in the project.

From Health Educator to Birth Attendant

The initial idea of the project management was that *murshidat* would be responsible for preventive health care and health education, while traditional birth attendants and midwives working in the hospitals would be responsible for assistance in childbirth. When the project management had been searching for a curriculum for *murshidat*, the Yemeni Ministry of Public Health had referred them to the curriculum of *murshidin*, which focused on health education and some curative care. One year later, when the first *murshidat* had graduated in Hodeida, the Yemeni Ministry had developed its own ideas about the training of *murshidat*. In the eyes of the Yemeni Ministry, *murshidat* had to be able to assist at childbirth and needed extensive training in doing deliveries. The project management argued that in the cities there was no need for *murshidat* to assist in labor because there were traditional birth attendants *(jadat)*, nurses, midwives, and doctors available. Yet in order to integrate the training of *murshidat* in Hodeida into the national policy, and to avoid problems with the employment of the women, the curriculum of the second training course was adapted to the ministerial requirements and deliveries were included.

According to the national norm, *murshidat* were expected to assist at twenty normal (uncomplicated) deliveries during the practical part of their training. The idea was that the *murshidat* would do these deliveries in the maternity ward of a hospital. But this requirement presented the project with a problem. In Hodeida, as elsewhere in Yemen, a limited number of births take place in the hospital because most of the women give birth at home in the company of female relatives or neighbors (see Bornstein 1974, 36; Kempe 1994, 115). Only complicated cases are referred to the hospital, and these deliveries are not suitable for training purposes. On top of that, a three-year training course for midwives had started in Hodeida in 1988, and these midwifery students also needed to attend births. The number of deliveries taking place in the two hospitals in Hodeida was far too small to give every student a chance to assist at twenty normal deliveries. The solution was that some of the *murshidat* went to Zabid to do their childbirth training.

The new *murshidat* were surprised when they heard that they would also have to assist at deliveries. Compared to the first group, they had a somewhat better idea about their future work, as they had seen the first group of *murshidat* working in the health center and in their area. They all knew that they were going to work in health care, and in particular in health education. Some said that they did not know they were supposed to do home visits and only learned about it during the practical training. But almost all of them were surprised when they heard about the childbirth training, and the ones who were unmarried were even scared. Because delivering babies was not part of the work of the first group of *murshidat*, the second group was surprised to learn that they were supposed to do deliveries. It was also rather unusual that young and unmarried women would assist at deliveries, in view of the fact that Yemeni women prefer to give birth in the company of older and experienced women, preferably from their own families (see also Buitelaar 1990; Scheepers 1991). The project members were acquainted with this fact but did not seem to have a choice. Although the initial idea had been to train married and mature women as *murshidat*, the women who were interested in becoming *murshidat* were young and unmarried. While it remained to be seen whether the community would accept these young women as health educators, the ministry required them to do deliveries.

For Samira, who was the only one in the second training course who had children, childbirth was not frightening. "Because I had children myself I knew what labor was, and how to treat the mother. I immediately learned to do deliveries, and I liked it." But most of the women needed more time to learn to assist at deliveries. Amal told me that it took a long time before she dared to assist a woman in labor on her own and that she was unable to eat after having delivered the baby. And Sa'diyya said that she used to hide when one of her sisters was in labor.

> But I was surprised that I became courageous when I attended the course. They even encouraged me to do deliveries at home. When I first started the course I could not imagine that I was really going to do that type of work. I found it very hard. But when I received training and had done twenty deliveries I noticed that I was strong and capable. I continued to do deliveries and I practiced bit by bit, and now the people in my area are all asking for my assistance.

Unintended and unplanned, the skill of assisting at childbirth turned out to be very important in the future lives of the *murshidat*. After finishing the practical training, and sometimes even before graduating, the *murshidat* were asked by relatives and neighbors to assist at childbirth. They had received a delivery kit, with all the necessary equipment to do home deliveries, and were able to assist women in the area. The word that they could assist at delivery spread quickly, and they were able to build up a clientele. They all told me that they assist at childbirth as a humane service *(khidma insaniyya)* and do not ask for money, but they often do get money, and that makes their work even more attractive.

The most interesting part of this development is that the age and marital status of the women did not seem to play as important role as had been expected. People in the community accepted the *murshidat* as birth attendants even though they were young and unmarried. How can this be explained? What strategies did the women use to make their work as birth attendants acceptable? And how did their identities change as a result of their involvement in childbirth? One of the main explanations for the quick acceptance of young and unmarried women as birth attendants is the fact that they had attended an official training course, which made them, in the eyes of the community, experts in health care. The title *duktura* is used very easily in Yemen, and almost anyone who has attended some kind of training course, like the traditional birth attendants who had attended a one-month course, is referred to as *duktura*. The exact contents of a course are not important, and especially in the past people did not know the difference between a nurse, a midwife, and a doctor. They were all "wearing white" and were regarded as experts in health care. That the *murshidat* had followed a very different training and that their tasks were not similar to those of nurses was often confusing for people in the community. For example, people did not understand why *murshidat* were not allowed to give injections. Moreover, the fact that people often saw them as midwives shows that professional training seems to decrease the importance of age and marital status. Whereas traditional birth attendants were asked to assist at deliveries on the basis of their age and their experience, *murshidat* were asked to assist on the basis of the professional training they had received.

Yet it is still remarkable that the *murshidat* were accepted in a domain that used to be restricted to adult women who had children themselves and that was surrounded by sensitivities and taboos (see Buitelaar 1990). Halima told me, for example, that her mother believed that it was *haram* (forbidden) for an unmarried woman to see the placenta because she would lose her fertility and not be able to get pregnant herself. "If you see a placenta, you may not see it again," her mother had told her. Halima became a very active birth attendant, but, as a young and unmarried girl, she had to use various strategies to be accepted.

> When a woman wants me to assist her, she asks me "You are still young, are you married?" Then I say "Yes," because I want her to accept the idea that I will assist at the delivery. And after I have finished I tell her "No, I am not married and I don't have children," to show her that it doesn't make a difference. She thinks that if I am not married, I won't know how to assist her. When she asks me "Do you have children?" I tell her that I have one child, because I am still young, and you can see that she relaxes. After she has delivered I tell her that I don't have children. I say to her, "In fact I am not married, why were you afraid?" And she asks me why I lied to her.

For Halima, not telling the truth is a strategy to be accepted as a birth attendant. She uses this strategy often, and not only when attending births. She told me that she also lies when she talks with women about family-planning methods. She says, for example, that she uses condoms herself when she is trying to convince a woman of the benefits, although she is not married herself. *Murshidat* often told me that they lied about their own family-planning method, when they were trying to convince other women to use a certain method. They recommended, for example, the benefits of IUDs by saying that they had an IUD themselves and that it did not cause them any problems. In reality, they did not use IUDs because they said that they did not like the idea of having an external object inserted into their bodies.

Although not telling the truth about the use of family-planning methods is fairly easy for married *murshidat*, as no one can check it, lying about one's age and marital status can only be done when *murshidat* are working in an area where their backgrounds are not known. The majority of the *murshidat* came from one of the two squatter areas (Ghulail or al-Mughtaribin), but they did not automatically work in their own area. Some *murshidat* who lived in Ghulail were working in al-Mughtaribin, and vice versa. Halima was a strong adherent of the idea that *murshidat* should work in areas other than the one they lived in. "The women will not accept someone whom they have known for years. They will say, 'She is younger than me so how can she know more than me?' But when you go to a woman you don't know, you can talk to her and she will say, 'She may know more than me so I have to listen to her.'" She noticed that women in Ghulail did not call her when they needed a birth attendant but that they asked someone from outside the area who was older. They say, "You are not married and you are young. We don't want a young girl." But she is convinced that they accept young and unmarried *murshidat* from outside the area as long as they do not know them. This choice may indicate that age and marital status are important factors when someone lives in the same area because an intimate experience is shared that is normally only shared with women who have given birth. When women become convinced that young, unmarried women can assist at their deliveries as well, they may accept them as birth attendants, but they prefer not to meet them in their daily life in the area.

Not all the *murshidat* are of the opinion that it is better to work in an area where people do not know them. Sa'diyya prefers to work in her own area. "The work is the same everywhere but it is better when you are a girl from the area [*bint al-hara*]. Then you know them and your relations are better." I asked her if the fact that she is not married is a problem when she is doing deliveries, and she answered, "They know that I am not married, but the people in the area like me very much. I also look older, and people tend to think that I am a mother myself. They only found out later that I am still unmarried but they had already gotten used to me and they wanted me to attend their births. They say, 'Ma sha Allah, you are a girl[5] but you know how to do deliveries, you are like us.'" So Sa'diyya's strategy is different from Halima's. Sa'diyya does not lie about her age and marital status; she convinces the women through her skills. The fact that she looks older also helps, as women often do not even ask her if she is married. They just assume that she is a mother herself. Iman, for example, is short and looks young, and although she is married, she is often seen as a young, unmarried girl.

The *murshidat* act as birth attendants in different ways. Some only do deliveries in their own families and among neighbors, whereas others assist anyone, in and outside of their own area. Nur, for example, has acquired a reputation as a birth attendant in and outside Ghulail. People even call her in the middle of the night and send a car to her house to collect her. She does not refuse. "I don't refuse, it is *haram*, especially at night when there is no one else who can help. Where can they go? They are looking around for someone to help, and the woman may be sick." But she added that she knows most of the people that come to her house and that they provide her with transport. Nur is married and has children herself, and that may also be why she can do deliveries at night, while young and unmarried *murshidat* do not. Their reputations will be harmed if they go out at night, as people may think that they are looking for distractions. But Nur is seen as a respectable woman who only leaves her house to serve other people.

Assisting at deliveries has become an important part of the identity of the *murshidat*. While the project team had not intended to involve the *murshidat* in midwifery services, as they saw them as health educators and not as birth attendants, Yemeni health administrators had a different opinion on the work of *murshidat*. In their eyes, as well as in the eyes of the *murshidat*, childbirth services were very important. Yet the training of *murshidat* as birth attendants meant that young, unmarried women became involved in work that used to be done by older women who had children themselves, and the *murshidat* had to employ

5. The Arabic word for girl *(bint)* is used for any woman who has not yet married and who is still a virgin.

various strategies to be accepted as birth attendants. Their professional training seemed to decrease the importance of age and marital status for assisting at deliveries, and as soon as they were accepted as birth attendants, their status in the community increased. Assisting at deliveries was more highly valued than giving health education and preventive health care. Moreover, being involved in midwifery also meant an improvement in the income of the *murshidat* because they received additional money for their private services as birth attendants. They saw the partial shift from health educator to birth attendant as a positive development and a contribution to their professional status.

Drivers and Driving Lessons

Another important way in which the positions of the *murshidat* changed was with regard to their contacts with men. The project staff tried to minimize the contacts between *murshidat* and unrelated men as much as possible because such contact would harm the reputation of the women and of their work. The women themselves often emphasized that their work was different from that of nurses because they only worked with women; "We are all girls" *(kulluna banat)*. Nurses work in hospitals and have to work with male patients, nurses, and doctors. The *murshidat* worked in a mother and child health-care center and "had nothing to do with men." But a closer look shows that this was not true; a male driver took them to and from work, the directors of the project were men, and men often visited the health center to accompany their wives or children. The home visits also challenged the ideology of gender segregation, crossing the boundaries of public and private life. In this section I want to take a closer look at the presence of male drivers working for the project, the problems this caused, and the ways in which the project management tried to solve these problems. The experience with male drivers offers an interesting case in the study of the changing positions of the *murshidat* and their changing status in the project as well as in the community.

   As mentioned before, the transportation that was offered to the *murshidat* was regarded very positively. It implied an increase of their status because a driver in a four-wheel-drive car took them to and from work. In the eyes of the *murshidat*, their relatives, and the community it was a sign of modernity; they were professional service workers employed by a foreign project. But the contacts with male drivers could also harm their reputations. Drivers were an ongoing source of problems, and most of these problems were related to gender. In the first place, the head of the health center was responsible for the driver. She could give the driver orders and she checked whether he had done what he was supposed to do. For the drivers it was hard to accept a woman as boss, and in particular a young woman. Moreover, not only the head of clinic was involved in their activities; the other *murshidat* were involved as well. In the morning the drivers had to pick them up from home and take them to the health center. They had to take them to the home visiting area and to collect them again. They had to drive them home again and sometimes collect them for afternoon work.

The *murshidat* were thus in daily contact with the driver, and there were often problems between them. The *murshidat* blamed the drivers for not listening to them and going their own way, while the drivers blamed the *murshidat* for ordering them around and behaving like a *mudira* (female boss). The drivers liked being in charge of a nice car, as it increased their status, and to drive around the city, but they didn't like the fact that young women were telling them what to do. It was humiliating and affected their masculinity. A second problem related to the presence of male drivers was the fact that most of the women did not want to sit alone in a car with a driver because doing so could harm their reputations. So the driver had to first pick up those women who did not mind being alone with him, or who rode together, like Saʿdiyya and her sister or Faiza and her sister. Another problem was who was going to sit next to the driver in the front seat. Most women preferred to sit in the back, but someone had to sit in the front seat. This was in most cases someone who did not mind sitting there, like Samira, who was divorced and did not worry anymore about her reputation, or Fatima, the supervisor, for whom sitting in the front seat was a way to distinguish herself from the other women.

But the major problem with male drivers was the fact that almost all of them had at some time made improper proposals to one of the *murshidat*. The intimacy of the daily car rides and the frequent contacts between the driver and the *murshidat* resulted sometimes in relationships. Fatum, a young woman from Ghulail who had encouraged many other women to join the second training course, fell in love with a driver. But he was married, and their relationship became a major problem for all parties concerned. The project management immediately dismissed the driver, and Fatum's parents sent their daughter to Taiz to distance her from the problematic situation. The female project staff tried to convince the family to allow her to come back to work, but to no avail. Fatum did not come back to work, and a new driver was employed.

In the following years a number of drivers were employed, but some of them were dismissed because they had approached the *murshidat* in an improper way. Finding appropriate drivers became more and more important, and being of irreproachable conduct was the main selection criterion. Yet the problems with male drivers continued, and at a certain point in time the project management was forced to seek another solution. The team leader at the time expressed it as follows:

> One must manage with what one has got, and make use of the limited resources. We had a few cars and we had a few drivers. But drivers were a problem because of the way they behaved. Several times drivers made improper proposals to the *murshidat*. Well, that was something we absolutely could not accept, in whatever way. And the way to avoid that was not to have a driver at all. So we said, "If the *murshidat* were able to drive themselves then we could get rid of this problem."

The idea to offer driving lessons was discussed with the *murshidat*, and the response was very positive. They discussed the idea at home, and almost all of them were allowed to learn to drive, which was remarkable in a society where driving was restricted to men and to a very small group of upper-class women.

Cars are a very important status symbol in Yemen, for almost all social classes, and every adult man will try to obtain a car as soon as possible. Young boys learn how to drive as soon as their legs are long enough. Women also value cars very much, as cars facilitate their mobility and they can avoid public transportation. Yet in the 1980s women's driving was in general seen as socially unacceptable because women who could drive were able to move around freely, challenging the boundaries of public and private domains and of gender segregation. With the modernization of Yemeni society, women's driving has become a modern phenomenon, and since the 1980s, in big cities like Sana'a and Hodeida, an increasing number of women, in particular professional and upper-class women, have started to drive. These women have become less dependent on drivers, previously a status symbol for upper-class families, and often have their own cars. Yet few middle-class and lower-middle-class women are able to drive, and they depend on their husbands and brothers as drivers, if the family owns a car.

In the mid-1980s, women driving in Hodeida were still rare, and my neighbor, a woman from a well-known family, told me that she was one of the first women to drive in Hodeida. The fact that a group of young women coming from low social classes learned how to drive was remarkable in this context, and a clear shifting of social and gender boundaries. There was a driving school in Hodeida, and most of the *murshidat* took classes. Only a few *murshidat* were not allowed to learn to drive, for example Hanan, Hawa's niece. Hanan had married her cousin soon after her employment as a *murshida*, and although her husband accepted her paid work, he did not allow her to learn to drive. The fact that most of the *murshidat* were allowed to attend the driving classes is a telling example of how they had gradually shifted gender boundaries, similar to how Hawa had gradually stretched the possibilities of what was culturally acceptable. Yet very few benefited from the classes and learned to drive properly, partly because they did not get enough chances to practice. There was only one project car available for them; the Dutch project staff and the only driver left used the other cars. Samira, who was one of the few who practiced enough to be able to drive around in Hodeida, said:

> I was already able to drive after ten days. The teacher saw me driving and he said, "You don't need two weeks. Ten days is enough for you."

There was only one car available for home visits, and those who were going on home visits took the car. One drove and the others would sit next to her. I was able to drive well, and I even took the car home with me and picked up the other women in the morning.

Unfortunately, this experiment did not last long. The car was old and needed spare parts and was handed over to the Health Office. A new car arrived, but also a new male driver. The number of *murshidat* who were able to drive, and more important, those who dared to drive, was too small to continue the experiment. Those who had learned to drive often referred to their driving experiences when they were sitting next to me in the car. "I also know how to drive," they often said, and I would ask them why they didn't do it. "I forgot" or "I didn't practice enough" were the standard replies. Without practicing, the few who had driven soon forgot how, and male drivers were back again. But the fact that so many *murshidat* had learned to drive was another example of their new position and identity, in which they were transgressing social boundaries. On one hand, learning how to drive prevented them from "negative" contacts with male drivers, which would hamper their reputation as respectable working women. On the other hand, the driving experience broadened their view and showed them that they were capable of doing things only upper-class women usually did. In their eyes, driving was a symbol of modernity, while in the eyes of the community it may have been seen as challenging gender boundaries.

During my visit to Hodeida in 2002, I visited Hanan, one of the *murshidat* who had not been allowed to learn to drive. Hanan had divorced her first husband and had married a man she had met at the health center shortly after her divorce. She continued to work. When I visited her in the health center, Hanan proudly showed me the keys of her car: "Four months ago my husband taught me how to drive, and I use the car wherever I want to go." And she drove me home and refueled on the way. Other *murshidat* asked me, "Have you seen Hanan? She has learned how to drive and drives everywhere in town!" They were clearly impressed that Hanan had acquired the skill of driving, while they had attended a driving course but had lost their skill.

"We Got Everything," or Becoming a Power Bloc

The driving lessons were only one way in which the project staff tried to protect and promote the *murshidat* and to strengthen their positions as professional health-care workers. The *murshidat* received support in many other ways and were clearly placed on a pedestal. During the training course they received all the material they needed, such as pens, notebooks, and white uniforms. On top of that, they received a monthly training allowance.[6] The project continued to pay their salaries until the moment they obtained government employment, which could take more than a year, as was the case with Badriyya and Sa'diyya. After training, the *murshidat* regularly received new uniforms and were supported in every possible way. They visited other health-care projects in Yemen, which for many *murshidat* was the first time they had traveled outside Hodeida or the Tihama.[7] In addition, as a kind of incentive, a yearly outing to the beach was organized for all the *murshidat*. The women who wanted to continue their education received financial support for their costs. Moreover, the health centers did not lack anything and were well equipped compared to other government health centers; even coffee and tea were available. Amal expressed the way in which the project staff treated them as follows, "When we had our weekly meeting on Thursday they often gave us cake and cold drinks. And when we were not in the mood for a meeting we would say, 'First you have to get cake and cold drinks and then we will start the meeting!' Really, we were spoiled. Anything we asked for they would give us!"

When the *murshidat* discovered that they were well respected and had a voice in the project, they began to make demands on the project management. The first sign of the formation of a power bloc was when the *murshidat* made clear demands concerning home visiting.

6. In 1988 the training allowance was YR880 per month. An average monthly salary was between YR2,500 and 3,000 (US$1 equaled YR11).

7. Morris (1991, 206–16) gives a vivid account of the trip he made with the *murshidat* from the project in 'Abs to other health-care projects in Yemen.

They accepted the idea that every *murshida* had to do home visits every other week, but they requested a "heat allowance" for home visiting during the hot summer months. The extremely hot temperatures in Hodeida of forty to forty-five degrees Celsius in the period from April through October, combined with a very high degree of humidity, turned home visiting into a torment no one looked forward to. As the health centers were air-conditioned, everyone preferred to stay inside, and every possible excuse not to go on home visits was brought forward. The *murshidat* suggested a financial compensation for home visiting during the summer months. The so-called heat allowance consisted of a monthly increase in their basic salary. Although the project management was not in favor of paying extra money to the *murshidat* because it could cause a problem when Dutch financial support to the project came to an end, the heat allowance was accepted as a way of getting the *murshidat* used to doing home visits. Another way of making home visiting more bearable during the summer was the introduction of umbrellas as sunshades. Some *murshidat* used the umbrellas, but they did not have the same encouraging effect that the heat allowance had.

Now that the *murshidat* knew that they were listened to and that they had a voice in the project, more demands were made. They requested a Ramadan bonus, one month's extra salary at the time of Ramadan. Ramadan was an expensive month, and the religious feast *'Id al-Fitr* at the end of Ramadan cost even more. The Ramadan bonus was another fringe benefit of working in the project. The project had paid overtime from the start, and thus three extra ways of increasing the basic government salary had come into being. Overtime was paid monthly on the basis of hours worked in the afternoon, the heat allowance was paid monthly during the hot summer months, and the Ramadan bonus was paid once a year before Ramadan. It is obvious that these financial advantages were a very attractive aspect of working as a *murshida* in the Hodeida Urban Primary Health Care Project, as were the other supports the project offered. One of the *murshidat* told me that she once spoke to a nurse working in the hospital who clearly envied her for working for the project. Although this nurse had finished intermediate school and had completed a three-year training course to be a certified nurse, she would have preferred to work as a *murshida* in a health center. "When they see that we are all women, that we go to the houses and visit mothers, then they say that they would prefer the work of a *murshida* over the work of a nurse. They say, 'You get courses and you learn to drive a car. And there are no men. You are all women. The project has really spoiled you.'"

Another example of the strong positions the *murshidat* developed in the project was their request for English-language courses. Although the project management did not see the need for these classes, as the *murshidat* did not have to use English during their work, it was seen as an incentive for the *murshidat*. The *murshidat* themselves were very outspoken about the need to learn English. They claimed that they were working in a foreign-financed project where English was one of the main languages, and where the Dutch team leaders did not speak Arabic.[8] In addition, many of the brand names of drugs were written in English, and they wanted to be able to recommend and hand out drugs, which would mean an increase in their status.[9] Moreover, they hoped that being able to speak English would help them further in the future, when the project came to an end. But what was probably more important was the fact that being able to speak English was a powerful symbol of modernity, which would also enhance their status in society.

Learning English was not as easy as many of the *murshidat* had thought, however, and within a short period of time the majority had dropped out of the course. Some of the *murshidat* are still disappointed that they did not have more chances to learn English and that only those who were quick learners succeeded. Halima was one of the few *murshidat* who was still attending English classes when I interviewed her in 1997. She seized every chance to benefit from the project. Although she planned to go to the university, she said, "The faculty can

---

8. The first two Dutch team leaders did not speak Arabic; the third team leader spoke Arabic fluently. The rest of the expatriate staff (the public health nurse, the midwife, and the anthropologist) all spoke Arabic.

9. Prescribing and handing out medicines carries a high status in Yemen, as in many other countries throughout the world.

wait. I am attending English classes now and I am attending the community midwife course, and both are paid by the project. If I study at the university I may lose the possibility of attending English classes and the community midwife course. But I want both." Halima was also one of the first *murshidat* to attend a computer course, and in doing so she evoked a lot of envy from other *murshidat*. Although the use of computers was in no way relevant to the work of the *murshidat*, they all regarded it as an important way to improve their professional status and as a possible way to find better work after the end of the project.

Conclusions

While the first group of *murshidat* came from relatively well-off families living in the city, the majority of the *murshidat* trained in the second and third group came from poor families living in the squatter areas. Moreover, almost all of them were young and unmarried. One of the main reasons different categories of women were trained and employed as *murshidat* was the rapid increase of educational levels among women in the squatter areas. In 1985, there were hardly any women living in Ghulail who had finished primary school, but in 1988 a large number of young women had a primary-school certificate. This rapid increase in educational levels was related to the socioeconomic and political situation in Yemen in the mid-1980s. Government efforts to increase the education of the population began to bear fruit, in particular in urban areas. The presence of a girls' school close to the squatter area of Ghulail had immediate results for the level of education among girls living in the squatter area.

Another difference from the first group of *murshidat* was that the women in the second and third group did not join the *murshidat* training course in order to continue their education. Instead they stopped their schooling in order to provide for their families. The poor living conditions of their families, and in particular the lack of income, was for a number of young, unmarried women the reason for becoming *murshidat*. Although they had hoped to continue their education and maybe even train as teachers, they decided to take up paid employment. One of the advantages of the *murshida* profession was that it offered the possibility of combining work with study. Not only was the *murshida* training a course of study in itself, but afterwards there were opportunities to continue studying. A number of *murshidat*, in particular from the second and third groups, were able to continue their education and obtained intermediate-school or secondary-school certificates. There were even some *murshidat* who were able to attend university. Yet the possibilities for continuing their education depended very much on their position in the family.

The fact that the second and third groups of *murshidat* came from lower social classes living in the squatter areas had important consequences for the status of the profession. Whereas it may have had a negative effect on perceptions of the profession in society at large, it did not affect the status of the profession negatively in their own areas. First of all, the women were working in areas where the majority of the population had similar backgrounds. Mainly rural migrants lived in Ghulail, while returned migrants from East Africa mainly inhabited the area of al-Mughtaribin. Joining a new profession with a modern status, and earning an independent income, meant an improvement in the social status of the *murshidat*, in particular in their own communities. Daughters became modern government employees providing for their families, which increased their decision-making power. Young women of mixed descent saw themselves as more modern and civilized than people born and brought up in Yemen. Their entrance into the *murshidat* profession was congruent with their notions of development and modernity. Women in both groups used their employment to improve their own situations, and some succeeded in continuing their education.

Moreover, the status of the *murshidat* profession improved because of developments that took place in their duties and in their position in the project. The establishment of a home-visiting system and the increased number of *murshidat* paying home visits in the areas of Ghulail and al-Mughtaribin led to home visits becoming more accepted. The *murshidat* began to see the positive impact of their home visits and built up intensive contacts with women in the area. This affected their own self-image and the image they had of the profession, and they began to value their work, which affected their identities positively.

Moreover, the fact that they were trained in midwifery improved their status in the community because this skill was more highly valued than health education services. Some of the *murshidat* became well-known birth attendants and earned an additional income with this service. It was remarkable that young and unmarried women became birth attendants in a society where deliveries were a domain restricted to mature women who had had children themselves. The *murshidat* had to employ various strategies to become accepted as birth attendants, but the fact that they had followed an official training course in childbirth assistance seemed to overshadow the importance of age and marital status. Owing to the positive reactions to their home visits and their additional tasks as birth attendants, the identities of the *murshidat* changed.

The position of the *murshidat* in the project changed as well. The number of *murshidat* increased, and the project team did everything to protect and promote this motivated group of women. The driving lessons were an example of the ways in which the project tried to improve the working conditions of the *murshidat*, and in doing so shifted social boundaries. The *murshidat* were aware that they were seen as an important group, and they made use of this regard to put forward their own demands. The heat allowance, the Ramadan bonus, and the English-language courses were examples of their successful demands. They improved their own position and status in and outside the project by making demands on the project, and other women working in health care envied them because of their advantageous positions. One of the main reasons that the *murshidat* were put on a pedestal and supported in every way possible was that the success of the *murshidat* experiment was seen as a golden opportunity that could yield a lot of positive results. It was the first time in Yemen that a large group of trained young women were going into the areas delivering professional health care. The wider implications of this experiment, for the health status of the inhabitants of the squatter areas, for the health sector in general, and for the *murshidat* themselves, could not have been foreseen, but the general feeling was that it could be the beginning of major changes in Yemeni society.

PART FIVE

Other Modernities

9

Dreaming of a Better Future

Women from the New Squatter Areas

Sara

WHILE SELECTING local health committee members, I worked closely with Sara. Sara was young, active, and very dedicated to her work. She was deputy head of clinic in the al-Mughtaribin health center. Sara wore a black *balto*, a black headscarf, and a black face veil, which she rarely lifted, and it was hard for me to recognize her at the beginning. "It's me, Sara" she would say when she realized that I had not recognized her. Later, when I got to know her better as we worked closely together, it became easier for me to recognize her. Sara was raised in Saudi Arabia and had returned with her family to Yemen in the early 1990s. She lived in Saddam Street,[1] one of the main streets running through al-Salakhana, the biggest new squatter area in Hodeida. When I asked Sara whether she wanted to tell me her life story, she was very happy because she had invited me several times to her house and I had only once accepted the invitation. I visited Sara on a Friday afternoon and had lunch with her mother and sisters. The family home consisted of a room built of concrete blocks, nicely furnished with Tihama couches and functioning as a guest room, a hut made of

---

1. The name of the street is a clear reference to the supportive attitude of the returnees toward Saddam Hussein in the early 1990s.

branches where her father was watching television, a kitchen, and a toilet made of corrugated iron. The compound was fenced in by corrugated iron, and in the corner stood a big tree, which had been planted when the family arrived from Saudi Arabia.

In this chapter I focus on the young women from returnee families (*mughtaribat*) who were raised in Saudi Arabia. Many of them joined the *murshidat* training courses in the 1990s and were employed in the health centers. I will show that in the first years after their return, their social status was low, and Yemenis who were born and had lived all their lives in Yemen (*muwatinin*) looked down on them. Later their social status improved, and they became more accepted in Yemeni society. Why did large groups of returnee women enter the *murshidat* profession? What was their social and educational background? What dreams and aspirations did they have in Saudi Arabia, and how were these dreams interrupted by the sudden return to Yemen? How do they try to reconcile the notions of development and modernity shaped by their lives in Saudi Arabia with their low status in Yemen? I decided to present Sara's story in this chapter because she is an example of a young and ambitious woman who returned to Yemen in her adolescence. Yet just like the other life stories I have presented, Sara's story is in certain ways atypical, in particular because economic need was not the primary reason for her becoming a *murshida*. Her story should therefore not be seen as a representative example of the entire group of *mughtaribat*.

When I asked Sara where and when she was born, she answered, "I was born in Saudi Arabia, in the city of Jedda, in 1976. My parents are originally from a village near Zabid. My father was forty years old when he married my mother; she was fifteen years old at that time. They came from the same village, but almost immediately after they married they went to Saudi Arabia." Sara's father had left his family and the village at a very young age because he did not like the rural way of life. He had worked from time to time in Saudi Arabia but only stayed there permanently when he married Sara's mother, in the early 1970s. They settled in the city of Jedda, where her father was employed as an inspector in the port, checking ships. Almost every year a child was born. Sara has five brothers and four sisters, two of her siblings having died in Saudi Arabia. Her oldest brother was twenty-four and her youngest sister was eight. Sara is the fourth child and the second daughter of the family. When I asked her about life in Saudi Arabia, Sara said,

> My family first lived for about fifteen years in the commercial area of Sabil, and then we moved to Hay al-Jami' [the area of the mosque], where we lived for eleven years. We lived in a big building on the first floor, and there were many different families living around us, Saudi families but also other Arab families. But we never played with the Saudi children; there were always problems between us. Saudi children played with Saudi children, and Yemeni children with Yemeni children.

All her brothers and sisters went to school, as it was compulsory, and her mother encouraged them to study. Her father did not really involve himself much. He worked during the day as well as in the evening. Sara was already interested in health care at a young age. "I liked school a lot. From when I was six years old, I wanted to become a surgeon; I liked to watch documentaries on television about operations. I don't know why, but I like that kind of thing. Now I also love to do deliveries." But there were no examples for a girl like Sara because neither Saudi women nor Yemeni women worked in hospitals. "When a Saudi girl finishes school she stays at home, and the Yemeni girls also stayed at home." Indian women were the ones employed as nurses in hospitals, and most of the doctors were Saudi or foreign men, not women, mainly from Bangladesh and from Pakistan.

Sara was attending the third class of intermediate school when the Gulf crisis started. "King Fahd said that he was going to send all the Yemenis out of the country. But my father knew someone at the port who said that he could get Saudi passports for us. So my family did not return to Yemen immediately in August 1990, when the majority of the Yemeni migrants went back. We stayed till 1992 and then decided to leave." Sara explained,

> My mother and my oldest brother did not want to stay in Saudi Arabia. They were afraid and said, "Let's go back to our own country."

Everybody around us had left, all our neighbors. We were the only ones left. We became strangers [*ghuraba*]. We had a hard time. Life was expensive and we had problems with the people around us. There were no other Yemeni girls at school and I stopped going to school.

Sara's family decided to escape the problematic situation and try their luck in Yemen. Sara said, "We were very happy about going back to Yemen. We had never seen Yemen." The family left by bus, together with two other families and all their personal belongings. "We took all our luggage. We traveled for three days, although it should have taken only one and a half days. But there were problems in Harad,[2] between Yemen and Saudi Arabia. They wanted to check the luggage. They checked both men's and women's bags. That is why we were delayed. We were on the road for three days."

When the family finally arrived in Hodeida in the morning, they had breakfast and sat down with their luggage at the side of the road. "When we arrived here and saw the country, we realized that it wasn't what we had expected. There was a lot of dust, and we sat by the side of the road and cried. Despite the fact that we knew people in the village, we stayed in Hodeida because life in the village is hard and we are not used to it." Sara continued,

We lived for a couple of months in a sort of tent on the side of the road, but then someone told us that all the other returnees were living in Saddam Street. He said, "We will give you a nice piece of land in Saddam Street. There are a lot of people there and there are shops. Try to go there." We went there and they showed us this piece of land. It was empty and we bought it for YR20,000.[3] The person who sold it was a returnee himself and in need of money, that was why he decided to sell part of his own plot.

I asked Sara whether her father started to work when they returned to Yemen, and she said, "My father hasn't worked since we

2. Harad is a Yemeni town at the border between Yemen and Saudi Arabia.
3. In 1992, US$1 equaled YR56.

came back from Saudi Arabia. He looked for work but he didn't find anything. He wanted to be a guard because he was not in good physical shape, but he didn't find work. He can only work as a guard and not as a porter[4] because he cannot carry things." At first the family was able to support itself with the money from Saudi Arabia. "Of course we had money from Saudi Arabia and we could live for a long time from that. We even built a room of cement blocks from that money." Soon after their arrival in Hodeida, Sara's oldest brother found a job in a car repair shop. "He met a Sudanese guy who had a workshop in Jizan Road, and he started to work with him, repairing cars. Now he can even repair big trucks. He travels to Sana'a and to Taiz to repair trucks." So Sara's brother was able to provide for the family. Then in 1994 Sara's oldest sister started to work as a teacher and brought in a second income. When they occasionally ran out of money, they sold some of their belongings. "We sold our gold, and five years ago we sold our washing machine."

Back in Yemen, all the children went to school again except Sara. She explained, "I didn't want to go anymore. I went to school for about six months, but I didn't like the way they taught us and I preferred to stay home." But that did not mean that she was sitting idly at home. Sara had plans to work in health care and looked around for possibilities in that direction. "I was interested in health care, so I asked people where girls who wanted to become nurses could get training. They referred me to the Health Office in Hay al-Tijari. I went there and I applied for the first *murshidat* training course but I did not pass the selection test." I asked Sara why she had not been accepted, and she said,

I was still too young. I was only fifteen years old and they wanted women over twenty. Then I went to the al-Tahrir health center

4. Many of the returnees worked as porters in the port. They waited for work as day laborers unloading ships or loading trucks. The fact that many returnees work as porters is an indication of their low status, as people of higher status do not take up this work unless they are destitute.

where I applied for another course, but again they did not accept me for the same reason. Then I applied for a third time in the same year. There were a lot of courses. I kept going to the Health Office, every day, every day. I had a very hard time, really, until I started the course. So I applied for a third time. And then I met Amina al-Khawlani,[5] who was responsible for all the training courses. I spoke to her and they interviewed me. When the list of women that were accepted was announced, my name was on it.

Was her age not important anymore? "I was still very young but they did not reject me. There were a few other girls my age. All of the participants were returnees, there were only a few girls who were born and brought up in Yemen [*muwatinat*]."

The course, which started in 1992, was financed by a British non-governmental organization and taught by a Sudanese midwife. Sara knew what to expect from the course, and what the work of a *murshida* was. "Before I started the course I went to the al-Mughtaribin health center and met some *murshidat*. It was the first health center I visited. I asked the girls there for information." Sara had an interest in health care and wanted to become a *murshida*, but she had more ambitious plans for the future. "I joined the *murshidat* training course because I liked this kind of thing, I knew that I would learn how to give injections and to assist at childbirth, but I also wanted to continue my studies." Earning money to provide for her family was not a reason, according to Sara, because her brother was working. Nevertheless, she spent her training allowance on the family. "I didn't buy anything for myself. But it was my own choice." The fact that it was not money she was after became clear when she told me that after graduation none of the new *murshidat* were employed. The Ministry of Public Health in Sana'a was not employing new *murshidat*, and only after a lot of lobbying by the administrators in the Hodeida Health Office were the twenty *murshidat* employed. "We worked voluntarily for a whole year.

5. Amina al-Khawlani was the head of Mother and Child Health in the Hodeida Health Office.

Twelve months." I asked Sara why she decided to continue to work even though she wasn't getting paid, and she answered. "Because I wanted to do this, I love the work. Even if there were no salary I would still work. I love my work very much. If I had to choose between my work and something else, I would always choose the work."

Sara liked the course but had to get used to the different environment of a new country. "Honestly speaking, we were not very happy here. We only started to like it after some time. We were not used to Yemen and the people. Their behavior was very different, and their language as well. Sometimes we didn't understand what they were saying until they explained it to us. We had difficulties in the beginning. But after a while we got used to Yemen and now we like it. We like it much better than Saudi Arabia." I asked her why and she said, "*Khalas*, that's it, we have found work, we have a house, and everything is okay now." So finding work and a place to live was very important to feel at home. "Everybody was surprised that I succeeded in getting a place on the course. And they all encouraged me, my parents and my brothers and sisters. They all knew that it was my wish to do this type of work." Sara explained that she did not have any responsibilities at home and could easily attend the course.

> I have never done any housework. Even in Saudi Arabia, I didn't do anything because I was sick; I could not walk and was feverish. Anyone who saw me thought that I would die. They never believed that I would survive. I only ate vegetable proteins. But when I went to the doctor he said that I was healthy. Whatever hospital I went to they always declared that I was healthy. They said that there was nothing wrong with me, but I couldn't walk. I only got better in Yemen. I didn't go to a doctor, I didn't go to anyone, but the illness disappeared by itself. People who know me from before and see me now are surprised.

According to Sara, Yemen offered her a new life, good health, a fulfillment of her dream to work in health care, and new perspectives. She liked the course, in particular doing deliveries, but her mother was not very happy about her assisting at childbirth.

My parents did not know that deliveries were included in the training course and the work of *murshidat*. When my mother heard that
deliveries were included she was worried about me. She thought that
I would get scared, that something would happen to me, because I
had never seen a woman giving birth. She did not sleep the night
before my first training session at the hospital because she was so
worried. She was afraid that I would make a mistake or that I would
get scared when I saw the baby or something.

But Sara liked to assist at deliveries and found it one of the most interesting parts of her work. Home visiting was in her eyes the most difficult part. "It is very hard to go out in the sun and to find doors closed
in your face." But she also liked it.

I got to know the mothers, I learned how to weigh children, and
when we encountered a new baby we told the mother to come to the
health center and have the baby vaccinated. There are mothers who
respond well and there are mothers who don't. I am happy when a
mother says to me, "Come in," and responds to us, unlike mothers
who say, "What do you want? Where do you come from?" and let
you stand in the doorway in the sun. That is frustrating.

Sara was a dedicated *murshida* and soon became deputy head of
the al-Mughtaribin health center. "I had been working as a *murshida*
for a year when they asked me to become the deputy of Riham, who
was the head of clinic. They asked me because I was very active.
When the driver did not come to pick me up I would walk to the
center. I was always one of the first to arrive, and I entered all the
rooms and prepared everything. I supervised the other *murshidat*
and the midwife." But not everybody was happy with Sara's dedica-
tion and commitment.

At the beginning the other girls did not accept me as a deputy because I was still young and new. They said, "Why has she been made
deputy? She is still young. There are girls who were trained before
her." They would have preferred one of them to be deputy head of
clinic. But some of the girls who were trained before were, you could

say, indifferent. Some of them didn't do their jobs well. But I am active, I come early.

Sara encountered a lot of problems with other *murshidat* in the center who did not accept her as deputy head of clinic. But she continued to work and was finally accepted.

Her age also hampered her activities as a birth attendant.

> The mothers say, "She is young and not married, how can she assist at a birth? She doesn't know anything." There was once a birth here in the area and when I went to see the woman, there was a *jada* [a traditional birth attendant] present; she was old, and she said to me, "Go away! Go away!" I said to her, "Why do I have to leave?" And she answered, "How can we let someone who is young and doesn't understand come so close to the birth." I said to her, "But I know how to assist at deliveries, I studied health care." I explained, but she was not convinced and they did not accept me. Then I left and went home.

But she also tried to overcome these obstacles. "There are also mothers who accept me and I assist at a lot of deliveries nowadays." Sara's dream is to become a certified midwife or even a doctor; she is not happy with her current status of *murshida*. That is the reason she decided to continue her education while working at the center. "They told us that there won't be any *murshidat* anymore in the year 2000, that the ministry will stop training and employing *murshidat*. In my view *murshidat* don't have any importance. A *murshida* only weighs and vaccinates children and she goes on home visits. It is not as important as the work of a midwife." Sara was therefore very happy when she had the chance to attend an upgrading course to become a community midwife, as the new policy of the Ministry of Public Health is to train community midwives instead of *murshidat*.

> They told us before that a community midwife is not like a certified midwife who has studied three years, and that a community midwife is more like a *murshida*. But now that we have done the course we realize that it's very different from the *murshida* training course. We have learned about social science, psychology, statistics,

management, a lot of things we never learned before. And the work will also not be the same. There are differences. There will still be home visits, but we will have more experience. Maybe we will work in the ante-natal room, in the family planning room, we will have more experience than a *murshida*.

But becoming a community midwife is not enough for Sara: she wants to finish secondary school and then go to the Medical Faculty in Sana'a. She is still young and does not think about anything other than her education. I asked her whether she wanted to get married, and she answered,

I don't think about getting married, really. The main thing is to finish my studies. That is the main thing for me now. Of course my father says that I have to get married. Marriage is obligatory. But my opinion is more important because it is my future. There are men who have proposed marriage but I refused, and my mother refused as well, although my father had agreed. We had an argument about it, but I did not give in. Someone else came to ask for my hand and I refused again.

In 1998, Sara successfully completed the community midwife course and returned to her job as deputy head in the al-Mughtaribin health center. When I visited her in 2002, she told me that she had finished secondary school a year before. Because of her work in the health center, she had not been able to attend classes in the morning and had to study at home *(manazil)*. She therefore could not choose the science option *('ilmi)*, as it was obligatory to attend classes for it, so she was forced to choose arts *(adabi)*. In order to go to the Medical Faculty, a secondary-school diploma in science was required, so Sara had to give up her dream of becoming a doctor. She decided to study Islamic law instead, at the university in Hodeida, and has already handed in her application with the required papers. She is still living with her parents in Saddam Street and gives half her salary to her mother. Her eldest sister and two brothers support the family as well. One of her younger sisters studies chemistry, and two others are still in school. With regard to marriage, her opinion has not changed. Recently someone came to ask for her hand but she refused again. She only wants to marry a man who can pay a dower of YR300,000,[6] who owns a furnished house, and who has a job. But such men are rare. "Nowadays men only want a woman who is earning an income" and "In Yemen women are providing for the men," she told me.

Another Group of Returnees

To Saudi Arabia and Back

In the previous chapters, I paid attention to rural-urban migration and overseas migration of Yemenis, in particular to Africa. Yet with the discovery of oil in Saudi Arabia and the Gulf States in the 1950s, a new destination for Yemeni migrants appeared. Even before the oil boom of the 1970s, Yemenis had migrated to the Gulf, established enterprises, and settled there with their families (ESCWA Secretariat 1993/1994, 110). But the sudden increase in oil prices in 1973–74 led to a new migration of Yemenis, mainly single men who went to work abroad on a short-term basis. As a result of the rapidly growing oil revenues, the governments of Saudi Arabia and the Gulf States started huge development projects in infrastructure, industry, and agriculture. The extremely limited number of inhabitants in these countries necessitated the "import" of a massive amount of labor (Swanson 1979, 55). Migrants were attracted from neighboring Arab countries but also from outside the Arab world. In Saudi Arabia, one of the largest groups of Arab migrants came from North Yemen. Migration to Saudi Arabia was very easy. In contrast to other foreign nationals, Yemenis could obtain a visa at any port of entry, they did not require a sponsor *(kafil)*[7] for work or residence permits, and they could have their own businesses (Addleton 1991, 514; Stevenson 1993, 15; Van Hear

---

6. In April 2002, US$1 equaled YR160.

7. For an elaborate description of the sponsorship system in Kuwait, which is similar to the system in Saudi Arabia, see Longva (1997).

1994, 20). Although precise information about the number of migrants is lacking because many were not officially registered, Dresch (2000, 131) speaks of 630,000 migrants in 1975 and 800,000 at the end of the 1970s, and Findlay (1994, 214) mentions a rise to between 850,000 and 1,250,000 migrants in the early 1980s. Riyadh, Dammam, Jedda, and Mecca were cities where many Yemeni migrants settled.

The majority of the Yemeni migrants were single men who migrated on a temporary basis. They worked as unskilled laborers in construction and agriculture. Migration was first and foremost a way to earn money in order to improve living conditions at home. Most Yemeni migrants accepted poor living conditions because they did not want to spend money on housing and tried to save as much as possible: "men are extremely reluctant to take their wives and families with them and remain committed to the idea that they will ultimately return home" (Swanson 1979, 56). In the 1980s, the demand for construction workers began to diminish, as many infrastructural projects were completed, but the demand for labor in the service sector increased (Findlay 1994, 209). In 1986, oil prices crashed after years of stagnation, which led to a crisis in the Saudi economy. Some Yemeni migrants then returned home, but the majority stayed in Saudi Arabia and accepted lower wages. Yemeni migrants moved from temporary employment in the construction sector to more secure employment in the service sector, for example as taxi drivers, gardeners, and shop-keepers (ESCWA Secretariat 1993/1994, 110).

The shift to more secure employment in the service and trade sector allowed an increasing number of Yemeni migrants to bring their families (Stevenson 1993, 16). In 1990 an estimated one-third of the migrant workers in Saudi Arabia were accompanied by their families (Stevenson 1993, 16). However, with the decline of oil revenues, the Saudi labor market shrank, and the presence of Yemenis in service and trade activities was increasingly seen as threatening job opportunities for Saudis.[8] Tensions between Saudi Arabia and Yemen were

---

8. The Saudi government tried to settle and integrate Saudi Bedouins into the economy, but many of these attempts failed because Yemenis (who were also

increasing, and the fraternal attitude that had once characterized their relationship began to change. In the late 1980s, the Saudi government attempted to introduce a law that stipulated that Saudis should own all unincorporated businesses. But North Yemen's president, 'Ali 'Abdullah Saleh, succeeded in securing a special exclusion for Yemenis (Stevenson 1993, 16). The unification of North and South Yemen in May 1990, and the subsequent democratization process, was another threatening development for Saudi Arabia. Moreover, the population of unified Yemen was greater than that of Saudi Arabia. When Iraq invaded Kuwait and the government of Yemen voted against a military attack by the allied forces in the UN Security Council, the Saudi government reacted by canceling the special conditions for Yemenis and imposing the same residence rights on them as on other migrants. From September 19, 1990, onward, Yemeni migrants needed a Saudi sponsor to obtain a residence permit *(iqama)*. The majority of the migrants decided to go back to their home country, even though some of them could have stayed. They had their pride and did not want to beg the Saudis for a permit when they had always had the freedom to come and go.

Within a month, around 800,000 migrants returned to Yemen. They brought most of their belongings with them, and came back by plane or in cars and buses. Those who had owned businesses had been forced to sell their property and possessions in Saudi Arabia, often for extremely low prices (Addleton 1991, 514; Stevenson 1993, 17). Most of these migrants returned to Yemen via Hodeida because it is the first big city after the border. Those with relatives in other parts of Yemen, especially single men, went back to their birthplaces and were rapidly reintegrated into society (UNICEF 1993, 37). However, those who had been away for a long time, and many who had been born in Saudi Arabia and had never been in Yemen, settled in camps around the main cities. In contrast to migrants coming from the Yemeni highlands, who often migrated only on a short-term basis, most of

---

unskilled and shared characteristics with the Bedouins) were occupying jobs in the unskilled service and trade sector (ESCWA Secretariat 1993, 111).

the returnees from the Tihama had been away for two, three, or even four decades (Van Hear 1994, 25). With the mass return of Yemeni migrants in August 1990, and in particular with their settlement in Hodeida, it became clear how many Tihami families had been living in Saudi Arabia. Having lived for years in urban environments, they were unwilling to return to the countryside (Stevenson 1993, 17). Sara had told me that her father refused to go back to his home village. He had left the village at an early age because he did not like the rural way of life, and he did not want to go back there now. Moreover, there was no work in the villages. Twenty years of labor migration had seriously affected the rural economy and made it dependent on cash income and new techniques such as pump irrigation (Ertürk 1994, 112). For many returnees the city seemed to offer better chances.[9]

Hodeida attracted most of the returnees who were originally from the Tihama, but returnees who originally came from other parts of Yemen also stayed in the city. One reason was that as a port, Hodeida offered more opportunities for work than elsewhere. A second reason was that some returnees planned to go back to Saudi Arabia as soon as the Gulf crisis was over and preferred to stay close to the border. This was especially the case for single men. They could easily cross the border illegally and take up their work as temporary laborers in Saudi Arabian border areas. The third reason many people decided to stay in Hodeida had to do with the land rights. As mentioned before, while most of the land in other cities in Yemen is in private hands, the government owns the land in and around Hodeida (Wenner 1991, 81). The land had previously belonged to the Imam and was expropriated after the revolution (82). Because most of the plots were not registered, they could easily be occupied when the government allowed it, as was the case in the late 1970s. Many people, in particular rural migrants, had occupied land around the city. In August 1990, the sudden influx of hundreds of thousands of

9. Like some of the migrants returning from Africa, returning migrants from Saudi Arabia and the Gulf States may have not wanted to return to their home villages because of arguments over property rights.

A wooden dwelling (sandaqa) *in a squatter area in Hodeida.*

people forced the government to accept squatting on a large scale (Lucet 1995, 31).

On the outskirts of Hodeida, large squatter areas appeared. These areas were regarded as temporary camps, and the government promised to provide housing as soon as possible. The hope was that the returnees would gradually integrate and that the camps would disappear. But the absence of clear rules regarding the occupation of land had the opposite effect. Returnees were in need of land and willing to obtain land in every possible way. At the moment of their return most returnees were not yet poor. They had come back from Saudi Arabia with their savings and all their belongings and had money to spend. Richer people, Yemeni residents as well as returned migrants, bought land and started to build. Although the land belonged to the government, and sale and purchase were prohibited, land tenure became a fertile black market (Qassim 1994, 15). Land was being occupied everywhere, for housing but also for the building of workshops, factories, and the like. No policy was followed to guide the integration of the returnees into the city (Nientied and Öry 1991, 7; Lucet 1995, 32;

de Regt and Ghailan 2007). From temporary camps these areas turned into permanent settlements where around 70,000 to 90,000 inhabitants live (Oldham et al. 1993, 2).

The living conditions in the new squatter areas were comparable to those in Ghulail in the 1970s and early 1980s. Fences made of corrugated iron or simply out of bushes masked the big, sandy compounds and poor dwellings. In the compounds one or two huts of straw (*'usha*) or wood (*sandaqa*) were built, depending on the financial situation of the household, to be replaced by rooms built of concrete blocks as soon as finances allowed. Water for cleaning was drawn from a well in the compound, and water for cooking and drinking was brought from one of the public taps.[10] Electricity was not available at first but soon (illegally) extended to the new squatter areas. Waste collection did not reach the squatter areas, and large heaps of refuse could be found on almost every street corner. There were no schools and no health facilities, and transportation facilities were poor. Because of the sandy roads, cars could hardly enter the areas, and taxi drivers often refused to go to the new squatter settlements. In the past ten years the situation in the squatter areas has improved considerably: electricity and water has been connected to many of the households (often financed by the returnees themselves), schools and health-care facilities have been opened, and access to the areas has improved. Yet the new squatter areas of Hodeida continue to be identified as poor areas, and the status ascribed to the people living in the areas is low.

The Social Status of Returnees

In chapter 7, the low social status of returned migrants who came back from Africa has been described. The conclusion that emigrants are highly valued in Yemen as long as they stay abroad is also applicable to labor migrants who went to Saudi Arabia and the Gulf

10. In 1994, the Dutch government financed the extension of the drinking water system in Hodeida to the new squatter areas.

States. While the remittances they sent home were the bedrock of the Yemeni economy, the migrant workers were not welcomed when they returned to Yemen; in fact they were discriminated against. This discrimination was first of all the result of economic conditions after the Gulf crisis. The returnees were blamed for the high unemployment levels, for price increases, and for the increasing number of crimes.[11] Yet although the deteriorating economic situation could partly be ascribed to the Gulf crisis, it was not the only cause. The growing pains of the new republic after unification, with its vague economic policy, contributed to the social and economic problems. Within a short period of time Yemeni residents had adopted the attitude that everything had been better before the arrival of the returnees, and they blamed the returnees for Yemen's problems. "Everything changed when the *mughtaribin* came," I often heard. A second reason for the discrimination and stigmatization of the returned migrants from Saudi Arabia and the Gulf States was that a relatively large group of the returnees that settled in Hodeida came from lower-status groups such as the *akhdam* and the *'abid*. For them, emigration had been a way to escape the low status ascribed to them in Yemen (Stevenson 1993, 17). Yet while they had been able to build a life abroad regardless of their social background, with the mass return to Yemen they were immediately stigmatized again.

The designation *mughtaribin* became a term of abuse, and returnees started to call themselves "*'a'idin*" instead (Oldham 1993, 4; Lucet 1995, 39). *'A'idin* literally means "returnees," while *mughtaribin* literally means "emigrants." The use of the term *'a'idin* was important because many Yemeni citizens questioned the ethnicity of the returning migrants. They accused them of being of non-Yemeni descent because the returnees who came back from Saudi Arabia and settled in

11. See the following *Yemen Times* articles: "Unemployment, High Cost of Living and Insecurity Drive the Low and Middle Class to the Streets!," Oct. 23, 1991; "We Are Overwhelmed by the Volume and Level of Crime," Mar. 25, 1992; "Returnees Stranded in Camps: Yemen's New Underclass," Aug. 12, 1992; "The Returnees: The Tragedy Continues," Aug. 22, 1993.

260 / Other Modernities

Hodeida were often dark-skinned and had African features, and they were accused of benefiting from the availability of land, employment, and educational and health-care facilities in Yemen. The returnees therefore preferred the term *'a'idin*, emphasizing that they originally came from Yemen.[12] Yet as mentioned before, many of the returnees who settled in the Tihama had been away for decades, and most of the *murshidat* were born and brought up in Saudi Arabia and had no relationship with Yemen.

Sara told me that she had been looking forward to going to Yemen: "We were very happy because we had never been to Yemen." But the dreams she had cherished about her motherland evaporated soon after she arrived in Yemen. Many of the *murshidat* coming from Saudi Arabia told me similar stories, recalling the shock they experienced when they arrived in Yemen, where they were forced to settle on empty pieces of land in areas without electricity, water, and sanitation facilities. When I visited them at home, they would always apologize for their poor living conditions and tell me that they had been much better off in Saudi Arabia. They told me about the houses they had lived in; the televisions, refrigerators, and washing machines they had owned; and the availability of air-conditioning. Almost all of them would speak with nostalgia about Saudi Arabia, and their stories made me curious. I wondered whether Yemeni migrants had really lived in such advantageous circumstances in Saudi Arabia, or whether their positive description of life abroad was a result of their bad living conditions in Yemen. I also realized that they felt the need to stress their own link with modernity with me, whom they saw as a representative of Western modernity. But their notions of modernity were different from mine, as became clear from their accounts of Saudi Arabia. For

12. Although many of the returnees prefer the term *'a'idin*, I will continue to use the term *mughtaribin* as this term is most common in Yemen. Whereas the term *mughtaribin* is a general term used for emigrants, and the returned migrants who came back from Africa in the 1970s were also called *mughtaribin*, in the 1990s the term was in general used for returning migrants who came back from the oil-producing countries on the Arabian Peninsula.

them modernity was associated with wealth and modern technology and also contained religious elements.

While many Yemenis looked down on the returned migrants and blamed them for the difficult social and economic situation in their country, the returnees themselves also looked down on the Yemenis (*muwatinin*). Just like the *muwalladin*, they rejected many aspects of Yemeni society and saw themselves as more "civilized" and "modern." But their notions of modernity differed in many respects from those of *muwalladin*. Although many *muwalladin* looked down on Yemenis because of their strict gender relations and emphasized that gender segregation in Africa was less strict and that men and women could freely intermingle, *mughtaribin* looked down on Yemenis because of the loose gender relations, which they denounced as "uncivilized" and "un-Islamic." In their view, there were too many possibilities to undermine gender segregation in Yemen, causing illicit relationships between women and men, and Yemenis behaved in an uncivilized manner. They regarded Saudi Arabia as the ultimate example of a modern Islamic society, which was based on the organization, prosperity, and efficiency of Saudi Arabian society in combination with conservative interpretations of Islam.[13] In her studies on the rise of Islamic fundamentalism in a Sudanese village, Bernal describes similar notions of modernity (1994; 1997). Labor migrants in Sudan who return from Saudi Arabia bring home new ideas about Islam and what it means to be Muslim. Their conservative interpretations of Islam are not so much a reaction against Western notions of modernity as a representation of "a vision of prosperity and civilization that is more compatible with their own identities and culture than the West can offer" (Bernal 1994, 42). These new understandings of Islam are particularly

---

13. Although the Islamist Islah party was established prior to the Gulf crisis, its following increased after the arrival of the returnees from Saudi Arabia. Sara also told me that many men living in Saddam Street were Islahis. Among the *murshidat* there was one woman active in Islah, and she was also a returnee. For information on Islah see Dresch and Haykel (1995); for information on women in Islah see Clark (2004); and for Yemeni adherence to Wahhabism see Weir (1997).

expressed through the redefinition of appropriate feminine behavior, emphasizing new forms of female seclusion and modesty. New types of houses were built in order to separate the domestic and the public spaces, and women began to dress differently, covering more parts of their body (Bernal 1994, 45–46).

In Yemen, changing dress codes among *mughtaribat* were also clear expressions of these new notions of modernity. Women who had lived in Saudi Arabia wore black *balati* and black face veils, which they rarely lifted, and sometimes black gloves and socks to cover their hands and feet, even in the extreme temperatures of the Tihama. While most of the *muwatinat* used their face veils in a flexible way, lifting them wherever possible, the *mughtaribat* lifted their face veils as little as possible. This clear expression of their adherence to Saudi-style covering, which they saw as the right Islamic way, can be interpreted as a way to show their "modernity" and to distance themselves from other Yemeni women who were in their eyes less strict and therefore less civilized and modern. By expressing themselves as "good Muslims," they developed a strategy to counteract the low status ascribed to them in Yemen and to maintain their self-respect.

Yet with the arrival of the *mughtaribat*, dress codes among *muwatinat* changed as well (see also Carapico 2001; Moors 2003). Already in the 1980s some women had replaced the *sharshaf*, which was the common dress for women in North Yemen, with Saudi Arabian *'abayat* (sing. *'abaya*), combined with headscarves *(hijab)* and face veils *(niqab)*. But with the arrival of the returnees in 1990, this way of dressing became common among the majority of young women in urban Yemen. First, the *balto*, *hijab* and *niqab* were seen as modern and more practical than the three-layered *sharshaf.* Second, the use of the face veil increased because male harassment was said to have increased with the return of thousands of migrants. I often heard women *(muwatinat)* complain that male returnees could not control themselves and harassed women who did not cover their faces.

In the past ten years the returnees from Saudi Arabia and the Gulf have become more integrated into society, and the relationship between *muwatinin* and *mughtaribin* has improved. During my visit to

Hodeida in April 2002, many *murshidat* said that there was no difference anymore and thus no discrimination. The integration process seems to have come from both sides. On one hand, *muwatinin* increasingly began to accept the *mughtaribin*, acknowledging that the arrival of returnees from Saudi Arabia and the Gulf had had positive effects as well. As I will discuss below, the education level of the children of the returnees who had been born and raised in Saudi Arabia was often higher than in Yemen. They had benefited from the educational system in Saudi Arabia, and they made use of their knowledge in Yemen. The supervisory team in the Hodeida Urban Primary Health Care Project consisted, for example, of seven midwives and one nurse who were born, brought up, and trained in Saudi Arabia. In addition, *mughtaribin* introduced modern practices that were new in Yemen. These new practices were, for instance, women's hairdressing shops, new ways of sewing and embroidery, and new henna decorations. *Muwatinat* were very interested in new styles, and many *mughtaribat* could make a living using these skills. On the other hand, *mughtaribin* also adopted Yemeni ways of living and working and began to feel at home in Yemen, as Sara also mentioned.

When I asked *mughtaribin* what the difference was between living in Saudi Arabia and in Yemen many of them answered that they had better living conditions in Saudi Arabia but that there was no freedom *(ma fish huriyya)*. In Yemen their living conditions were bad, but they liked the personal and political freedom they had. Many *mughtaribat* told me that they had grown accustomed to Yemen and did not want to go back to Saudi Arabia anymore. For them, the fact that they were not restricted in their mobility was of major importance. In Yemen they were able to go out on their own, meet friends, go to the *suq* and to weddings and parties—things they had not been able to do in Saudi Arabia.

Young and Ambitious

Sara is an example of a young and ambitious woman who is eager to work in health care. Although her story is in some respects atypical, in particular because she was not obliged to seek paid employment to provide for her family, as many daughters of returned migrants were, her Saudi Arabian background gave her particular possibilities for realizing her ambitions. First of all, one of the striking side effects of the mass influx of returnees to Hodeida was the sudden presence of large numbers of young and well-educated girls. When I discussed the difference between *mughtaribat* and women who had always lived in Yemen, a number of words were used repeatedly: they were said to be educated *(muta'allimat)*, smart *(dakiyyat)*, and developed *(mutataw-warat)*. Being born and brought up in Saudi Arabia meant that basic education had been compulsory, and almost all Yemeni boys and girls who grew up in Saudi Arabia had, regardless of their social background, attended primary school. Until 1960, there had been no public schools for girls in Saudi Arabia, but some of the oil revenue was invested in the development of the education system. In 1960 the first primary schools for girls were opened, and gradually a full-fledged system of girls' education emerged. Free schooling from the primary to the doctoral level is now provided (El-Sanabary 1993, 1332). However, non-Saudis were not allowed to attend secondary or university education. The Yemeni women who were born in Saudi Arabia had benefited from the well-organized educational system and had already completed a couple of years of primary school before they got to Yemen. Most of the *mughtaribat* registered at Yemeni schools and had to adapt to a different school situation. Sara told me that she was so disappointed with Yemeni schools that she stopped going to school altogether. She had gotten used to the Saudi education system and did not want to spend her time in overcrowded classrooms that lacked basic teaching equipment and had poorly trained teachers.

The daughters of returnees had been acquainted not only with a well-organized education system but also with highly advanced forms of health care. In addition to education, the Saudi government had invested massively in expanding health care, and an astronomical growth in health-care facilities and personnel had taken place. Public and private hospitals offering high-quality and specialized services had mushroomed. From the 1980s, the Saudi Ministry of Health emphasized

the importance of preventive health care, and massive vaccination programs, environmental health and hygiene programs, health education,
early screening, primary care, and mother and child health care received major support (El-Sanabary 1993, 1333). El-Sanabary mentions
that there were 1,650 primary health-care centers in the country in
1989. For Yemeni women like Sara, primary health care was thus not
a new phenomenon, and she was also acquainted with well-equipped
hospitals and highly trained personnel. But Yemeni women living in
Saudi Arabia and interested in health-care professions did not have
many role models; almost all the health cadre in Saudi Arabia consisted
of foreigners, doctors as well as nurses. Because of the low status of
nursing, the country relied heavily on expatriate nurses from Western
and Asian countries such as India and the Philippines. El-Sanabary
discusses the background of the low status of nursing in Saudi Arabia
and argues that the work conditions, in particular the night shifts, and
the intermingling of men and women are the main factors that prevent
the participation of Saudi women in nursing (1333).

Jamila, one of the supervisors at the project who was born in Saudi
Arabia, told me that Saudi women teachers from the Health Institute visited her class when she was still at intermediate school in Saudi
Arabia. They actively promoted the Health Institute and the nursing
courses and hoped to recruit new trainees. Yet Jamila was the only one
interested in going to study at the institute. Although she had never
thought of nursing before and had never even visited a hospital, she
liked what the women told her about the course and decided to register. She discussed it with her parents, and they both approved. Jamila
explained that her parents were open-minded. In addition, she decided
to specialize in mother and child care so as to minimize contacts with
unrelated men. During her internship she worked in a mother and
child hospital and found employment there after graduating as a public health nurse. The parents of some of the other girls of her class
did not allow them to become nurses and work in a hospital, mainly
because of the intermingling with men.

Because very few parents allowed their daughters to take up paid
work in Saudi Arabia, in particular in health care, it had surprised

Jamila that so many *mughtaribat* entered health care after their return to Yemen. According to her, the Yemeni government played a crucial role in encouraging women to enter health care. Although the country still relies heavily on foreign health cadres, and the government has in that sense not done enough to encourage women to enter health-care work, in the 1990s a relative improvement in government policies toward the female health cadre could be observed. The Islah Minister of Public Health and his successor paid explicit attention to training a cadre of female Yemeni health workers. The important role foreign donor organizations play in the formulation of health-care policies, and in particular in the training and employment of Yemeni women as health-care workers, is an additional reason the government takes the training and employment of women health workers more seriously. The presence of a large number of educated young women in Yemen, resulting from increased access to education for women in urban areas and the return of migrant families from Saudi Arabia and the Gulf States, facilitated the training of female health-care workers as well.

The fact that many *mughtaribat* joined the *murshidat* training courses can be explained by two factors. First, for many *mughtaribat* the *murshidat* training course was one of the few routes to paid employment. Like the young women who attended the second and third *murshidat* courses, they were in need of paid employment because their male relatives were unable to find work. The training led to government employment and was seen as respectable work (*'amal sharaf*), in particular because it was related to mother and child health care. As mentioned before, mother and child health-care services were closely linked to women's child-rearing duties and easily reconcilable with practices of gender segregation. By emphasizing that they were working with mothers and children, and not in contact with unrelated men, the *mughtaribat* were downplaying what were considered negative aspects of women's employment in health care. In chapter 10, I will show that in the case of the *mughtaribat*, the picture they presented of their work as not challenging gender ideologies did not fully correspond with the reality. The second factor leading to the entry of the

mughtaribat into the *murshidat* profession is that the daughters of returned migrants benefited from their education and their experiences
with professional health care in Saudi Arabia. Attending the *murshidat*
training course was not difficult for them because they were used to
studying. Moreover, most of them already knew a lot about preventive
health care because of health education messages that were spread by
the mass media in Saudi Arabia.

One of the *mughtaribat* who entered the *murshidat* training course
out of economic necessity was Arwa, a young *murshida* who assisted
me during a small-scale study on nutrition and child-feeding practices among the poor inhabitants of Hodeida in 1993. A number of
murshidat accompanied me on my visits to families in the squatter
areas, but Arwa was the most dedicated, and we got on very well. She
soon invited me to her house, in the middle of the new squatter areas,
and I met her mother and her seven brothers and sisters. Arwa had
grown up in Saudi Arabia, and her family had returned to Yemen at
the time of the Gulf crisis. After their return to Yemen, Arwa's father
tried to find work but failed to do so. Arwa decided to leave school
and attend the *murshidat* training course. She graduated in 1993 and
was employed in 1994. Since the early years of her training she had
been the main provider for her family. During the day she worked
as a *murshida* in a government health center, and in the evenings she
served as a nursing assistant in one of the private hospitals in Hodeida. She covered the daily expenses of her family and paid for the
schooling of her younger siblings. With assistance from relatives still
working in Saudi Arabia, the family was able to finance the building
of a number of rooms on the compound. When I visited Arwa in
2002, her two oldest brothers had finally found work, one as a traffic
policeman, the other as a police officer in the Security Office, and
they also contributed to the household expenditures. Moreover, more
rooms had been built, and the family had even been able to buy an
adjacent plot of land. Since her brothers were also bringing in money,
Arwa decided to leave her work as a nursing assistant in the hospital,
where she often had to work night duties, and took up an easier afternoon job in a nearby private clinic.

While Arwa became a *murshida* out of economic need, Sara said that there was no immediate need for income in her family because her brother had been working since the family had returned to Yemen. Yet although Sara said that there was no economic need to work, she still gave all the money she received as a training allowance to her family. Every Yemeni riyal brought into the family was used. She was also able to work voluntarily for one year, awaiting her official government employment, which was extraordinary. For many of the newly trained *murshidat*, the fact that they were not immediately employed was a downright disaster, as their families were dependent on their income. Arwa's family, for example, had a hard time when Arwa graduated as a *murshida* but lost her monthly income. Foreign donor organizations financing the training courses of *murshidat* had decided not to pay the salaries of the *murshidat* after they had graduated because that was seen as the responsibility of the Ministry of Public Health. In the past, the Hodeida Urban Primary Health Care Project had paid the salaries of the *murshidat* who had not yet been put on the government payroll. But the experience was judged counterproductive, as the Ministry then saw no urgency in employing the *murshidat*. For the Yemeni government it was much cheaper to allow foreign donor organizations to employ the *murshidat*, but its reluctance can also be interpreted as a lack of commitment to the training and employment of primary health-care workers. The Yemeni Ministry of Public Health preferred to spend the already meager government budget for health care on curative services and advanced technology, which is telling for its notion of development.

Sara said that she did not mind not being paid for her work. The financial situation of Sara's family was better than that of many other *murshidat* who were in immediate need of money. But even they continued to work voluntarily, as their main hope was to be accepted into government employment. They were afraid that they would lose their chance of government employment if they stayed at home in the meantime. Another reason Sara could put a lot of effort into finding a place in a training course was that she did not have many responsibilities at home because of her illness. For Sara the return to Yemen signified a turning point in her life: she was cured and she had the chance to work in health care. Her parents and brothers and sisters supported her in her efforts to become a health worker and did not impose household tasks on her. Her situation can be compared to Badriyya, whose story I presented in chapter 7 and who returned with her family from Sudan to Yemen. As daughters of returnees they both benefited from the new possibilities the return offered. Although they came to a poor and un-known country where the education system and the opportunities to develop themselves were in general worse than in the countries where they had been brought up, they succeeded in taking advantage of the opportunities that were available. In addition, Sara was of low social status, just like many other returnees living in the squatter areas of Hodeida. After a long period abroad many of them denied their low social status, in particular people of *akhdam* background. They had been able to attend school, they had acquired new skills, and they had replaced their low social status with a higher economic status. Becom-ing a *murshida* was one of the opportunities for improving their eco-nomic status, and many low-status women joined a training course.

For women of low social status, return migration thus offered op-portunities for change. Yet there were also many *mughtaribat* for whom the return to Yemen did not create possibilities for self-development but ushered in new forms of social control and dependency. Like Arwa, many returnee daughters felt obliged to take up paid work as *murshidat*, and sometimes their parents even forced them to seek em-ployment. Moreover, their parents did not leave the spending of their income to their daughters but forced them to hand over their money, which is in contradiction to Islamic law entitling women to spend the money they earn according to their own wishes. Amira, a *mughtariba* working in the al-Salakhana health center, does not dare to go home without money because she knows that her father will beat her; he does not work himself but needs money to buy *qat*. Amira tries to stay away from home as much as possible and spends most of her time with friends. The crucial contribution unmarried daughters make to the family income is in some cases the reason parents do not allow their daughter to get married. They are in need of her salary and do not want to lose it. Even a clause in the marriage contract stipulating that the woman will continue to support her parental family financially is not enough for some parents. They do not want part of their daughter's salary; they want her entire salary. I heard several stories of *murshidat* who wanted to marry but whose parents did not approve of their marriage plans. Their employment as *murshidat* is only to a limited extent for their own benefit. In her study about Palestinian families in a refugee camp on the West Bank, Rosenfeld (2002, 537) also describes how (eldest) daughters were often forced to postpone their marriages in order to provide for their families and to finance the schooling of their younger siblings. These women were, however, highly uncritical of their families and explained their situation in emotional terms such as obligation, loyalty, and sacrifice. The fact that their situation had been of a transitional nature and that they had eventually started their own families is a plausible explanation for this attitude (537). The *murshidat* I encountered had, however, not often yet crossed that stage and felt caught in an exploitative situation.

When I spoke about these issues with some of the heads of clinic, who were acquainted with many of the *murshidat*, they said that it was hard to generalize about which families do and which families do not force their daughters to hand over their salaries. They emphasized that it depends on the mentality of the family members. Yet it is very common that *murshidat* voluntarily support their parents, even after they are married, and their support is often more substantial than that of their (married) brothers. Young women seem to feel much more responsible for their parental families than do young men. I also encountered a number of cases in which boys stayed home and did not continue their education or look for paid work as long as their sisters were working as *murshidat*. The fact that there is hardly any work was given as explanation. Fathers, brothers, and husbands who do not work but stay at home are particularly common among *mughtaribin* families. The fact that many *mughtaribin* had been employed as unskilled laborers in Saudi Arabia made it difficult for them to find work in Yemen.

But returnees who were educated and who had acquired skills abroad were also often unable to find work in Hodeida. Hayat's husband, for example, had a secondary-school certificate, but he was not able to find work when they arrived in Yemen in 1990. Together with their four children, Hayat and Mohamed returned to Yemen at the time of the Gulf crisis, even though they could have obtained a residence permit. Hayat's parents have Saudi citizenship and could have been their sponsors, but Mohamed refused. "He is too proud to accept other people's help," Hayat said. They settled on an empty piece of land in Hodeida, built a dwelling from waste material and lived for some time in very poor circumstances. From an acquaintance Halima heard about the possibility of becoming a *murshida*, and she registered for a training course, even though she did not know what the work implied. She liked the course and the work and became the sole provider for her family. Her husband took care of the children, but he could not accept that he was unemployed. "He is mentally depressed" Hayat told me when I visited her in 2002. "He shouts at me and says that I want to be the man in the house, because I provide for the family. But what can I do? He doesn't have work so I have to work." I asked her why her husband does not go back to Saudi Arabia and try his luck there again,[14] but Hayat answered that he was too proud to show her family in Saudi Arabia that he had not found work in Yemen. The fact that male returnees had been employed in Saudi Arabia and the Gulf States, and had often been the sole providers for their families, may explain why it was so difficult for them to accept their unemployed status in Yemen.

A similar explanation is applicable to the reaction of the young, female returnees who took up paid work as *murshidat*. Many of them emphasized that circumstances had driven them to take up paid work. While the need to find paid work was similar to the situation of the young women in the second and third groups, the way in which they presented their choice to become a *murshida* was different. They often emphasized that being a *murshida* was not enough for them: they were

14. Several male returnees go back to Saudi Arabia on a short-term basis. They cross the border illegally and are illegally employed in construction projects near the border. I heard several stories of men who provide for their families through temporary work in Saudi Arabia.

capable of achieving higher positions. For at least some of them, the fact that they had to take up paid work as *murshidat* was lowering their status, and they saw it as downward social mobility. In Saudi Arabia they would not have taken up paid work because female employment was negatively valued, with the exception of professions with high status, such as teachers or medical doctors. Yet for the women who were trained during the second and third courses, the training as *murshida* meant an improvement in their social status. They came from social backgrounds where women's paid work was not so negatively valued but could even mean upward social mobility. The daughters of rural migrants came from social groups in which women's paid work was also less negatively valued. They grasped the opportunity to take up paid work as *murshidat* and in doing so started a process of upward social mobility because it was the first time that young women of lower social classes had entered professional employment. The daughters of mixed parentage came from societies where women's paid work was more acceptable, and therefore they did not present their choice to become a *murshida* as a sacrifice. Moreover, for these last two groups, being trained and employed in a foreign development project was another positive factor, while the relationship with Western notions of development impressed the returnee daughters from Saudi Arabia and the Gulf States less. They emphasized that Saudi Arabia was a very "developed" society, and they did not need to associate themselves with Western modernity.

10

The Last Phase of the Project,

1993–2002

SARA WAS TRAINED during one of the training courses organized after the sudden influx of thousands of returning migrants from Saudi Arabia and the Gulf States during the Gulf crisis of 1990–91. The massive arrival of returnees had immediate consequences for the health-care situation in Hodeida, and subsequently for the training of *murshidat*. The existing health centers were unable to respond to the increased demand for health-care services, and an expansion of health centers was needed. Many development organizations had withdrawn from Yemen, but some countries, including the Netherlands, and NGOs had continued their aid. In addition to the Hodeida Urban Primary Health Care Project, other donor organizations built and opened health centers in the city, and in the squatter areas in particular, and set up training courses for *murshidat*. Many young women from returnee families, raised in Saudi Arabia, joined these courses and were employed in the health centers. Their training and employment meant that again another group of young women entered the *murshidat* profession, with backgrounds different from the previous groups. In May 1993 it was decided to bring all primary health-care activities in Hodeida under the umbrella of the Hodeida Urban Primary Health Care Project. This expansion of the project had several consequences, not least for the *murshidat*.

In this chapter I focus on the changing position of the *murshidat* in the last phase of the Hodeida Urban Primary Health Care Project. On one hand, they experienced a strengthening of their position, as some of them were promoted to heads of clinic, and *murshidat* gained an important role in cost-recovery and community-participation activities. But on the other hand, this change led to new tensions. The expansion of the project, the integration into the Health Office, and the new policy of the Yemeni Ministry of Public Health to train community midwives instead of *murshidat* affected their privileged position. Worries about the future were the immediate result. In the last section of this chapter, I describe developments after the Dutch funding ended.

The Consequences of a Citywide Program

More *Murshidat*, Different *Murshidat*

One of the first consequences of the citywide program was that all *murshidat* working in Hodeida became part of the same program. The *murshidat* who had been trained and employed in the Hodeida Urban Primary Health Care Project were distributed across the thirteen health centers in Hodeida, and some of the *murshidat* who had been trained and employed by other foreign donor organizations came to work in Ghulail and al-Mughtaribin. The result was a mixing of *murshidat* trained by different organizations, with different work experiences and coming from different backgrounds. In August 1993 there was a total of ninety-six *murshidat*, sixty-one of whom were not yet officially employed by the Ministry of Public Health (Hodeida Health Office 1993). The government had employed none of the *murshidat* trained after 1990. Sara told me how she worked voluntarily for a year, waiting for official employment. Foreign donor organizations wanted to guarantee sustainability, and government employment of the *murshidat* was seen as one of the main ways to do that. Once the *murshidat* were employed, there was a better chance that they would continue their work when the foreign funding ended. As mentioned before, foreign donor organizations in Hodeida began to refuse to pay the salaries of the *murshidat* once training was completed because experience had shown that the Yemeni government did not employ the young women while they were on the payroll of a foreign organization. As a result of continued pressure from the Health Office in Hodeida, the *murshidat* were employed in the following years, but gaining government employment remained a problem for every new group. And it became increasingly difficult after 1995, when the government initiated a structural adjustment program and there was a general freeze on new government posts. Although health care and education were officially excluded from the temporary freeze, as these sectors were still in need of personnel, it became very difficult to obtain a government contract without an intermediary[1] and the necessary money to pay bribes to people assisting in the procedures.

Some *murshidat* were officially employed, but others were not, and there were other differences between the various groups of *murshidat* who were now working together. First of all, the selection of *murshidat* had been different for each training course, and the selection criteria as applied by the Hodeida Urban Primary Health Care Project were not necessarily applied by other donor organizations. Sara, for example, was accepted into the training course although she was too young and had already been rejected twice because of her age. She was not an exception; the *murshidat* trained during the 1990s were in general much younger and less mature than the ones trained during the 1980s. While age had been one of the main selection criteria in the late 1980s, in the next decade the age restrictions became less strict. Although there were a larger number of young women willing and able to be trained as *murshidat* than in the 1980s, and therefore courses could afford to be more selective, the restructuring of the program neglected the selection process. "Anyone can become a *murshida* nowadays," I often heard in the interviews with the *murshidat* trained during the first training courses. The main difference in the selection was that less attention was paid to the women's motivation, and the need for income became a sufficient reason to gain a place. The number of families in need of money had increased dramatically after the Gulf crisis, and many returnee families were unable to keep

1. For an elaborate study on the *wasta* (intermediary) system, see Cunningham and Sarayrah (1993).

their heads above water. Unlike Sara, who voluntarily dropped out of school and was therefore an atypical example, the majority of returnee daughters felt forced to leave school and look for jobs as their fathers and brothers were unable to find work in Hodeida.

Not only the selection criteria but also the selection procedure changed. While in previous courses young women living in the area had come to the health center to apply for a training course, or were approached by the heads of clinic and the *murshidat*, now young women from all over town came to the government Health Office and put their names down. The Mother and Child Health Department at the Hodeida Health Office was responsible for all *murshidat* training courses in urban Hodeida and the surrounding rural areas, and everyone could go there to register for a course. Sara told me how she went almost daily to the Health Office, to talk her way into a course. The fact that managers at the Health Office were now in charge of the selection procedure also meant that less attention was being paid to the motivation of the young women. Muna expressed it as follows, "We used to contact young women in the area, whom we knew from the home visits. But now they don't do it like that anymore. They select the women directly. In the end God knows who is good and who is not good." And Hayat said, "Some of the *murshidat* are not suitable to give health education but they let them work as *murshidat*, despite the fact that they don't understand the work. Why? Because the persons in charge want to help them, as their family situation and their financial situation is bad. The demand is so great, so what can they do?"

Another result of the changes in the selection procedure was that having the right contacts in the Health Office became increasingly important, and the use of *wasta* became gradually one of the few ways in which young women could get a place in the course. From the time of the Gulf crisis in 1990 and the subsequent social, economic, and political problems in Yemen, corruption and nepotism have flourished (see Dresch 2000, 183–214). Because salaries are so low, every opportunity to earn extra money is used, and the *wasta* system has entered almost every area of society. For women like Sara, who lack the right contacts, the only way to get what they want is to go daily to the Health Office until they find someone who will take an interest in them. The result is that young women continuously approach managers at the Health Office to gain access to a training course. Yet these health managers are often unable to select the right women because they do not understand the exact nature of the work, or what is needed from the women.

Another reason for the differences between the previously and the newly trained *murshidat* was the way in which they were trained. Although there was some kind of an agreed national curriculum, every organization interpreted it according to its own ideas. In some courses more emphasis was put on curative care and the use of drugs, while in the Hodeida Urban Primary Health Care Project courses focused on preventive care and home visits. For the *murshidat* trained in the project during the 1980s, it was frustrating to realize that the *murshidat* trained in later courses sometimes knew more about drugs. Also, not every trainer paid the same attention to home visits or to communication skills. Muna said that the newly trained *murshidat* did not learn how to communicate with the mothers and to be patient and explain things slowly to them. "They have not learned it in the same way as we learned it because there are no good teachers who understand and who sit with the *murshida* and show them how to do the work." Muna referred here to the close supervision she received while she was working in the health center. The *murshidat* of the Hodeida Urban Primary Health Care Project had been supervised and trained on the job for a number of years. With the enlargement of the program a supervision team had been established, consisting of eight midwives and one nurse (all returnees). Thera de Haas and Fatima Salem were placed in charge of the supervision team, and a system was developed to oversee the thirteen health centers in the city. Yet the close supervision that had been carried out in Ghulail and al-Mughtaribin did not continue, which also explains the differences in work attitude and motivation.

It is clear that the restructuring and expansion of the project, and the increase in the number of *murshidat*, led to a kind of "generation gap" between those trained before and after 1990. On one hand, there were the *murshidat* trained during the first three courses in Ghulail and al-Mughtaribin, who were referred to as "the old ones" *(al-qadimat)*. On the other hand, there were the new *murshidat* (called *al-judud*) trained in various courses organized after the Gulf crisis. I have explained the differences between the two groups on the basis of the changing selection procedure and selection criteria, on the basis of the contents of the training course and the trainers, and on the basis of the limited supervision given after the training. But I have not yet touched on the different backgrounds of the *murshidat* trained after the Gulf crisis, and these different backgrounds were also a source of tension. Almost all of the new *murshidat* came from returnee families and had been born and brought up in Saudi Arabia. The influx of *murshidat* with returnee backgrounds had various consequences. Some of the previously trained *murshidat* looked down on the young and ambitious *mughtaribat* and blamed them for the social and economic changes taking place in Hodeida. But envy also inspired their attitude because the older *murshidat* felt threatened. As I have mentioned earlier, most of the young women who had been born and brought up in Saudi Arabia had attended school and had often finished intermediate education and sometimes even secondary education (see Van Hear 1994, 29). They were well educated and were able to pick up new things quickly. For most of them, the tasks they carried out as *murshidat* were not difficult, and they often aspired to more. Some, like Sara, became heads or deputy heads of clinic within a short period of time, while women trained in earlier courses had to gain much more experience before they were allowed to take up such a position. These differences led to tensions between *murshidat*.

Another consequence of the fact that *mughtaribat* became *murshidat* is related to the status of the profession, which was relative and depended on the neighborhood and the background of the *murshidat*. In general, the *murshidat* were more easily accepted in the poorer areas of town than in the city center and the commercial area. In these areas people were less interested in preventive health services and more suspicious of letting strangers into their homes. The low status of the returnees in Hodeida, in particular the darker women, affected the status of the *murshidat* profession negatively. Hawa, for example, told me that people in the older parts of the city would treat a *murshida* with a dark skin differently than they treated her. Although they would allow her to come in, they would not offer her a glass of water and would probably also take her health messages less seriously. The majority of the inhabitants of the squatter areas, however, were themselves returnees and came from low-status groups, and they did not look down on the *murshidat* because they shared the same background. Hawa also said that it was much easier for low-status women to work in areas where people of similar status were living. As mentioned before, many returnees encouraged their daughters to take up paid work, and being trained and employed as a *murshida* was one of the few possibilities. Because *murshidat* worked with mothers and children and did not have many contacts with men, returnee families preferred this to other types of work, such as factory work and office work. Interestingly, the expansion of the project led to an increase in the number of men involved in the work of the *murshidat,* and the ideal of gender segregation was undermined. The increasing involvement of men and the consequences for the reputation of the *murshidat* profession will be discussed below.

Murshidat as Heads of Clinic

The Gulf crisis had led to the official appointment of Muna and Riham as heads of the health centers in Ghulail and al-Mughtaribin, respectively. In Hodeida the designation *mas'ulat al-markaz,* literally "responsible for the center," was used to refer to "heads of clinic." Muna and Riham were the first *murshidat* to become heads of clinic. Before their official appointment in 1990, they had already been managing the health centers, but Thera de Haas and Fatima Salem assisted them on a daily basis. From 1990 onward they were officially in charge of the health centers, although they were still closely supervised. The head of clinic is responsible for the work of the *murshidat.* She checks that all employees are at work on time and prepares work schedules, fills in attendance lists, and reports leave and absenteeism to the management in the Health Office. She supervises the *murshidat* during their work, makes sure that all the necessary equipment and materials are present, and orders new materials when necessary. She checks the register books and compiles daily, weekly, and monthly statistical forms, which are sent to the Ministry of Public Health. She solves problems between the *murshidat*, between *murshidat* and drivers, and between *murshidat* and clients. She is responsible for the car and driver assigned to the health center and organizes transportation, in particular for home visiting. Once a week she chairs a meeting with all the *murshidat* of her center in order to discuss the running of the center, any problems, and possible ways to solve them. She is responsible for the implementation and supervision of special programs, such as the food program and the sewing and literacy classes for women (HUPHC 1995, 29). In short, being a head of clinic involves a good deal of responsibility.

Both Muna and Riham said that they did not find it difficult to move into this position. They emphasized that they had gradually taken on more responsibilities and that they were continuously assisted and advised by Thera de Haas and Fatima Salem. Muna said, "Thera was always beside me and she encouraged me a lot. She taught me step by step and said with everything I did, 'Don't be scared.'" Riham had the same experience with the Yemeni supervisor Fatima; "Fatima was always assisting me. I was not involved in management in the beginning. I calculated the statistics with the girls, I went on home visits, we mapped the area, we gave health education, but Fatima did the administrative work." Riham gradually became more involved in the administrative side of the work and eventually took over the responsibility for the center from Fatima. The gradual way in which Muna and Riham were trained as heads of clinic has affected the way they view their own position. They both emphasized that the work of a head of clinic is not so different from the work of the *murshidat*. "I like any work I do," and "There is no difference," they both said repeatedly when I asked them how it is to be a head of clinic.

Yet emphasizing that their work was not different from the work of the other *murshidat* was also an important strategy to make their position acceptable to others. The appointment of female heads of clinic, and in particular the appointment of *murshidat* as heads of clinic, was a radical development in Yemen. *Murshidat* were seen as the lowest category of health-care workers, as they had completed only six years of basic education and a one-year training course in preventive health care. Management positions were highly valued and restricted to people with a high status in society, based on their family background, their economic class, or their level of education. Managers were supposed to be men, and only in limited cases did women achieve a management position in Yemen.[2] *Murshidat* did not fit this picture at all, as they mostly came from low-status families and were not highly educated. Hamid Hassan, the Yemeni director of the project, had not been in favor of appointing *murshidat* as heads of clinic. When the expatriate staff left the project in the first half of 1991, called home as a security measure in view of the Gulf War, both Muna and Riham had the chance to prove that they were capable of managing the health centers, and after the Gulf War he approved their appointments.

Muna and Riham had been working as heads of clinic in the relatively safe surroundings of the project, but with the expansion of the project to all governmental health centers in Hodeida, the appointment of *murshidat* as heads of clinic became an issue that had to be discussed with the Hodeida Health Office. In the eyes of the project management, the *murshidat* were the best informed and the most experienced in setting up a primary health-care system and therefore most suitable as heads of clinic. But in the eyes of the Health Office management, heads of clinic had to be highly educated, preferably (male) doctors. In Hodeida there were five centers with a male director, often an older man who had been trained as a nurse but who considered himself a

---

2. In the gender analysis of the Yemeni Ministry of Public Health and Population, Martin (2001, 23) mentions that in 2001 there were very few female staff in the ministry at the institutional level above the grade of administrative or secretarial staff. There were no female deputies and no female director-generals except for the director-general of the Reproductive Health Department, who also promoted the appointment of female staff in Reproductive Health Departments at the governmental level.

doctor. These male directors had built up authority in the area and were not willing to give up their positions as health center directors. Discussions and negotiations between the project management and the management of the Hodeida Health Office followed, and a compromise was reached. The *murshidat* became responsible for MCH services and were called "responsible for the center" (*mas'ulat al-markaz*), and the male nurse or doctor became responsible for curative services and was called the technical director (*mudir fanni*). The result was that some centers had a director and a head of clinic, which in English may sound redundant, but in Arabic the difference was clear: these centers had a *mudir* (male director) and a *mas'ula* (responsible female). The fact that the *murshidat* did not become female directors (*mudira*) was not accidental; the different words were important to show the hierarchy between the two positions with the *mudir* having the highest status and the *mas'ula* being his subordinate.

The selection of female heads of clinic was left to the staff of the foreign development projects, in particular to Thera de Haas and Fatima Salem. They had a fairly good picture of the female staff working in the health centers of Hodeida and decided who was suitable to take on these responsibilities. The head of clinic needed to be dedicated to the work, intelligent, and mature, and she had to be able to work in the afternoon. In the centers where *murshidat* had been trained, one of the *murshidat* was selected. In the centers where a midwife or a female nurse was managing the center, she was selected as head of clinic. And in the centers where a male director was in charge of the center, a *murshida* was put in charge of MCH services. Some *murshidat* were disappointed that they had not been selected as heads of clinic, but others were happy that they did not have to take on extra responsibility. Hanan, who had been trained during the first course in Ghulail, felt passed over when she was not selected because the other three *murshidat* of the first group, Muna, Riham, and Hawa, all became heads of clinic. There were doubts about her ability to carry the responsibility of managing a health center; she was seen as too young and fickle to become a head of clinic. The same was true for Halima, who had been trained during the second course and was an active and intelligent *murshida*. Although Halima was surprised that she was not selected, she said that she did not mind because she was busy with her studies in the afternoon, and heads of clinic often had to work in the afternoon as well. There were also women who were active and dedicated *murshidat* but did not want the responsibility of being a head of clinic. "I don't like the administrative work," Sa'diyya told me, and Nur said, "I didn't want the responsibility because if something happened it would be my fault." Sa'diyya and Nur both loved the home-visiting side of their work and were very much involved in home deliveries. For them, becoming a head of clinic would have meant a shift of emphasis from practical work in the community to administrative work in the health center, and they liked the practical side of their work better. Although most of the heads of clinic liked to emphasize that their work was not very different from the work of the *murshidat*, there was a clear difference.

Almost every time I asked the heads of clinic how they felt about occupying a management position in the health center, they immediately responded that there was no difference between their work and the work of the other *murshidat*. Iman said,

> I don't see a difference between the work of the heads of clinic and the *murshidat*. The head of clinic works like a *murshida*. The only difference is that she prepares the statistics, that she is in charge of the center, that she gives the girls the work schedules, and that if anyone comes from outside to visit the center the head of clinic speaks to them. But the way we do the work is the same. Even a *murshida* can learn how to do the statistics, and then she can take over. Anyone can be in charge.

There are several reasons that most heads of clinic trivialized the importance of their position. The main one is that they tried to make the fact that they had taken up a responsible position acceptable to themselves, to their relatives and acquaintances, and to their colleagues. As I explained earlier, female managers are rare in Yemen, and management positions are closely linked to one's family background and educational level. It was therefore very likely that there would be resistance to this development, and the heads of clinic developed strategies anticipating this resistance. One of their strategies was to trivialize the importance of their position. When I asked Muna how her acquaintances reacted to her becoming head of clinic, she answered, "What is the difference? There is no difference. I didn't tell them. They see it themselves when they come to the health center. When they come to vaccinate their children they say, 'Oh, you don't work with the other *murshidat*? So you are the head of clinic?'" Muna did not even tell her husband that she had been promoted to head of clinic. "He knew it by himself. When he saw for example the keys of the health center with me, and when he noticed that I could not be absent, that I had to be early at work because the keys were with me. I didn't say 'I am head of clinic,' he just knew it after a while." Muna's decision not to tell her husband about her new position as a head of clinic is in line with the strategies I discussed previously. The *murshidat* gradually shifted the boundaries of what was socially acceptable by not drawing attention to their activities and in doing so created room to maneuver and avoided conflicts. Their relatives accepted their work as long as they were not openly confronted with it.

In the interviews, all the heads of clinic emphasized that they were working together with the other *murshidat* instead of "playing the director" and giving orders. They told me how they were teaching new *murshidat*, not by telling them what to do but by sitting next to them and showing them the work. Hawa explained the fact that she liked to be a head of clinic as follows,

> I like the responsibility, I really like it. You know why? Because I know the work of the *murshida* and what is lacking in the work of the *murshida*, and I know what I can do, I know which things I should improve. But if I had been responsible directly, without having done the work myself, there would not be any improvement. When someone knows the work, even with regard to appointing the workers, one needs to have a feeling for the work. I know that when a worker is ill, I can't let her work. And if I feel that she does not want to do something, I won't say that she has to do it. Because carrying the responsibility does not mean that you have to be in power. The girls and I, we are equal.

A weekly meeting of the heads of clinics.

Samira even said, "I was not working in the health center as a head of clinic, but as a cleaner," to stress that she was doing those tasks in the health center that were the least valued. She called this way of working explicitly "a democratic way of management" *(idara dimuqratiyya)*, a word she had learned during a supervision course. And many of the heads of clinic said that they learned to manage the health center from Thera de Haas and Fatima Salem, who were said to work in a democratic and nonauthoritarian way. They were both important examples for the first three groups of *murshidat*, as they trained them on the job with very close supervision.

Yet there were also conflicts between the heads of clinic and the *murshidat* working in the health centers, which shows that the heads of clinic did not always work in a democratic way. Their emphasis on equality and democracy can also be explained by the fact that the heads of clinic were all originally *murshidat* themselves and used to have the same position as the other *murshidat*. In order to be accepted as heads of clinic by the others and in order to avoid problems, emphasizing equality was an important strategy for them. Sara, for example, told me that she had a lot of problems with the other *murshidat* when she was appointed deputy head of clinic, which happened a year after she had started to work as a *murshida*. The *murshidat* who had been working in the health center before did not accept her, as she was much younger and still relatively new in the health center. In addition to age and length of experience, there were other reasons that the *murshidat* did not always accept the head of clinic appointment. Muna told me that she was not accepted as head of clinic by two *murshidat* who were trained during the same course as she was, while Riham was not accepted by a number of *murshidat* who were older than she and who were married and had children. She even stayed at home for a while because the problems in the health center had become too stressful. Tensions between the *murshidat* and the heads of clinic usually led to the transfer of one of them, and in most cases it was the *murshida*.

So despite the emphasis on equality, which most of the heads of clinic expressed, there was clearly power and status involved in being a head of clinic. Carrying responsibility implies recognition of one's authority. One of the *murshidat* who had been promoted to head of clinic said, "It is an honor to be head of clinic" and continuously talked about how she built up "her center." When she was attending a one-year upgrading course to community midwife, another *murshida* replaced her, but she did everything to come back to "her own center."

There were also many *murshidat* who were not interested in becoming head of clinic and who were much happier doing the practical work. For them power and status were not so important, and they easily accepted another *murshida* as head of clinic. However, contact with men, which had been the main reason Hawa had initially decided not to become a head of clinic, was no longer mentioned as a problem, which showed that gender boundaries had gradually shifted in society at large.

More Men Make Their Entry

One rationale with which the *murshidat* defended their work in health care was that there were very few men involved in their work. They delivered MCH services, so they worked with women and children. And with regard to their colleagues they repeatedly emphasized that "we are all girls" *(kulluna banat)* and that there was little mingling with men *(ma fish ikhtilat)*. In the previous chapters, I have already shown that this picture was not a complete reflection of reality. There were male drivers working for the project and the *murshidat* were in daily contact with them, which often caused problems. They went on home visits where they also met men, albeit in the context of the family. And the director and codirector of the project were men. With the expansion of the project, more men became involved in the work of the *murshidat* at different levels. They now had male colleagues, they met male patients, and they had to work together with male community members. Gradually the picture began to change.

The involvement of men was most evident in the three main health centers, where curative services were also delivered.[3] In these centers a male doctor, a male laboratory technician, a male pharmacist, and sometimes a couple of male nurses worked in the curative part of the center. Tensions and frictions between the *murshidat* and the male staff were the order of the day, in particular in those centers where the male director did not accept a *murshida* as head of MCH services. As I mentioned before, the fact that *murshidat* with only basic education and one year's training in health education were given authority as heads of clinic was sometimes met with resistance, especially by the male health cadre working in the centers. Hawa was one of the few *murshidat* who did not mention problems with the male staff in the health center. Hawa is an intelligent and mature woman with children, whom everyone respects. Other *murshidat* had to fight for the respect

---

3. As mentioned in chapter 4, in the governmental health centers in the city, mainly curative services had been delivered before these centers became part of the citywide program. The al-Tahrir health center was the main health center in town. In addition to al-Tahrir, the Ghulail health center was designated a main center in order to cover the southeast of Hodeida, and the newly built health center in al-Salakhana, in the middle of the new squatter areas on the northeastern outskirts of town, became the third main center.

and recognition of the male staff in the health center because they were young or did not have "natural authority," or because they came from low-status backgrounds.

With the expansion of the project, the duties of the heads of clinic also began to change. In the previous project phase, the project management and the female supervisors had maintained contact with the managers in the Health Office, but now the heads of clinic had to visit the Health Office on a regular basis. The project management and the supervisors used to have two rooms in the Health Office, but now a special department for Urban Primary Health Care was established, and the project management and the supervisors became an integral part of the Health Office. So the lines of authority started to change, and the director-general of the Health Office had the final say over the activities in the health centers. A much closer contact between the project management, the director-general, and the different departments of the Health Office resulted.

For the *murshidat* working in the health centers, this change did not affect their daily work, but for the heads of clinic the new citywide approach and the integration into the Health Office meant a major change. Weekly meetings were organized in the Health Office to discuss the work. They became responsible for the financial administration of the center and had to deal with the Financial Department of the Health Office. And in case of problems they were called to the office to discuss possible solutions. In short, their contacts with the managers in the Health Office increased considerably after the expansion of the project, and these managers were mainly male. The head of the Mother and Child Health Department was a woman, and the members of the supervision team were all women, but the rest of the heads of department and the director-general were male.[4] For many *murshidat* it was a new experience to deal with men in a formal setting, outside the family. And while the male project directors treated them with respect and dignity, and the *murshidat* often referred to them as

4. The number of staff working in the Hodeida Health Office was around 150 (although many more people were on the payroll).

"being like a father," they had to get used to the different approach of the men in the Health Office. In the Health Office they were not put on a pedestal, and their words were not always listened to and respected. It was a totally different environment from the relatively safe surroundings of the health center.

A third reason contacts with men increased after the expansion of the project was related to the newly developed cost recovery and community participation programs (see chapter 4). For the heads of clinic and the *murshidat*, the cost-recovery and community participation programs entailed a number of extra responsibilities and increased contacts with men. First of all, they were responsible for the formation of the local health committee and the selection of committee members. Organizing and attending focus group discussions, interviewing suitable candidates, making sure that the right people were selected, and bringing the committee together were all responsibilities of the head of clinic. She could delegate activities to the *murshidat* in her center, but she had the final responsibility. The male directors sometimes got involved in the selection of committee members by proposing acquaintances or friends, but they rarely went into the neighborhood to attend focus group discussions. After the final selection of committee members had taken place, the heads of clinic were the ones who organized the monthly meetings of the committee. They contacted the community members and chaired the meetings. The male directors always attended the meetings of the local health committees, but they did not get involved in the organization of the meetings, at least in the first years of the cost-recovery and community participation programs. On most local health committees, male community members did most of the talking and dominated the discussion. For the heads of clinic it was an entirely new experience to chair meetings with men, but during the first five years of the project they had learned to make their views known, as part of their new positions in the project. Now they benefited from these experiences in their contacts with men, and most of them stood firm. But their work had not become easier, and they were confronted on an almost daily basis with problems they had to solve.

Another new responsibility for the heads of clinic was the financial management of the cost-recovery and revolving drug fund. The heads of clinic had to check the money and take it on a fixed day of the week to the accountant at the Health Office. The responsibility for finances was for many heads of clinic a heavy burden, and some of them withdrew from their posts because they did not want that responsibility. Amal, for example, was held responsible for a missing YR3,000 lost during her absence. She had to pay the money back, which took her half a year. After that experience she refused to be in charge of the money paid for drugs. "I said, I will be responsible for everything in the center except for the drugs. Honestly, I don't want that responsibility anymore. Who is going to help me when there is a deficit? No one helped me this time. I paid it all by myself. And my salary is only YR5,000. I couldn't buy anything for my brothers and sisters this month because I had to pay back the deficit."

Many heads of clinic complained about the heavy responsibilities they took on after the introduction of cost recovery, but none of them mentioned the increased contacts with men explicitly when discussing the consequences of the citywide program. This is a sign of the gradual change in gender boundaries, which had taken place in the past ten years. In the first project phase (1985–93), the *murshidat* had been able to build up confidence and to secure their positions, in the company of their female colleagues and supported and protected by the project management. In the second project phase (1993–99), they had to leave the two health centers, as they were distributed across the other health centers in town, and had to cooperate with men in the Health Office. Yet the fact that they managed to keep their positions and continue their work as *murshidat*, or even as heads of clinic alongside male directors, was a sign that the pioneering phase was over and that their presence was more or less accepted.

The Other Side of Integration

The *murshidat* had been protected and put on a pedestal in the first project phase, but after 1993 they had to work together with people who were less supportive and sometimes obstructed their work. Among the male managers in the Health Office, most of whom were trained as medical doctors, pharmacists, or paramedical personnel, there was often little respect for the poorly educated women working in the health centers. In addition, very few of the male managers knew what primary health care was. They often valued curative activities more highly than preventive health care, and they saw the *murshidat* as the lowest level of health personnel and only necessary while Yemen did not have sufficient female nurses and midwives. While the project team continued to emphasize the importance of the work of the *murshidat*, as they were the only ones working in the community, the managers in the Health Office were unconvinced and continued to look down on the *murshidat*.

Some *murshidat* were very disappointed and pessimistic about the future when they heard how some of the male managers in the office talked about the *murshidat*. Kelthum told me that one of the deputy directors of the Urban Primary Health Care Department had insulted the *murshidat* by saying that their place was at the door of the director's office, waiting for his orders and bringing him his coffee.[5] The *murshidat* felt so insulted that they called for a meeting with the director to discuss this incident, but they never received a serious response to their request. One of them said,

> When I heard the insults, I thought "I want to work somewhere else." I thought about going to Sana'a, to apply for any type of work, in any place. I was fed up. We have been working for eight years, giving everything, and this is what we get. They could at least have said, "Thank you for your work as a *murshida*." We don't even want a financial reward. We want a word of thanks, or a certificate

5. Morris (1991, 245) describes the similar attitude of a doctor newly appointed as director who refused to employ the *murshidat* because they did not have sufficient training or experience to become salaried health workers. He, or other doctors, would deal with delivery cases instead. While the training of *murshidat* had been one of the few successes of the project Morris worked in, local (male) health managers obstructed the achievements of the project.

of appreciation because we have made a huge effort. When something like this happens I get very angry. He drives his air-conditioned car and sits in the office. He is happy because he is the director. But he should not forget that he is filling that position because of us, because of the *murshidat*. If there were no *murshidat* he would not have achieved this position!

The fact that the management of the Urban Primary Health Care Department did little to defend the *murshidat* was a sign of the increasing gap between the management in the Health Office and the female health staff working in the centers. In the first project period the *murshidat* had been protected and promoted by the management, but now they had to fight for themselves. The gap increased even more in the second half of 1994, after the civil war, when Richard Simons became the team leader. Simons saw the integration of the project into the Hodeida Health Office as his main task and focused on establishing contacts with the Health Office managers. Yet his approach led to frictions with the Yemeni director and with the female supervisors, who had the feeling that he was not protecting the established system.

In addition, in 1995 the director-general removed Hamid Hassan, after continuous tensions and problems, and a much younger and less experienced doctor replaced him. The totally new management team started to follow a different approach than the *murshidat* and the female supervisors had been used to. Within a short period of time two camps were formed: on one hand the male managers and on the other the women health workers. The frictions between the two camps increased dramatically and were never really resolved. Instead of a process in which the previous project approach was integrated into the Health Office, the opposite happened; the new project management adopted the ways in which the male managers in the Health Office dealt with women, and with *murshidat* in particular, and the *murshidat* lost the respect and recognition they had received before.

In addition, although the project was in certain ways integrated into the Health Office, the Hodeida Urban Primary Health Care Program continued to be regarded as a foreign project with a lot of money, and the differences with other departments in the Health Office remained substantial. The building of a fully furnished separate wing to the Health Office for the program in 1996 accentuated these differences. The shift of a project approach to a program approach was in the eyes of the project management a way to integrate the project activities into the Yemeni public-health sector and, in doing so, achieve sustainability. Yet in the eyes of Yemeni health managers, integration mainly meant sharing in the assets of the project.

The *murshidat* lost many of the (financial) advantages they had had in the project. While they used to receive compensation for afternoon work, a Ramadan bonus, and a heat allowance for home visiting during the hot summer months, all these financial benefits disappeared at the start of the citywide program. In the name of "sustainability," the project management decided to stop these financial benefits because the Health Office would not be able to continue to pay them after donor support had come to an end. Amal told me how difficult it was to get used to the new approach in the beginning. "We were shocked when the project expanded, because we had been spoiled. We had always received everything we asked for, but now that was impossible because there were thirteen centers to take care of." One of the consequences was that afternoon work was less attractive because there was no overtime paid anymore. Many *murshidat* accepted other jobs in the afternoon, working as health assistants in private clinics and private hospitals, just as Arwa did. Because of the deteriorating economic situation, their government salaries were not sufficient to live on, and they were forced to look for other sources of income. Having two jobs, a government job in the morning and a job in the private sector in the afternoon, is very common in Yemen and for many people the only way to survive, in particular after the start of the structural adjustment reforms in 1995.[6] Afternoon activities diminished, yet the home visits continued.

---

6. The reform measures taken included cuts in subsidies on gasoline, electricity, and heat; cuts in the number of government employees; and a devaluation of the Yemeni riyal. The immediate result was a rise in the cost of living, and one salary no longer sufficed. For the particular consequences of structural adjustment programs for women in the Third World, see Afshar and Dennis (1992) and Rai (2002, 121–58).

I already mentioned that there was an increasing gap between the management of the Urban Primary Health Care Department and the female health cadre in the centers. But the distance between the female supervisors and the *murshidat* also increased. In the first years of the citywide program, a team of thirteen young midwives supervised the activities in the health centers.[7] These supervisors were very committed to their work and visited all the centers on a regular basis. They trained the *murshidat* and heads of clinic on the job, spending whole days in the center and assisting wherever possible. The two female supervisors who had been in charge of supervision in Ghulail and al-Mughtaribin guided this supervision team. But in 1997 many supervisors left to become trainers in community midwife courses. As trainers they could earn more; foreign donor organizations financed the community midwife courses, and the salaries were paid in dollars. Gradually the supervision team was dismantled, and the MCH Department of the Health Office became responsible for supervision. Fatima Salem was appointed head of the newly established Quality Assurance Department,[8] which meant that she was no longer actively involved in the activities in the health centers. For the *murshidat* in the centers, and in particular for the heads of clinic, the changes taking place at management level had an immediate impact on their work. There was less close supervision, and they were left to their own devices. Iman complained about the lack of attention paid to the activities in the health centers. "I want supervision, I want someone who presses me and encourages me to do things in the right way. If they do not come to supervise it will affect the work, honestly. A human being is not perfect. We all make mistakes. There has to be supervision."

Another important consequence of the lack of supervision was the fact that problems were no longer solved at the level of the center; the

7. For a life story of one of these midwives, see the interview with Khadija in Paluch (2001, 129).

8. In the second half of the 1990s, quality control became a new phenomenon in public services.

heads of clinic felt obliged to take every small problem to the Health Office. The result was that small problems were blown up, and the management became involved in the petty details of the work. Almost all the interviewed *murshidat* complained about this development and blamed the newly trained *murshidat* for not knowing how to solve problems among themselves. In short, the integration into the Health Office led to increasing differences and tensions between the *murshidat* themselves and between male and female health cadres, in the health centers as well as in the Health Office. Instead of more equity, stronger hierarchies were the result of the restructuring and expansion of the program. The announcement of a new policy to train community midwives instead of *murshidat* was another source of tension.

From *Murshida* to Community Midwife

A New Policy

Sara wanted to continue her studies in order to obtain a higher certificate because she had heard that the Ministry of Public Health had decided not to train and employ any more *murshidat*. "In the year 2000 there won't be any *murshidat* anymore," she said, and she decided to prepare herself for this gloomy future. The reason for her pessimistic view was that the Ministry of Public Health had launched a new policy in 1996, in which it proposed to train community midwives *(qabilat al-mujtama')* instead of *murshidat*. The immediate cause for this policy change was a national field survey carried out in ten governorates to identify the need for training centers and Health Manpower Institutes, to assess the opinion of the community on MCH services, and to identify its subsequent needs. The main outcome of the survey was that MCH services were inadequate, even in those places where *murshidat* were present. The report stated that people did not use the services of the *murshidat* because "most of them are very young and their short period of training does not qualify them to deliver quality services" (Ministry of Public Health 1996). This survey was carried out almost exclusively in rural areas because around 75 percent of Yemen's population lives in the countryside, and the health status of people in rural areas leaves a lot to be desired.

Although it was difficult to train women health workers in villages because of high illiteracy rates, women's heavy workload, and cultural notions limiting women's paid labor, in particular in health care, an increasing number of women had become *murshidat* by the 1990s. Yet despite these *murshidat*, the level of MCH services remained low in rural areas. *Murshidat* did not have the knowledge or equipment to assist at difficult deliveries and could often do no more than refer women to the nearest hospital. In many cases it was impossible to reach the hospital in time because of long distances and lack of roads, which sometimes caused the infant's death as well as the mother's. In addition, the *murshidat* received very limited support from the Ministry of Public Health. They often lacked basic equipment and a regular supply of essential drugs and contraceptives, and they received hardly any supervision (Hassan and Amer 1997, 51). *Murshidat* were therefore unable to decrease infant and maternal mortality rates.

One of the new strategies introduced by the Ministry of Public Health was the training of community midwives. Community midwives receive two years of training after finishing intermediate school.[9] They are more highly educated than *murshidat* but less trained than certified midwives, who have attended a three-year midwifery course at a Health Manpower Institute. Another difference is that community midwives are explicitly trained to work within their own communities and not in a health facility. Community midwives are linked to a health center in their area, but they are supposed to work from their own homes. They do home visits to check the health status of women and children and to identify their needs. They give health education, and they assist at home births. The actual work of community midwives does not differ much from the work of the *murshidat*, but community midwives are better trained to carry out midwifery tasks, in particular when dealing with complications in labor.

9. For detailed information on the community midwife training in Yemen, and in particular the training of trainers, see Penney (2000).

The initial idea was that the majority of the community midwives would not be employed by the government but would generate an income from their services in the community. They would be a new category of private practitioners, but closely supervised by the health center personnel in the area. For the government, community midwives were thus a cheap solution to a big problem. But experts in the field of health care immediately recognized the risk of allowing people to earn an income via private practice. Community midwives might be tempted to deal with health problems beyond their capabilities and might run the risk of worsening the health situation in rural areas. The Yemeni government then decided to employ the community midwives. The Dutch government funded the community midwife training program, a typical example of the shift from project aid to program aid.[10]

In the cities, and in Hodeida in particular, the situation differed from that of the rural areas. The presence of health centers, hospitals, and private clinics, and the availability of highly educated personnel such as nurses, midwives, and doctors, had improved infant and child mortality rates.[11] Urban *murshidat* focus on preventive health services and contribute in that way also to a better health status for the population in general, and of mothers and children in particular. But the *murshidat* themselves were not satisfied with their position in the Yemeni health establishment. Almost all of the *murshidat* emphasized that they wanted to upgrade their qualifications and change their status of *murshida* to the status of midwife or nurse. Nurses and midwives were more highly valued because they were better educated and because their activities focused on curative care and midwifery

10. The project was called "Community Based Reproductive Health Through Training of Midwives." The project was planned for the period November 1997 until November 2000, with a total budget of 5.2 million euro. UNFPA would implement the activities (Hardon et al. 2002, 26).

11. In 1997, infant mortality rates were 63.4 deaths per 1,000 live births in urban areas and 78.8 in rural areas, and child mortality rates 17.8 deaths per 1,000 live births in urban areas and 36.0 in rural areas (Central Statistical Organization 1998, 99).

The graduation of a group of murshidat *upgraded to community midwives.*

services, whereas *murshidat* were "only weighing and vaccinating children." From the beginning of the project a discrepancy had existed between the desires and ambitions of the *murshidat* and the opinion of the project team. In the eyes of the project team, the *murshidat* filled an important role in their communities, and upgrading their qualifications to midwife had not been one of the priorities. Yet most of the *murshidat* saw their training as a first step in a career, and they aspired to continue their education and to attend as many courses as possible, preferably to become midwives or nurses.

From 1997 onward, almost every foreign donor organization involved in health care started to organize and finance community midwife training courses in rural and urban areas. Certified midwives were trained as trainers, and often left their regular job to teach a two-year training course because the salaries were paid in dollars and were much higher than their regular salaries. As mentioned before, many of the midwives who were working as supervisors in the Hodeida Urban Primary Health Care Program decided to become community midwife trainers because of the money they could earn but also because their work as supervisors was gradually becoming less important. Sara was right when she said that the Yemeni Ministry of Public Health did not want to train and employ new *murshidat* anymore and focused on the training of community midwives instead. An exception was made for those areas of the country that did not yet have any female health personnel, and where the number of women with an intermediate school certificate was too small. Hodeida was anything but a remote and isolated area, so the training of *murshidat* came to a halt. The last group of urban *murshidat* was trained in 1997.

Providing for the Future

For the *murshidat* in Hodeida the announcement of this new policy led to a lot of unrest. Most of the *murshidat* were already worried about their future, in particular in view of the coming end of donor funding in 1999. The integration into the Health Office did not go smoothly, and the *murshidat* were confronted on a daily basis with the disadvantages of "integration." A different way of managing urban primary health care, lack of money, lack of communication, and an increasing feeling of disrespect for their work were a constant thorn in their flesh. They feared for the future, and the announcement that "there won't be any *murshidat* anymore in the year 2000" added to their worries. What was going to happen to them? Were they going to be dismissed? And if not then, what about in the future when Dutch funding for the program would end?

One of the solutions for ending these fears and making their position more sustainable was to give *murshidat* a chance to upgrade their qualifications to community midwife. The Hodeida Urban Primary Health Care Program took the initiative to organize so-called upgrading courses for *murshidat*. Instead of a two-year training course, the *murshidat* could become community midwives with one year of extra training. While the project management initially proposed that the *murshidat* of the first two groups should get the first chance to be upgraded, the Ministry of Public Health did not approve of that idea. The main requirement to being accepted into the course was that the *murshidat* should be in possession of an intermediate-school certificate. And that happened to be an obstacle for many, particularly for "the old ones." As I have explained before, combining paid work and study was not an easy thing to do. Household responsibilities, lack of money, the need to work in the afternoons, and inability to pick up things quickly were among the main obstacles to continued study. The project management decided to financially assist *murshidat* who were unable to pay the school fees and, in this way, to encourage them to finish intermediate school. But still only a select group of *murshidat* were able to obtain intermediate-school certificates and register for the upgrading course to community midwife.

The first upgrading course was planned to take place in 1996, but because of discussions and negotiations with the Health Manpower Institute in Sana'a, the preparation of the course curriculum was delayed, and the course only started in 1997. The fact that the project had taken the initiative to organize an upgrading course, and had not awaited the approval of the Yemeni Ministry of Public Health, was one of the reasons the curriculum was not ready in time and the course was delayed. According to Thera de Haas, this situation was similar to what had happened ten years ago, when the project had organized the first *murshidat* training course without the official approval of the ministry. The result was that the ministry had not immediately employed the first *murshidat*, in order to show "the Dutch" that they were obliged to stick to government policies. In 1996 that was the case again; by delaying the preparations for the curriculum the ministry showed its power and the dependency of the project.

For most of the *murshidat*, the upgrading course was one of the few chances to improve their position. Twenty *murshidat* started the course in 1997, among them Hawa, the only "old one" who had been able to obtain her intermediate-school certificate. Three *murshidat* trained during the second training course also participated in the course. The rest of the students were *murshidat* trained in later courses, and often after 1990, like Sara, who also joined the first upgrading course. They all left their work in the center for a year in order to attend the course, but they were told time and again that they would return to their centers and take up the same work they had been doing before. Obtaining a higher certificate, and a higher position in the governmental pay scale and maybe a higher salary, were presented as the only benefits of attending the course.

In addition to upgrading their certificates to safeguard their positions, the *murshidat* were also interested in improving their knowledge and becoming better health-care workers. Those who were active birth attendants were longing for more knowledge about deliveries and related issues, and those working as heads of clinic wanted to upgrade their skills in order to be better able to supervise the staff in the health centers. Hawa, who was head of clinic in al-Salakhana, found it difficult to supervise and assist the midwives in her center. "Sometimes you have the feeling that those you are responsible for have more knowledge than you have. That is frustrating. It is true that I have more experience and that I can teach them a lot, but sometimes they ask me things which I don't know, and that is difficult." In fact, most of the *murshidat* aspired to become certified midwives instead of community midwives, but they did not have the choice. In order to become certified midwives, they had to attend a three-year course at the Health Manpower Institute. The fact that they were already experienced *murshidat* did not make any difference in the length of the course: three years remained three years. So enrolling in the community midwife course was the only alternative they had.

The feelings about the first upgrading course were mixed. Some *murshidat* found it useful and said that they learned many new things, while others complained that there was not much difference from what they had learned before. "There is only a small difference with what we learned as a *murshida*. We learn a bit more about diseases." Yet Sara noticed many differences. "We learned about social sciences, psychology, statistics, management, a lot of things we had never learned before." The course was clearly more focused on curative care than on preventive issues, which had positive and negative aspects. Curative care was highly desired, as it improved the status of their work, but some *murshidat* missed the preventive part. They thought that it would be good if *murshidat* and community midwives

302 / *Other Modernities*

could complement one another. "Community midwives are like *murshidat*, but they lack the health education aspect. But the *murshidat* can teach the new community midwives health education. If they also received the information we received, that would be good." Three upgrading courses to community midwife have taken place, and around sixty *murshidat* attended. After graduation all of them went back to work in the health centers. Most of them work as midwives, but they combine their work with the activities they carried out as *murshidat*. Moreover, their salaries have increased slightly.

Losing Out?

Becoming a community midwife was the best chance a *murshida* had to upgrade her qualifications and to safeguard her future. But what about those who were not able to attend an upgrading course? Muna and Riham, two of "the old ones" and heads of clinic in Ghulail and al-Mughtaribin, had never tried to continue their education and obtain intermediate-school certificates. Neither had a good head for study, and they liked the practical work in the center much better. They were competent managers, good health workers, and inspired many people around them. Moreover, responsibilities at home had prevented them from finishing intermediate school. Other *murshidat* were not interested in joining an upgrading course because they did not see the difference between the work of a *murshida* and that of a community midwife. "The work is the same," I often heard. Some also emphasized that they were government employees, and that was most important for them. "I am a government employee so I am not afraid of losing my job," they answered when I asked them whether they were not afraid of losing out if they remained "only *murshidat*." In addition, a number of heads of clinic did not want to attend an upgrading course because they were afraid they would lose their positions as heads of clinic, which is a responsible position and therefore has a higher status than that of *murshida*.

While Muna wanted to stay as head of clinic, Riham thought that it was time for a change. "I have worked for ten years now, I know the work, I know the system. It would be nice to change and improve my position. As long as a person is young and can learn, they should learn and develop themselves." Riham's hope for change can partly be explained by the fact that I interviewed the *murshidat* in 1997, and donor assistance was only planned to come to an end in 1999. Many *murshidat* expressed the hope that they would still get a chance to attend a course that would be beneficial and help them to improve their positions. The *murshidat* trained during the first two training courses, especially, continued to press the project management for such courses. From the very beginning of the project they had had happy dreams about the future, with the prospect of upgrading courses, English-language training, and maybe even courses abroad. This hope had been inspired by promises made by the project management, in particular during the first project period, when the *murshidat* had been put on a pedestal. In the meantime they had visited other projects, had attended short training courses, and had been given the chance to learn English, but their position had not changed. They were still *murshidat*, and many of them were disappointed about that. Riham saw the chance to attend a course as a way of showing respect to the *murshidat*. Iman, on the other hand, emphasized the importance of a longer training course to improve their knowledge. The requests for more training did not yield much success. In the following years, 1998 and 1999, the management of the Hodeida Urban Primary Health Care Program had to spend the budget allocated for training before Dutch financial assistance would come to an end. But instead of sending *murshidat* for training courses abroad, three male doctors got a chance to study for a master's degree in public health in Egypt, and many other people benefited from longer and shorter training courses in Yemen. After enormous pressure, in particular from Thera de Haas, who was the only foreign "expert" left,[12] a group of nine *murshidat* paid a one-week visit to Egypt in April 1999. Muna, Riham, and Hanan, three of "the old ones" who were

---

12. In October 1997, Richard Simons, the British team leader of the project, died suddenly and was not replaced by a foreign adviser. In December 1997 my contract finished.

unable to attend the community midwife course because they did not have intermediate-school certificates, were part of the group.

In September 1999, Dutch funding for the Hodeida Urban Primary Health Care Project came to an end. The project activities had been integrated into the Hodeida Health Office; personnel had been trained and the cost-recovery and community participation system was supposed to partly finance the activities. As described in chapter 4, a closing conference in June 1999 officially marked the end of the Hodeida Urban Primary Health Care Project, yet a new Dutch-funded project started in September 1999: the Hodeida Primary Health Systems Support Project (HPHSS). This project was supposed to build upon the achievements of the Hodeida Urban Primary Health Care Project and implement health and socioeconomic activities in both urban and rural Hodeida. It was decided to use a strategy that includes both curative and preventive health-care interventions, integrate health-care and non-health-care activities, and involve governmental, nongovernmental, and the private sector in "carrying out activities that will strengthen the health-care system and raise the economic status of poor members of society in both urban and rural Hodeida" (Stolba et al. 1998, vi). The project duration would be five years in total and consist of two phases.[13]

"I am afraid," Muna often answered me when I asked her about the future. "I don't know what will happen" and "the future will be difficult" she replied when I asked her why she was afraid. She experienced the change in approach after the integration into the Health Office as a gradual loss of what had been built up in the ten years before and foresaw more problems after the end of donor funding. Most of the *murshidat* found it hard to accept the idea that Dutch funding would come to an end. They had gradually grown accustomed to foreign support and protection, and they feared the future. They wanted to secure their positions and upgrade their qualifications, but even then

13. The first phase would run from September 1999 until September 2002 (three years), the second phase would run from September 2002 until September 2004 (two years).

they found it hard to imagine how they were going to work without Dutch funding. Thera de Haas, who had worked for the project since 1984 and who was still there fourteen years later, was a key person in the project. She was the only expatriate member of the project staff left in 1998, and she supported the *murshidat* whenever she could. Her departure was for some of the *murshidat* hardly imaginable. But Thera continued to stress that the new project would continue to support the *murshidat* and that there would be new foreign advisors who would assist them in their work.

"The Days of the Project Are Over"

Political Changes

Soon after the project ended, a new director-general was appointed to the Hodeida Health Office, replacing 'Abdelhalim Ramzi, who had been closely involved in the Hodeida Urban Primary Health Care Program. The main reason for his replacement was the fact that he had been offered a place in a master's course in public health in Amsterdam in 2000–2001 (paid as an incentive by Dutch development aid). However, he was not willing to hand over one of the project cars, the Toyota Land Cruiser that had caused a problem at an earlier stage of the project.[14] The Dutch embassy decided to give him a choice: he had to give back the car or he would lose his right to attend the course. Interestingly he chose to keep the car, which underlines the important symbolic value of cars. In addition, his choice meant that he had to leave the Hodeida Health Office, and after eight years of close involvement in public health care he became director of a private hospital.

The new director-general, Husein Ahmed, was a medical doctor who had been director of one of the main hospitals in Hodeida. He did not have a background in public health and had not shared the

14. In chapter 4, I described how the Yemeni project director Hamid Hassan lost his position because he did not want to hand over the Toyota Land Cruiser to the director-general.

history of the Hodeida Urban Primary Health Care Project. One of his first actions was the replacement of almost all departmental heads, as the existing ones were in his view too closely linked to 'Abdelhalim Ramzi. Nepotism is a general feature of Yemeni politics: when 'Abdelhalim Ramzi had been installed, he had also changed almost all the department heads. He appointed people who, like him, were members of the Islamist Islah party and came mainly from the area around Taiz. Husein Ahmed appointed friends and former colleagues from the hospital, members of the ruling PGC party and of Hodeidi background. They did not necessarily have a background in public health, but neither did the previous ones. The result was that managers of different backgrounds, and consequently with different notions of health-care development, replaced those who had previously influenced the project. The previous department heads, all of them male, found other positions outside the Health Office. Some of them started to work for foreign donor organizations, others for private hospitals. But they all kept their government salaries.[15] The only two women who had held responsible positions during the project period continued to work in the same departments. They were already in position when the previous director-general came to power and were therefore not seen as part of his "clan." Fatima Salem continued to be head of the Quality Assurance Department, and Amina al-Khawlani became deputy head of the Reproductive Health Department.

When I visited the new director-general of the Hodeida Health Office in April 2002, and told him about my research, he said firmly "there are no *murshidat* anymore" because they were all upgraded to "nurses." I found this expression a telling example of the attitude of the new Health Office management toward *murshidat*. First, he did not seem to know that there were still many *murshidat* working in the health centers and that less than half of them had managed to

---

15. As mentioned before, government employment in Yemen is a guarantee for life; a government contract is almost never ended and even people working in the nongovernmental sector or the private sector can at the same time be government employees.

upgrade their qualifications. Second, he called the newly trained community midwives "nurses," which showed his lack of knowledge as well as his preoccupation with curative care. Yet the end of the project did not mean the end of the employment of the *murshidat;* they all continued to work, but their work had changed. During the project years the *murshidat* had been promoted as primary health-care workers, focusing on preventive health-care services but also able to treat minor diseases among women and children, such as diarrhea, coughing, and nose and ear infections. Every woman and child who entered the health center had been obliged to visit one of the *murshidat* first before seeing the doctor (if there was a doctor). After the end of Dutch funding, almost every health center had a doctor, at least in the afternoon,[16] and people immediately visited the doctor instead of the *murshida.* The work of the *murshidat* in the health centers became limited to weighing and vaccinating children, which meant a devaluation of their work and status.

Moreover, many other changes took place in the primary health-care system; there were no family cards, prenatal cards, and growth-monitoring cards anymore to hand out to the patients; there were shortages of contraceptives; there was no supervision anymore; and the heads of clinic sometimes had no access to money from the cost-recovery scheme. The home visits, which were an essential part of the work of the *murshidat,* were only carried out to a limited extent and did not have the same impact as before. Only three health centers still had access to a car that could be used for home visits. In the other centers the *murshidat* could only go to areas at a walking distance from the center. The consequence was that they often visited the same families, and people grew tired of listening to the health messages without obtaining drugs or contraceptives. A field study carried out in April 2001 showed that families were less interested in home visits because the *murshidat* no longer had access to contraceptives, some essential

16. Nowadays every government health center in Hodeida offers curative services in the afternoon, paid for by merchants who are at the same time Members of Parliament and who hope to increase their following.

drugs, oral rehydration salts, and the like (Hardon et al. 2002, 53). The fact that the *murshidat* only came to weigh children and give health education made their work less interesting to the community.

On the other hand, in the fifteen years that *murshidat* had been trained in Hodeida and in other parts of the country, their work had become accepted and recognized. Although there were still people who did not know what a *murshida sihhiyya* was, in particular in cities where there were no *murshidat* working in health care,[17] the majority of the Yemeni population in the countryside and in Hodeida knew about their work. During a focus group discussion with community members in Hodeida in 2002, several men asked why the *murshidat* were not going on home visits anymore, as the community felt that home visits were an important service. The DGIS evaluation of the impact of the Hodeida Urban Primary Health Care Project, two years after financial support had come to an end, was also relatively good (Hardon et al. 2002). The work of the *murshidat* had become known, and community members recognized its importance. The main issue is therefore not so much the limited value people attach to preventive health services but, more important, the undermining of the work of the *murshidat*, who used to combine preventive health services with limited curative care. The fact that these small curative services have been taken out of their hands means a devaluation of their work.

I often heard the phrase "The days of the project are over" during my visit to Hodeida in April 2002. The female health staff used this phrase to make clear to me that things had changed in the past two years. And the new male managers in the Health Office used the phrase to show that the project was something of the past, and that the related systems, structures, and personnel belonged to the past as well. According to many women health workers, the main motivation for replacing previous systems and persons was self-interest. A certain group of people had benefited (technically and financially) from the

17. Hodeida and Dhamar are the only two cities where urban *murshidat* have been trained. Not surprisingly the health services in these two cities were both supported by Dutch development aid.

previous Dutch project, and now another group of people was going to benefit. The new managers in the Health Office accused the previous staff of the Hodeida Urban Primary Health Care Project of "licking honey for years," and openly said that it was now their turn to benefit. "Development" was in the eyes of the new health managers not an end in itself but the means to accumulate wealth. The economic situation in Yemen and the dependence on foreign aid has resulted in serious competition over scarce resources, and therefore over development projects. Health managers who were not involved in the Hodeida Urban Primary Health Care Project believed that they had a right to benefit, just as the people working in the health centers and in the project had benefited before.

The new Dutch project in Hodeida was seen as such an opportunity, and Husein Ahmed built up a close relationship with the new project manager. Training courses for community midwives, for medical doctors, for anesthetists, for nurses, and for certified midwives were set up in rural and urban areas. A system of so-called "white huts," where local people could obtain essential drugs, was established in villages without health-care facilities. In Hodeida three local health committees were encouraged to become nongovernmental organizations and initiate income-generating projects for the people in their area. One of Husein Ahmed's personal projects was to establish a computer network linking all the health centers and health units in the Hodeida governorate and facilitating the processing of statistics, even though a well-organized health information system was lacking. His preference for sophisticated technology is in line with the notions of modernity of health managers on the national level as described in chapter 3. While their policy priorities focus on the improvement of public health care, the requests they make to donor organizations are mainly for sophisticated technology in curative care.

The sustainability of the activities established during the Hodeida Urban Primary Health Care Project was thus limited, and there was little sense of "ownership" of the project activities among the new health managers. This lack was understandable in view of the fact that most of them had not shared the history of the project and did not have experience with primary health care. While decentralization, ownership, and good governance, the celebrated terms of development discourses in the late 1990s, were stated elements of Yemeni health sector reform policies, the interpretation of these concepts was far from unequivocal. All actors involved in (health-care) development—international donors, national governments, and people working at local levels—had their own interest in interpreting these concepts differently. The health managers in Hodeida, who benefited from the "feudal administrative system" (Dresch 2000, 164, 179) and had personal interests in the private health sector, used concepts such as decentralization and ownership to safeguard their own positions instead of sustaining the public primary health-care system.

The women health workers employed in the Health Office and in the health centers complained that they did not receive any support from the new project. "While the previous project focused on women, the new project focuses on men," they told me. They had the feeling that their work, preventive services at community level, was not valued anymore, and that they were being punished for having been part of "the old project." Fatima and Amina, who had been closely involved in "the old project" and who had long-standing knowledge and experience in primary health-care services, lacked the means to carry out their responsibilities and sat empty-handed behind their desks. "Everything has been taken out of our hands," they said. Other staff in the Health Office interfered in their work while they themselves did not have a budget to carry out their duties, and the project cars, which were handed over to the Hodeida Health Office on the condition that they would be used in the Quality Department and the Reproductive Health Department, were taken away. They were being used for the new management team.

In addition, corruption increased. Health workers, who for example earned an additional income as teachers or trainers, had to hand over a percentage of their salary to managers in the Health Office. Moreover, the cost-recovery system and the revolving drug fund were easy targets for those interested in increasing their incomes. The local health committees, which had been in charge of managing the health center's income and functioned independent of the Health Office, lost their de-cision-making power. The health managers in the office were interested in the large amounts of money that came through the health centers. Whereas local community members used to have a say in the manage-ment of the health center's income, now community participation was reduced to the community participating by paying money for health services. New people replaced the health managers who had been in charge of the revolving drug fund during the project, and the *murshidat* lost their influence on the financial management of the drugs.

The level of bureaucracy increased dramatically, and all the people involved in this bureaucracy developed their own ways of earning an ad-ditional income on top of their government salary. In particular, heads of clinic complained that they spent a lot of time going to and from the Health Office to arrange supplies or money for the health center. At the time of the project they had sorted out the requests in one day, but now they needed three or four days. "I spend most of my time in the Health Office," the heads of clinic told me. In addition, the fact that the new managers often did not know the background of certain systems and activities frustrated them very much. "I have told them a hundred times that things should be done differently, but they do not listen to me," said Hawa. Some of the new managers admitted that they lacked the knowledge and experience to sustain the activities as established in the project period, and they asked for more support from foreign donor organizations. The fact that I was seen as a representative of Dutch de-velopment aid inspired their requests; they hoped that I would be able to obtain more donor support for Hodeida. Fifteen years of support from various donor organizations to the governmental health services in Hodeida appeared to be insufficient, as a new group of medical doc-tors lacking knowledge and experience in primary health care replaced those who had received support and training.

One of the basic elements of the health sector reform is decen-tralization, which means handing over responsibility to lower levels of organizations, from the ministerial level to the governorate level and from the governorate level to the district level. The aim of decen-tralization is to improve efficiency, management, and responsiveness of governmental health services. Yet as Al-Dubai (2000, 20) argues in his master's thesis on health sector reform in Yemen, decentralization may also lead to more inefficiency and inequity. The management capacity at lower levels of the health service in Yemen is weak, and the majority of the current health personnel are curative rather than community oriented (10). Moreover, health sector reform implies a redistribution of power and is therefore threatening for those who are benefiting under the old system (vii). This threat is particularly so for health managers who also have private interests in health care, being linked in one way or another to pharmaceutical companies and medical equipment manufacturers (9). Al-Dubai also points out the political character of reform policies, and the risks involved in political changes such as the replacement of ministers or of other health professionals who were committed to reform (9). Thus, while decentralization is one of the basic elements of health-sector reform, the experiences in Hodeida show that decentralization increased bureaucracy at the level of the Hodeida Health Office.

No More *Murshidat?*

The end of the project did not mean the end of employment for the *murshidat;* they all continued to work. In addition, many *murshidat* took up work in the private sector, working as nurses in private clinics and hospitals, which has subsequently led to an increase in their status, as curative care is much more highly valued than preventive health care. The fact that they can earn an additional income in the afternoon has also increased the status of their work. Government employment has become increasingly scarce owing to the current economic situation in Yemen. Many women who are more highly educated than the *murshidat* envy them their government contracts. A famous saying in Yemen is "it is better to work for the government and earn less than to work in the private sector and earn more."[18] As mentioned before,

---

18. "*Shibr ma'a al-dawla wa la dira' ma'a al-qabila*" (literal translation: 15 cm with the government instead of 58 cm with the tribe).

it has become very hard to obtain government employment because of the economic measures taken as part of the structural adjustment program, and only in the education and health-care sector are people still being employed.[19] People need *wasta* and money to pay everyone involved in the procedures. The selection of women for community midwife training courses is almost completely based on the *wasta* system, as is their employment. Many of the newly trained community midwives told me about the difficulties they encountered in obtaining government employment. In April 2001, only 48 of the 143 who graduated in 1999 (34 percent) were employed (Hardon et al. 2002, 36). The *murshidat* were therefore happy that they had obtained government employment at a time when it was not as difficult as it is today. It gave them the security of a monthly salary for the rest of their lives, which in many cases has led to a feeling of autonomy.

The undermining of the work of the *murshidat* could also have led to their replacement as heads of clinic, but that did not happen. When I asked a number of heads of clinic whether they were accepted by the new health managers in the Health Office, they said, "They all know that there is no one who knows the work in the health centers as well as we do. That is why they don't replace us." In particular the vaccinations given to infants under one year of age were of crucial importance for the Health Office, as coverage rates for vaccinations were an indication of the effectiveness of the health-care system. In the first period after the end of Dutch funding, a number of male doctors working in the health centers had proposed that the *murshidat* should be replaced as heads of clinic, but the new director-general rejected this request. Yet when I said that I was happy to see that they were still in place, most of the heads of clinic answered that they would not mind being replaced. "Being a head of clinic is no fun anymore; I have sleepless nights because of all the problems I encounter in the health center due to mismanagement in the Health Office," one of them said to me.

19. As part of the Health Sector Reform, it was decided that no new students would be accepted for technical training courses, with the exception of community midwives and primary health-care workers *(murshidat)*.

And another one said, "The girls that are working as *murshidat* just do their work and do not suffer as much as we do. I would not mind being a *murshida* again, in fact it would save me a lot of problems." Muna sometimes thought about giving up the responsibility of managing the health center: "I have enjoyed my work tremendously in the past fifteen years, but now it is giving me a headache." Hawa tried to convince her that she should not give in and should continue her efforts to maintain the system, but Muna answered, "I know I should be happy with those fifteen years we had, but it is hard to accept that things have changed so much." In particular the *murshidat* who were trained during the first years of the project had difficulty accepting the changes. They had derived their identities and authority from working for the project, whereas the *murshidat* who were trained in the 1990s entered the project much later, had invested less, and therefore adjusted quickly to the changes.

Conclusions

The influx of thousands of returnees from Saudi Arabia and the Gulf States to Hodeida had important consequences for the health-care situation in Hodeida and subsequently for the training of *murshidat*. First, because of the increased health needs in the city, in particular in the new squatter areas, other donor organizations started to offer primary health-care services and began to train *murshidat* as well. Second, because of the arrival of thousands of young, educated women born and brought up in Saudi Arabia and in need of work, it was no longer difficult to find women willing to be trained as *murshidat*. Third, because of the proliferation of primary health-care services, the project activities were expanded over all thirteen governmental health centers in the city, which led to a restructuring of the project and subsequent changes in the position of the *murshidat*. One of the results of these developments was that new notions of development and modernity ("other modernities") were introduced.

Many of the young women who became *murshidat* would not have entered a health-care profession in Saudi Arabia and probably would not have taken up paid work at all. Because of the impoverishment of their families, they felt forced to leave school and find paid work. Although they liked their work, they also expressed the wish to improve their skills and obtain higher diplomas. They were not satisfied with being *murshidat*. The fact that they were brought up in Saudi Arabia, where paid work for women, in particular low-skilled work, was negatively valued, contributed to their wish to upgrade their qualifications. For many of the *mughtaribat*, their paid work was a dubious blessing; on one hand they liked their work and it meant an improvement in their status, while on the other hand their (male) relatives forced them to work and some had to hand in all the money they earned. Instead of becoming more independent from their (male) relatives, in some cases their dependency increased, and they were sometimes not even allowed to marry. The return migration to Yemen offered opportunities for change, but also introduced new forms of social control.

In addition, the return to Yemen was seen by many of the *mughtaribat* as downward mobility. Their living conditions in Yemen were bad, they were blamed for the social and economic problems in the country, and they were perceived to have a low status. By emphasizing that they had lived in a modern, and "developed" country, they tried to counteract this low status. One of their strategies for maintaining self-respect was to combine a belief in modern services and technology with a Saudi interpretation of Islam, inspired by their long stay in Saudi Arabia. Moreover, they had benefited from the well-organized education system in Saudi Arabia and used their study skills to upgrade their qualifications. Young female returnees, in particular, aspired to make use of their knowledge and education. They often introduced new skills, which were received enthusiastically by *muwatinin*, as they were seen as modern and new. Yet the presence of a large group of educated women could also be threatening. Some of the *murshidat* felt threatened by this new group of young and ambitious women.

At the level of the project, other notions of development and modernity also made their entry. With the restructuring of the program and the expansion to other health centers in town, new male health managers became involved in urban primary health-care activities.

These health managers had not shared the project's history and the project's notions of health-care development. Curative services and the provision of drugs were central to their notions of health-care development, and they had little interest in preventive care and community health services. On one hand, the status of the *murshidat* in the project decreased because of the restructuring and expansion of the program; they gradually lost the protection of the project team and were confronted with negative attitudes regarding their work. On the other hand, the *murshidat* profession became more established as they were placed in every health center in the city; they became regular health-center staff; and some of them even became heads of clinic. In addition, the *murshidat* had the chance to become community midwives, which was an important upgrading of their qualifications.

After the end of the Hodeida Urban Primary Health Care Project, again other notions of development and modernity made their entry. A new group of health managers replaced the previous management at the Health Office. The primary health-care system built up during the project was from that moment onward seen as a thing of the past. New people were appointed, and new systems and structures were introduced. Yet while decentralization and restructuring are part of the national strategy of health sector reform, at the local level of Hodeida it has led to a reproduction of patterns of inequality and a strengthening of hierarchies, in particular with regard to gender relations. The *murshidat* find themselves at the bottom of the health-care ladder, where preventive health services are no longer highly valued. In addition, their pioneering role in making paid employment for women in health care acceptable has been fulfilled, and increasing numbers of women of different backgrounds are trained and employed as health-care professionals. While this is on one hand a positive development, on the other hand it has meant that the *murshidat* have lost some of the benefits of their pioneering role.

Conclusion

I BEGAN THIS STUDY with a personal introduction in which I described my experiences as a development worker in Yemen, first in the rural town of Rada' and later in the city of Hodeida. From my very first encounters with Yemeni women who were working as extension agents *(murshidat)* for foreign-funded development projects, I was interested in their backgrounds and motivation. Like many other foreign development workers, I saw the women as pioneers who moved out of their houses to take up paid work in health care and in doing so challenged dominant gender ideologies. Yet in the course of my stay in Yemen, I began to question the pioneering and presumably liberating aspects of training and employing women because I started to realize that these women were simultaneously confronted with new forms of social control as a result of their training and employment.

My own initial view on the *murshidat* as pioneers is an example of the assumption that women's education and employment are automatically emancipatory. This notion was also present in Kuhnke's (1990) account of the Egyptian School of Midwives and in Dutch discourses on women and development. Yet in the past decades it has increasingly become clear that education and employment are not always liberating. The overly optimistic evaluations of women's education and employment have been questioned by studies that emphasize the use of women as symbols in "larger" political debates, the disciplinary side of their training and employment, and the forms of social control they entail. Fahmy's (1998) critical analysis of the School of Midwives is an example of such a study. In a similar vein, the anthropology of development has created a critique of the optimistic accounts of foreign-funded development projects as emancipatory projects. The political interests behind development aid and the unintended consequences of these projects, which often lead to a reproduction of power inequalities, have been criticized, for example, by Escobar (1984) and Ferguson (1990).

However, because these critical perspectives have often been developed as a critique of approaches emphasizing agency and notions of emancipation, they have tended to neglect the ways in which these projects may also be enabling. This neglect is perhaps especially problematic when dealing with women in the Middle East, where there is such a long tradition of seeing them as victims of their own society. In this study I have therefore started with the more nuanced formulation that development and modernization projects ("projects of modernity") may have both disciplinary and enabling aspects for women (see Abu-Lughod 1998b). In order to analyze these two sides of "development," I made use of the actor-oriented approach of development as formulated by Long (1992), an approach that deconstructs planned intervention by looking at the various ways in which social actors manage, interpret, negotiate, and challenge new elements in their life worlds. I distinguished three main actors in the Hodeida Urban Primary Health Care Project: Yemeni state institutions, the Dutch donor organization, and the women trained and employed as *murshidat*. A close analysis of the agendas and activities of these three actors showed that none of the three could be viewed as a homogeneous entity, but that they instead consisted of individual people with different ideas and ambitions.

State and Donor: The Politics of "Development"

In chapter 2 I briefly described the Egyptian School of Midwives established in the nineteenth century as an example of the contradictory effects of the policies of Mohamed 'Ali. Whereas low-class women gained the opportunity to study and enter public service, they were simultaneously used as "agents of discipline and regulation" (Fahmy

1998, 63). Fahmy analyzed the School of Midwives as a "project of modernity" by unraveling the interests of the state in training and employing women as midwives and the backgrounds, duties, and experiences of this newly trained group of health professionals. In spite of the fact that the School of Midwives and the Hodeida Urban Primary Health Care Project were enacted at different historical moments and in different locations, his analysis was an important source of inspiration for my study of women health workers in Yemen.

In both cases the training and employment of women health workers were part of state-directed political projects, albeit in different ways. Fahmy (1998) argues that the main impetus for the establishment of the Egyptian School of Midwives was the creation of a healthy climate for the army, part and parcel of the Mohamed 'Ali's efforts at modernization; the "emancipatory" effect of training and employing local women was a side effect of the school. The Hodeida Urban Primary Health Care Project was a bilateral project of the Dutch Ministry of Development Cooperation and the Yemeni Ministry of Health aiming at improving the health situation of the population of Hodeida, and in particular of the people living in the squatter areas. The provision of health care was an important political tool for the Yemeni state; by providing health care, the state established a positive image of its regime, while people's dependency on these services underlined the state's authority and guaranteed social cohesion (Van der Geest 1986, 246). The training and employment of women as health workers were also in this case side effects of the project, and not its main goal. Yet, as in the School of Midwives, it was an important side effect that was used in different ways in by the state and the donor.

For the Yemeni state, training and employing women had both a practical and a symbolic value. In the first two decades after the establishment of the Yemen Arab Republic, there was a need for labor because a large part of the male population had migrated to Saudi Arabia and the Gulf States. Mobilizing women became therefore a national priority. Yet, despite the government's rhetoric in which education and employment of women were put forward as important for Yemeni state building and development, there was initially little support for the training and employment of *murshidat* at the national level (for similar cases elsewhere in the Middle East, see Kandiyoti 1991; Moghadam 1994). The actual implementation of progressive policies was hampered by the state's dilemma of on one hand wishing to promote development and modernization, and on the other hand not wanting to alienate conservative groups that would consider changes in women's position as a threat to Yemeni cultural authenticity (see also Rassam 1984; Kandiyoti 1991; Moghadam 1994; Seif 1995).

The fact that few women were interested in becoming health workers is also the effect of the negative image of this work in the Middle East. While health care is often seen as an area of employment that is suitable for women because it is interpreted as an extension of women's domestic roles, this does not mean that women's health-care activities have a high status. Women have a long tradition of involvement in midwifery and in "traditional healing," but the women involved in these activities often came from lower social classes (see Towler and Bramall 1986; Donnison 1977; Shepherd McClain 1989), and their work was sometimes associated with evil and hence seen as threatening (for cases from the Middle East, see Jansen 1987; Doumato 2000). The Egyptian School of Midwives had, for example, great difficulty in finding women willing and able to be trained and employed as midwives. Few girls joined the school of their own free will, and those who did were mostly orphans (Fahmy 1998, 48). In the case of nursing, an additional problem is that women working as nurses often have to work with male doctors or male patients, challenging existing practices of gender segregation (Badran 1995, 181). Hence nursing was one of the most difficult types of work to offer women in the Middle East. Nursing still has a very low status in Egypt (see Salib 1998) as well as in Saudi Arabia, where, despite government policies aimed at increasing the number of female nurses, relatively few women are interested (see El-Sanabary 1993). Public health, and in particular mother and child care, is one of the few areas of health care Middle Eastern women are interested in. Also for the first cohort of *murshidat* the fact that their work focused on mother and child care was an important reason to accept their employment, and they underlined, albeit selectively, that their work differed from the work of nurses.

Not only was the status of their work ambiguous, the symbolic role the *murshidat* played in the politics of development was ambiguous as well. Political motivations inspire many development interventions. The Dutch development relation with Yemen was for example established because of the need to have political allies in the Middle East after the oil crisis in the 1970s. In addition, Dutch development discourses and approaches changed continuously depending on the political climate in the Netherlands. For the Dutch donor organization, training and employing women as primary health workers fitted well into Dutch development discourses, in particular in the early 1990s when "Women in Development" became an official spearhead of Dutch development policies. Both the focus on primary health care and the employment of women were important for the project's political recognition. Yemeni state support for primary health-care projects and the training and employment of *murshidat* was at least in part brought about because of the pressure of donor organizations (see Van der Geest, Speckmann, and Streefland 1990).

The political agendas behind development and modernization efforts are not new; Fahmy and other scholars showed how (health-care) interventions before and during colonialism were politically inspired (see for example Fahmy 1998; Vaughan 1991; Arnold 1993; Packard 1997; Ali 2002; Mitchell 2002). However, placing too much emphasis on the politics behind development discourses and interventions runs the risk of neglecting the role individual people may play in social change. Development discourses are not all-encompassing schemes that govern the lives of individuals but instead are subjected to the agency of individual people. Speaking of discourses or interventions of *the* Yemeni state or of *the* Dutch donor organization is not very useful (see Long 1992; Grillo 1997; Crewe and Harrison 1998). States and donor organizations consist of individuals who together "have the means of reaching and formulating decisions and of acting on at least some of them" (Hindess 1986, 115). National and international discourses of development can therefore be very different from local discourses and interventions on the level of a project, as social actors on the local level have different interests from those on the national and international level. In the past two decades, numerous studies have appeared that have analyzed the interaction between different social groups and individuals engaged in development practices in Asia, Latin America, and Africa (see for example Justice 1986; L. Stone 1986; Ferguson 1990; Pigg 1992; 1997; Porter, Allen, and Thompson 1991; Long 1992; Villareal 1994). Yet the use of an actor-oriented approach in studies on development discourses and practices in the Middle East is remarkably absent, so the agency of people, and particularly women, in this region is often neglected.

The fact that development aid is not only a top-down process but is subjected to the ideas and activities of key individuals at the local level is best illustrated by the start of the Hodeida Urban Primary Health Care Project. Primary health care did not have a high priority on the national level in Yemen in the early 1980s when the project was just established; infrastructural improvements, such as the building of clinics and hospitals, were seen as more important. The local director-general of the Ministry of Health in Hodeida, however, was convinced of the importance of primary health care and even suggested the training of women as health workers instead of men. He played a major role in the first project phase, which affected the project to a large extent because the training of *murshidat* became an essential element. While in the fifteen years of the project's existence the attitude of the national government became more supportive of primary health-care activities, the recognition of primary health care and the essential role of women health workers depend to a large extent on key persons, both in the local government and in donor organizations.

Employing a historical perspective also brings to the fore the idea that Yemeni state institutions are not static but need to be seen in a continuously changing field of national and international power constellations. Many states in the Middle East have been confronted with the rise of Islamist opposition movements with ideologies that strongly argue for the social control of women (see Kandiyoti 1991; Moghadam 1994). In Yemen, after the first democratic elections in

1993, the Islamist party Islah became part of the government and has remained one of Yemen's main political parties. While Islah supported conservative interpretations of Yemen's personal status law (see Würth 2003), legislation around women's employment was not affected (see Carapico and Wuerth 2000, 265), and Islah even played a positive role in the training of women health workers in the mid-1990s, when the Ministry of Public Health fell under its responsibility (see Worm 1998). Also, in this case one person may have made a difference; the Minister of Public Health himself pushed women to take up paid work in nursing, with the argument that "this profession was fully in accordance with Islamic values" (Worm 1998, 21). Still, the fact that Islamists can be supportive of women's training as health workers, especially when responsible for government policy, also comes to the fore in Hoodfar's studies about volunteer health workers in Iran (1997, 1998); the Islamic Republic of Iran has a highly successful population program, thanks to the efforts of the state to train women as health workers. While women's labor participation in other sectors has not been encouraged, reproductive health and family planning are seen as an extension of women's role in the family and therefore acceptable to the Iranian government (Hoodfar 1997, 228).

In Yemen, as in many other Middle Eastern countries, the rise of Islamism coincided with the introduction of structural adjustment policies, imposed by the World Bank and the International Monetary Fund and forcing the government to restructure the public sector. Economic and political liberalization policies have affected the training and employment of *murshidat* in different ways. On one hand, as a result of the deteriorating economic situation, a growing number of women in need of paid labor have taken up employment as health workers, a type of work that has increasingly become recognized as a suitable job for women by progressives and conservatives alike. On the other hand, the restructuring of the public health sector has led to a reproduction of gender inequalities and a strengthening of hierarchies at the local level, with the *murshidat* finding themselves increasingly at the bottom of the health-care ladder. Thus, while this particular group of Yemeni women has been integrated into the labor market, they have simultaneously been marginalized within it, a process that has been described extensively for other developing countries (see Afshar and Dennis 1992; Afshar and Barrientos 1999; Rai 2002).

The Women: Three Cohorts of *Murshidat*

"Particular development intervention models (or ideologies) become strategic weapons in the hands of those charged with promoting them. Nevertheless, the battle is never over since all actors exercise some kind of 'power,' even those in highly subordinate positions." (Long 1992, 24). By studying the Hodeida Urban Primary Health Care Project over a longer period, I revealed how development discourses and practices have changed, as well as the power relations between the various actors. Development projects have both enabling and disciplining aspects, but they work out differently for different groups of people. "Development" is not a unilinear movement but consists of periods in which the changes or interventions that occur may work out positively for certain groups of people, while these same changes or interventions may have a negative impact on the lives of others. While the previous section focused on the political projects of the Yemeni state and the Dutch donor, the two actors occupying positions of power, in this section I turn to the women trained and employed as *murshidat*. Instead of seeing them as "puppets on a string," as objects in dominant discourses on women and development or as the means to achieve better health care in discourses on health-care development, I look at the *murshidat* as active participants in the process of "development."

Listening to and analyzing the life stories of the *murshidat* was crucial in this respect. In studies about women's paid labor, the ways in which women's labor stories are interrelated with historical developments have often been overlooked. Fahmy (1998), for example, has pointed to the low-status backgrounds of the first women trained in the School of Midwives, who were former slaves and orphaned girls. Yet his material did not allow him to further investigate the impact of their social status for the status of their work, nor trace the possibly changing backgrounds of the *hakimat* over time. My study, based on extensive topical life stories of the *murshidat*, shows the intricate ways in which individual life trajectories are related to social, economic, and political changes in society at large, and the ways in which this relationship has affected women's education and employment. Similarly to Rofel (1999), I have distinguished three cohorts of women trained and employed as *murshidat* that mark particular moments in Yemen's social, political, and economic history: the women trained in the first course (1985–86), the women trained in the second and third courses (1988–90), and the women trained after 1990. Yet while there is a strong relationship between the cohorts and the socioeconomic status of the families of these women, other differences, such as those of age and marital status, intersect with the socioeconomic status as well.

The main difference between the three cohorts was the particular historical moment in which the women were born and brought up. The women of the first cohort were born in the 1960s and inspired by revolutionary discourses promoting education as the road to development. All of them were longing for education, which they saw as an important way to self-development. Their motivation is in some sense comparable to the motivation of higher-class women in Egypt in the first half of the twentieth century (see Badran 1998) or in the Gulf States in the second half of the twentieth century (see Al-Mughni 2001), who fought for the right to education and employment for the sake of personal and social fulfillment, rather than because of economic need. Women's education and employment were not valued highly in their families, and they had to overcome many obstacles before their schooling and work were accepted. The fact that the women of the first cohort succeeded in attending literacy classes at the Yemeni Women's Association in Hodeida, sometimes after marrying and a period of staying at home, shows their agency. Despite doubts about the acceptability of women's education in their own social circles, but supported by a political project in which education was promoted, they succeeded in obtaining primary-school certificates. Most of them saw the *murshidat* training course as a next step in their educational trajectory. Taking up paid work was not their goal, but when they had the chance to be employed they seized the opportunity with both hands, even when their (male)

326 / Pioneers or Pawns?

relatives were against it. Although most of the women of this cohort did not become *murshidat* out of economic need, in the years that followed their salaries became more important to sustain their families, especially in the 1990s, when the economic situation deteriorated seriously and many families, even those who had been relatively well off, became impoverished.

The young women of the second cohort were born in the early 1970s and can be divided into daughters of rural migrants and daughters of returned migrants from Africa. Despite the poor living conditions of their families, the daughters of rural migrants had benefited from the improved educational facilities that were established after the 1960s civil war, in particular in urban areas. Yet, after reaching a certain level of education, these young women felt obliged to leave school in order to provide for their families, a situation comparable to that of many (eldest) daughters in lower-class families elsewhere (see, for the Middle East, Jansen 1987, 240; Moors 1995, 274; Rosenfeld 2002, 534). Emphasizing that it was their own choice to become *murshidat*, they "sacrificed" their education to support their families and often to finance the education of their younger brothers and sisters, gaining more say in family affairs in the process. The return migrants from Africa arrived in the mid-1970s, forced by the changing political climate in the countries of migration and encouraged by the call to return after the establishment of the Yemen Arab Republic. The fathers of the young women had often been conservative with regard to women's education and employment in the countries of migration, but the return to Yemen made them loosen the reins and accept their daughters' education and employment. The experiences they had gone through abroad, and their contacts with other societies, had affected their attitude toward women's education and employment positively. Women of mixed parentage *(muwalladat)* were often the first to take up paid employment in Yemen, as evinced by the relatively large number of *muwalladat* among the first cohorts of *murshidat*.

The third cohort arrived in Hodeida in 1990, an important year in the history of Yemen because of the unification of North and South Yemen and the start of the Gulf crisis. The optimistic atmosphere after unification disappeared quickly with the arrival of thousands of Yemeni migrants from Saudi Arabia and the Gulf States. Although these women would not have taken up paid work in Saudi Arabia, where only paid work that requires a high level of education such as teaching or medicine was seen as respectable, they felt forced to enter paid employment in Yemen because of the impoverished condition of their families. Not satisfied with their position as *murshidat*, they emphasized that they wanted to upgrade their qualifications to achieve higher positions; already better educated, they often managed to continue their education alongside their paid work. Their fathers, often not in favor of women's paid employment, were forced to accept their daughters' work as they were unable to find work themselves. The deteriorating economic situation in the 1990s, resulting from the Gulf crisis, the 1994 civil war, and the introduction of structural adjustment policies, led to a greater overall need for income, and increasing numbers of women took up paid work.

The strategies women of each of the three cohorts employed and the ways in which they experienced their work intersects with the socioecononomic status of their families. As discussed before, women's work in health care generally did and does not have a high status in the Middle East, and women of the higher classes were not interested in working as midwives or nurses. Indeed, the first women trained at the Egyptian School of Midwives were orphans and former slaves (Kuhnke 1990, 124; Fahmy 1998, 47). The first *murshidat*, however, did not come from low-status families. This was largely the result of the way in which they were selected, which had an element of contingency, but also points to the effects of attempts of professionalization. The project management was looking for women who were able to read and write and approached women who had finished literacy classes at the Yemeni Women's Association. While the male relatives of these women had accepted their pursuit of literacy, they were not in favor of their employment as *murshidat*. In order to make their work acceptable to them, the first *murshidat* emphasized that they were only working with women and had no contact with men, and in addition stressed the value of their newly acquired skills for the benefit of their own families. Their experiences and strategies were comparable to those of women in Egypt in the first half of the twentieth century, who promoted jobs for women in sectors like education and health care, where women could serve women (see Badran 1998, 170).

For the second cohort of young women, who mainly came from low social-status groups living in the squatter areas of Ghulail and al-Mughtaribin, the training and employment as *murshidat* signaled a process of upward social mobility. By becoming *murshidat* they were able to improve the living conditions of their families as well as their own social status (see Walters 2001). Important elements in this process of upward mobility were the fact that they were trained on a foreign development project and employed by the government. For them, working on a foreign development project was positive, because of the (assumed) availability of money and facilities and the link with development and modernity. Government employment was valued as a relatively secure form of employment, with a lifelong contract and secondary benefits such as the right to sick leave and maternal leave.

For some women of the third cohort, in contrast, working as *murshidat* was a form of downward social mobility. These young women were born and brought up in Saudi Arabia and would not have taken up paid work if they had stayed there. Some of them were coming from low social-status groups such as the *'abid* and the *akhdam*, and were stigmatized again after their return, while they also were often blamed for the social, economic, and political problems in the country in the 1990s. In response to such negative attitudes, the young women of returnee families emphasized that they had lived in a modern country, had attended high quality education, and were acquainted with sophisticated forms of health-care delivery. They were less impressed with Western notions of development, but instead associated Saudi Arabia with a better form of modernity because it combined its prosperity with holding on to Islamic values (for a similar association of Saudi Arabia with modernity, see Bernal 1994, 1997).

The cohorts also differed from each other in the ways in which they positioned themselves in relation to the project. The first cohort was very committed to the project and had internalized project notions on health-care development. They were convinced of the importance of preventive mother and child care and stressed the obstacles they had to overcome before their work was accepted, both the resistance of certain (male) relatives and that of the people in their areas of work, who were sometimes suspicious of their activities. They clearly saw themselves as pioneers, providing a new form of health care, and their identities were closely linked to the success of the project. This attitude is similar to what Macleod (1991, 68) describes for the first cohorts of women who entered government employment in Egypt in the 1960s. These women also saw themselves as pioneers in opening up new spaces for women, were convinced of the importance of women's employment, and were strongly committed to their jobs.

The second cohort of *murshidat* in Hodeida was also very committed to the project although in a different way. Coming from lower social-status groups, they had benefited in many ways from their training and employment. They had not only become government employees but had also gained the opportunity to develop new identities and take on new positions as modern, professional workers with important tasks in their communities, especially because of their training as birth attendants. The support they received from the project in combination with powerful symbols of modernity, such as the project car and English language classes, affected their status positively. These seemingly unimportant side effects of their training and employment were of crucial importance for their identities, a process that is comparable to the one described by Freeman in her study on women workers in Barbados (2000).

The third cohort was relatively less committed to the project, which can, to some extent, be explained by the fact that they were trained by different donor organizations involved in urban primary health-care activities in Hodeida after 1990. The extension of the project to all government health centers led to an increase in scale, and consequently to a weaker link between the project management and the women working in the health centers. Moreover, the women of the third cohort did not benefit from the financial advantages of working for the project, such as the Ramadan bonus and the heat allowance, because these benefits were removed with the expansion of the project activities to all health centers. Increasing numbers of women were trained as health-care workers by different organizations and institutions, and working as a *murshida* was increasingly becoming an ordinary job. For the third cohort, upgrading their qualifications and improving their positions was the main concern. In contrast to the younger women in Macleod's study (1991), their first goal was not to get married and leave their jobs but to safeguard their future by obtaining secure jobs.

Differences in age and marital status also had an impact on women's experiences as *murshidat*. Although the project's intention had been to train adult women who already had children because they would be better able to build up relations of trust with mothers living in the squatter areas, the majority of the women trained were young and unmarried. The fact that young and unmarried women were recruited had consequences for their status as professionals because people sometimes questioned their knowledge and experience, particularly with regard to midwifery. Yet the fact that the young women had attended a one-year training course in health education and midwifery, were employed by the government, and worked for a foreign-funded project contributed to their professional status, and their acceptance in the areas of work. In addition, while a number of unmarried women in the first cohort stopped working after getting married, very few of the women in the following cohorts did. This can partly be explained by the economic changes that have taken place in the country and the increased need for women to work even after they are married, as government salaries are low and families increasingly need two or more salaries to make ends meet, a situation comparable to Egypt (see Macleod 1991; Hoodfar 1999). But it is also an indication of the increased acceptance of women's employment among all layers of society and of women's wish to continue their paid work out of personal fulfillment.

The Work: An Ambiguous Profession

In the previous sections I have discussed the training and employment of women health workers as political projects and have focused on the backgrounds, motivation, and strategies of the women employed. I will now take a closer look at the work of the *murshidat*, which will give further insight into the ways in which their employment was enabling as well as disciplining. Fahmy concluded that the duties of the women trained in the Egyptian School of Midwives were of a dubious character. Instead of emancipating women from low social classes by offering them professional work, the state used the *hakimat* as "agents of discipline and regulation" (1998, 63). Are there parallels with the work of the Yemeni *murshidat?* And if so, how did they deal with the ambiguities of their work?

While the School of Midwives was a state project, set up with the help of foreign experts, the Hodeida Urban Primary Health Care Project was first and foremost a foreign development project, which gradually, in the course of the fifteen years of the project, became an integrated part of the Yemeni state apparatus. This foreign sponsorship affected the status of the work of the *murshidat* in different ways. In the early project years, the attitudes of the local population toward foreign development projects were ambiguous. For some the project symbolized outside influences that could threaten Yemen's cultural authenticity, which discouraged them from allowing their daughters be trained as *murshidat*. Other people saw the project as a symbol of development and modernity that stood in positive contrast to other (modern) work settings for women, such as factories, hospitals, and government offices. They expected their daughters and wives to be "more protected" on the project, and they therefore accepted the employment of their female relatives.

Yet gradually, material aspects became more important in people's assessments of working for a foreign development project. The availability of bonuses and other financial advantages, of project transportation, and of better working facilities such as well-equipped health centers, was much appreciated. As has been argued for development projects elsewhere, the opportunities these projects offer to individual people can be more important than the actual project activities. In her article on villagers and the discourse of development in Nepal, Pigg states that "from the local people's perspective, the

332 / Pioneers or Pawns?

tangible advantages of *bikas* (development) lie less in receiving the benefits of programs . . . than in becoming one of the salaried workers who implements *bikas*" (1992, 511). While these personal benefits also played a role in the motivation of some *murshidat*, especially among the third cohort, they were particularly present among the male health administrators who became involved in the third phase of the project. There were clear gender differences in the motivation behind working on a foreign development project.

For most of the *murshidat*, obtaining government employment was more important than working on a foreign project. In studies on women's paid labor, little attention has been paid to public sector employees, although the public sector is often the main employer of women. Hijab (1988, 88; 2001, 50) states that the public sector offers the most trouble-free and respected employment for Arab women. In Yemen, and in many other countries in the world, public-sector employment has a relatively high status because it guarantees a monthly salary, a lifelong contract, and secondary benefits such as the right to sick leave and maternity leave. In the early 1970s the Yemeni state was in need of manpower, and people with an intermediate-school certificate were automatically state-employed. Yet it soon became more difficult to obtain government employment because the number of government employees had increased rapidly. The fact that the *murshidat*, who had only finished primary school, obtained government employment was an important reason an increasing number of women were interested in entering this new profession. In the 1990s the status of government employment decreased, mainly as a result of the worsening economic situation and the subsequent inflation, but government employment is still desired because it offers one of the few opportunities to a low but secure income. The *murshidat* are in this sense better off than many other Yemenis who may have higher education but little chance of finding (government) employment. As mentioned before, in Egypt similar processes have taken place, and many lower-middle-class women who were the first in their families to obtain government employment adhere to their government jobs despite the relatively low status of their work (see Macleod 1991; Hoodfar 1999).

The *murshidat* in Hodeida were the first in their families to secure government employment, and they had to negotiate their participation in training and employment with their (male) relatives. The fact that the *murshidat* profession was a new phenomenon in the mid-1980s gave the first cohort ample opportunities to present their work to their relatives in a way that facilitated their employment. These issues became less important for the next cohorts as the profession became gradually more accepted. The pioneering aspects of the work of the *murshidat*, which had greatly contributed to their sense of self-development, gave way to health care becoming an acceptable form of employment for women from different layers of society. Yet while the profession became more accepted in society at large, the *murshidat* found themselves increasingly at the bottom of the Yemeni health-care establishment.

Salaried work may create opportunities for self-development and for the improvement of one's situation, but it can also engender new forms of social control. Some *murshidat* underlined that they benefited from their status as salaried workers, as it increased their say in family affairs (see Salaff 1981; Moors 1995). But others became more dependent on their relatives, who forced them to start, continue, or stop working or prevented them from marrying because they were in need of their income. This situation is similar to that of educated Palestinian women living in refugee camps in the West Bank, who often married late because they were the sole providers in their families and their salaries were badly needed (Moors 1995; Rosenfeld 2002). And that did not mean that after marriage the *murshidat* no longer felt obliged to support their parental families; in a number of cases their support was more important to their families than what their brothers provided.

Providing primary health care in itself can have multiple meanings and potentially divergent effects. Health care, and in particular Western health care, is an important political tool in the spreading and consolidation of state power. The *murshidat* were employed to carry out primary health-care activities, with a special focus on mother and child care, activities that at first may seem apolitical and by definition positive (see

Van der Geest 1986). Yet a closer look at the agendas of the Yemeni state and of the Dutch donor showed the political importance of introducing primary health care. The duties of the *murshidat* underline this political importance, and show the ways in which their work re-created power relations in Yemeni society. The introduction of primary health care was not only a means of improving the health situation of the population of Hodeida, but was also a way to discipline the community. Squatter areas were "organized" by dividing them into sections and blocks, in order to facilitate home visiting and to create order in apparent chaos. The strong focus on mother and child health care meant that women were only approached in their roles as mothers, and, simultaneously, "modern" notions on good motherhood were introduced. The boundaries between public and private in Hodeida shifted, and women's bodies increasingly became public because of the attention paid to women's reproductive and child-care activities in the governmental health centers and through the home visits of the *murshidat* (for a similar case, see Shami 1997). This invasion of privacy is part of the process of disciplining imposed by the state and supported by a foreign development project, and has a strong relationship with the larger project of modernity (see for example Ali 2002; Kanaaneh 2002). As state-employed health workers, the *murshidat* were thus in a sense also "agents of discipline and regulation," and the difficulties they encountered during their home visits may in part be linked to this agency.

In his analysis of the School of Midwives, Fahmy emphasizes that the duties of the *hakimat* had negative consequences for certain sectors of society and were therefore of an ambiguous nature. While the *hakimat* benefited from their training and employment, they were also confronted with opposition from various groups in society. I take his argument a step further and argue that the ambiguous position of the *murshidat* was related not only to the disciplining effects of their activities for others, but also to the fact that their duties contained both enabling and disciplining aspects for the *murshidat* themselves. Certain aspects of their work that offered them new opportunities simultaneously introduced new forms of social control. The enabling and the disciplining aspect were two sides of the same coin.

The home visits are again a good way to illustrate this ambiguity. Professional home visiting was a new phenomenon in Yemen, and the young women had to challenge social boundaries as part of their work. Entering a squatter area, knocking at the doors of unrelated families, and facing resistance from community members was very difficult at first. They had to learn how to be "good health educators," which included training on how to behave properly, how to approach women, and how to pass on health messages. Only after they had acquired these new skills did they start to feel comfortable with home visiting, seeing it as a form of self-development. There are interesting parallels here with Najmabadi (1993, 489), who argues that higher-class women in early-twentieth-century Tehran could only claim a place in the public sphere after they had acquired the right language, a disciplined body, and the correct scientific sensibilities.

This ambiguity can also be seen in the ways in which the *murshidat* dealt with contacts with unrelated men. While the *murshidat* emphasized that they were "all women" in order to defend their work, in practice they were in contact with men drivers, colleagues, and community members. In order to protect their own respectability and the respectability of their work, the women were subjected to strict rules and regulations. They were taken to and from work in order to facilitate their mobility without challenging practices of gender segregation; they were not allowed to meet unrelated men at work; they were not allowed to make and receive phone calls; and women who had relationships with men at work were fiercely punished. Yet gradually the contacts with men at work increased, in particular after the restructuring and expansion of the program, and, once the *murshidat* had internalized modes of "decent" behavior through a process of self-discipline and had become used to their new roles, the strict measures were loosened (see Najmabadi 1993).

The *murshidat*'s training in midwifery also shows the enabling effects of self-discipline. The large majority of *murshidat* were young and unmarried and therefore not acquainted with childbirth; many of them faced difficulties during their training in midwifery. In addition, after finishing the course, they encountered resistance from community members who did not automatically accept young, unmarried women as birth attendants. Midwives used to be older and experienced women who had gone through childbirth themselves (see Buitelaar 1990; Scheepers 1991). The *murshidat* therefore had to make a real effort to be accepted by the local population. Yet if they succeeded, it was their involvement in childbirth services that led to an improvement in their status in the communities. Midwifery services were valued highly and could, in fact, become an additional source of income for the *murshidat*.

The effects of the promotion of some *murshidat* to positions as heads of clinic were also in some ways ambiguous. Placing young women with only six years of basic education as managers of health centers definitely marked a shifting of class and gender boundaries, and the fact that these heads of clinic are still functioning is a real achievement. Yet the female heads of clinic were also confronted with new forms of social control. Many Yemeni health managers did not value the work of the *murshidat*, and, specifically at the time of the restructuring and expansion of the project, gender hierarchies were (re-)introduced. Male health managers, trained as medical doctors and pharmacists, valued curative care more than preventive care, whereas the women working in the centers were trained in and appreciated preventive health care. Instead of being supported, they had to defend their way of working, and they were regularly obstructed in their work, in particular after the end of the Hodeida Urban Primary Health Care Project.

The fact that the *murshidat* profession was a new phenomenon in Yemen gave all the actors involved, the Dutch donor organization, Yemeni state officials, and the women trained and employed as *murshidat*, the opportunity to interpret the status of the profession differently. Dutch development workers emphasized the ways in which the *murshidat* shifted gender boundaries and introduced new types of health care. For the Yemeni government, the training and employment of *murshidat* was part of a general process of modernization, in particular of the health-care sector. Yemeni state officials emphasized that the *murshidat* were only a temporary solution to the shortage of female health cadres, and that more highly educated women needed to be trained in curative care. The women trained and employed as *murshidat* stressed on one hand the benefits they had gained through their training and employment, but on the other hand complained about their low status in the Yemeni health-care establishment.

A Comment on Development Projects

The Hodeida Urban Primary Health Care Project thus not only provided new opportunities for the women trained and employed as *murshidat* but also introduced new forms of social control. The politics of development behind the Dutch support to Yemeni health-care services underline these new forms of social control. As mentioned before, the political interests of both the donor and the receiving governments mainly inspire development relationships and development aid. "Development" is thus not a value-free process but instead a process infused with power, which automatically raises questions about development aid and its "good intentions." Based on my experiences in Yemen, I end with some comments about development projects.

First of all, this ethnography of a development project shows that despite the shifting development discourses and approaches among donor countries, which are formulated to improve sustainability, Western notions of development continue to determine the direction and contents of development aid. Concepts such as equity, transparency, good governance, and ownership are imposed on receiving countries, whereas the way in which these concepts are translated at local levels often differs greatly from the actual content. Moreover, the content of these concepts is far from unequivocal: the actors involved in development projects, including the donor organization, all interpret these concepts in their own interest.

In addition, development policies are changing quickly and new concepts and approaches are constantly being introduced. These changes can be explained by the imperative to stay "modern"; in order to be acceptable to the public, development discourses have to change regularly. Yet the need to change concepts and approaches affects the implementation of policies at local levels. The Hodeida Urban Primary Health Care Project was first and foremost designed as a health-care project, not as a women's project. The goal of the project was to improve the health status of the people living in the squatter areas of Hodeida, and the training and employment of *murshidat* was one of the main ways to achieve this goal. The fact that training and employing women fitted well into Dutch development discourses, in particular in the early 1990s when Women in Development became an official "spearhead" of Dutch development policies was therefore more an additional advantage than a planned goal.

Second, Western financed development projects and development policies are based on the idea that social change can be effected by interventions from the outside. Little attention is paid to all the other processes of change that take place simultaneously. My study shows that the influence of development policies and projects is far more limited than presumed, and other factors, such as changing international relations, are much more important in their effect on processes of social change. The Gulf crisis and the subsequent return of thousands of migrants is an example of an international event that had major consequences for the project in Hodeida. The presence of young, educated women in need of paid work was one of the results of the crisis; whether the project would have been so successful without their presence will remain an unanswered question. Another example is the introduction of the structural adjustment program in 1995, which led to the restructuring of the economy and an increased need for income at all layers of society.

Third, development projects often reproduce social inequalities instead of reducing them. While the main goal of the Hodeida Urban Primary Health Care Project was to improve the health-care situation in the squatter areas through the training of women as health-care workers, the side effects of the project were as important. The presence of the project may have worked toward more equity in the provision of health-care services, but it also contributed to increasing power differentials among people working within the health-care sector, in particular because of the material assets associated with the project.

The fact that the *murshidat* had been protected and promoted during the project also had a "negative" side because they were accused of having had material benefits for years as a result of their involvement in the project. These inequalities, coupled with a so-called "feudal administrative system" where the right political connections guarantee access to the cash economy, gave rise to corrupt practices.

Fourth, Western notions of modernity are often inconsistent with the notions of development that are imposed on aid-receiving countries. An example is the discrepancy between the importance Western donor agencies attach to preventive health care and the preference for curative care of Yemeni women and Yemeni health managers. Western modernity is characterized by the power it attaches to science, knowledge, and technology, and this has had major implications for the way in which health and health care are viewed. The fact that highly advanced curative care is a powerful symbol of modernity explains its high status in developing countries. The promotion of primary health care in developing countries by Western donor organizations is therefore a kind of contradiction in terms. Moreover, the primary health-care approach is essentially developed *for* developing countries and has not been implemented in Western countries. The inequality that ensues from these contradictions is obvious: developing countries aim primarily at improving curative services in order to achieve a modern status and satisfy their population, but their dependence on Western donor aid forces them to prioritize preventive services. Health-sector reform programs try to bridge the gap between these different notions of development and combine curative and preventive health care as much as possible, but the success of these programs is still very much dependent on the willingness of the actors involved.

Although I was aware of "the politics of development" before embarking on this research project, my personal views have altered in the course of the research. I have become much more critical of the ways in which development aid is "given" and development projects are formulated. Yet I have not lost my belief in social change and in the ability of people to work toward social change despite structural forces limiting their space for maneuvering. We must continue to criticize dominant discourses of "development" because of the politics that inspire them, but we should not dismiss the strength of people, and particularly women, to shape their own lives despite powerful social structures. By placing the Yemeni women working for the project at the center of analysis, I gained insight into the ways in which they use their agentive power to judge, negotiate, and accommodate social change. The ways in which the *murshidat* in Hodeida strategically made use of the opportunities available to them will continue to inspire me.

Epilogue

The Politics of Ethnographic Research

IN THE PAST DECADES it has become clear that doing ethnography is in itself a political endeavor. Questions about modes of representation, objectivity and accountability, relativism and ethnocentrism have been raised in the discussions about ethnographic writing, and new forms of doing ethnography have been introduced (see for example Clifford and Marcus 1986; Marcus and Fisher 1986; Abu-Lughod 1991; 1993; Behar and Gordon 1995; Fabian 2001). One of the reasons ethnographic research has been scrutinized is that anthropologists are increasingly being confronted with the responses of those they write about (see Brettell 1993). In particular, anthropologists who do research at home, or in societies where access to their writings is relatively easy, have to take the possible responses and effects of their ethnographies into account. But those who do research in societies where access to academic literature is more limited also have to deal with questions of representation and accountability. Native scholars have become an important and critical audience for ethnographies written by foreign anthropologists while, as a result of debates about the ownership of research, research results are increasingly being "given back" to the informants. Inspired by the above-mentioned debates, I decided to look for ways to make the results of my research accessible to the women I have written about as well as to non-English speakers in Yemen and beyond. In this epilogue I elaborate on the complex issues involved in translating and publishing the book and the reactions of some of the women involved.

Getting the Book Translated

From the very first moment I started my research I intended to translate the book into Arabic so that the women health workers in Hodeida would be able to read it. During the years that I had been working on the Hodeida Urban Primary Health Care Project I had become used to the fact that almost all reports were translated from English into Arabic, and the other way around. The women health workers, who did not speak English, were in this way to a large extent involved in the discussions in the project. I also wanted them to be involved in my research as much as possible. During one of my visits to Hodeida, I showed the table of contents to a number of women and discussed the translated life stories with the women whose stories were going to be presented in the book. While I was afraid that they would not approve of such a detailed description of their lives, they felt proud that I had selected their stories, and their comments were restricted to small details. I asked them if they wanted me to use pseudonyms and if so, which name they preferred. One of the four women did not want me to change her name, two others selected their own pseudonym, and the fourth one left it to me. I changed all the names of people involved in the project in order to protect their privacy.

When my dissertation was finished, I took a number of copies with me on a visit to Yemen and proudly showed my friends and former colleagues the final result. The women health workers congratulated me with my degree and quickly glanced through the book, looking at the few pictures that were included but unable to read the text. They asked me for the Arabic translation, and I promised that I would do my best to find funds to realize the translation. Friends and family in the Netherlands were willing to donate money to cover the translation costs, but their contributions were not sufficient, so I had to look for other sources. Fortunately, the Department of Central Programmes and the Netherlands Organization for Scientific Research (NWO) were willing to fund the translation, and I could use the donations to cover the publication costs. Mohamed 'Abdelhamid, a Sudanese friend and professional translator who lived for ten years in

Yemen, was willing to translate the book, and Dar Muhajirun in Cairo agreed to publish the translation.

The First Reactions

In the summer of 2004 the first draft of the translation was ready, and I decided to show this draft to some of my former colleagues in Hodeida. I wanted to make sure that they would approve of its contents because the book would be sold in bookstores in Yemen. I gave four women health workers who were closely involved in my research copies of the draft translation. I emphasized that they had to imagine that the book would be available in bookstores in Hodeida, and anyone interested would be able to buy and read it. Which parts needed adjustment and what could stay as it was? I returned to Sana'a, where I was doing fieldwork for my postdoctoral research, and called the women regularly to ask whether they were reading the manuscript. They all work full time and are responsible for child care, cooking, and other domestic chores and therefore have little time for reading. But I was happily surprised when I heard that some of them had started reading the draft and enjoyed it.

When I returned to Hodeida six weeks later, Jamila was the first to give me her comments. Jamila was closely involved in the project as a supervisor. Her first reaction was that she had never read a book like mine, a book in which a detailed description was given of the lives of women in Yemen and in which the entire history of the project was laid down. She said that she had read the manuscript with a lot of interest and that she was impressed by my writing style. I was very pleased with her remark because I had always had the women health workers in mind when I was writing the book. I had tried to write as accessibly as possible so that nonacademics, and in particular the women health workers, would be able to read the book, and it seemed that I had succeeded in doing so. But Jamila also had some critical comments, which mainly concerned the level of detail, in the life stories as well as in the description of the project. "You really wrote down everything," and "You dug up everything about our society!" were some of her reactions.

I explained to her that this level of detail was necessary in academic research, but I also realized that the information we, as anthropologists, are interested in may have a very different value for the people we write about. While I had consciously used life stories, quotations and detailed ethnographic descriptions of everyday practices to make my informants come alive and make the book interesting for a wider audience, this style of presenting data happened to be problematic in the eyes of the people involved (see also Davis 1993, 31).

With regard to the life stories, Jamila wondered whether the four women would accept such an explicit description of their lives and advised me to show them their stories again now that the book was translated. One of the issues the women might, in her view, feel particularly uncomfortable with was the fact that I had written in detail about their social backgrounds. Most women health workers come from the lower social classes and prefer not to talk about their social background while I had explicitly referred to it in my book. I agreed and decided to give copies of the life stories to the four women. Again they all approved of the stories as I had presented them and only made minor changes. Even when I emphasized that the book would be available in bookstores in Hodeida and anyone would be able to read their stories, they did not object. "You changed our names so I don't see a problem" and "There are many girls with similar life stories as me" were some of their comments. Only Hawa, who comes from a strict family, changed a number of details in order to make herself less recognizable. "I don't want my brother to buy the book and find out that he is reading the story of his sister," she said. One of the women read the whole book after it had been published and criticized my elaboration of the social background of women health workers. In her view I had generalized too much.

Jamila's second remark concerned my detailed description of the state of affairs in the Hodeida Health Office after the project had come to an end. The clear references to the increased level of bureaucracy, the corruption, and the lack of support of the women health workers were in her eyes problematic. "Everyone will know that we are the ones who told you about the current situation, and we will be blamed for talking to you." She was afraid that she and her colleagues would encounter problems when the governmental health administrators in Hodeida would read what I had written. They might lose their job or in other ways be confronted with the fact that they had been my key informants. The other women who had read the manuscript agreed that it was better not to write about it in such an explicit way. Fatima was even afraid that the political security would find out that they had talked to me and advised me not to publish the translation of the book. Muna had locked herself in her office for a whole day in order to finish reading the book and said that everything that had happened in the past twenty years had passed through her mind again. She advised me to change the end of the book, but her motivation was different: she was not afraid of losing her job or of being persecuted but said that I could not write about the developments in the past few years because I had not worked on the project myself anymore. "You did not experience it yourself but only heard about it from us." I answered that there were many other things I had not experienced myself, and that this is often the case when doing research. Yet she still advised me to adapt the end of the book.

Only when receiving the reactions of the women did I realize that there is a big difference between translating one's research results for a selected number of people and publishing the text so that it becomes accessible for a wider audience. While I had thought that I had done my informants a favor by having the book translated, I realized that publishing the translation could harm them. As a result of their reactions I decided to change the end of the Arabic version. I deleted clear references to persons, even though I had used pseudonyms, and direct quotations, but I did not change my main line of argumentation.

Presenting the Book

In February 2005 the Arabic version of the book was published in Cairo and distributed to bookstores in Egypt and Yemen. In order to announce the publication publicly, I organized a book presentation in a cultural center in Sana'a, but only after having had serious doubts whether a public presentation of the book would work out positively or negatively for the women involved. On one hand I wanted to draw attention to the book, but on the other hand I was afraid that this attention could have a negative impact on the women health workers in Hodeida, and in a broader sense put development work in a negative light. Just like Hilhorst (2003, 231), who used ethnographic methods to study the everyday politics of a Philippine NGO and was confronted with the critical reactions of the people she had written about, my research itself might become part of political struggle. Encouraged by the women themselves, who told me not to worry because I had changed the end of the book, I decided to organize the book presentation. I invited Hawa, Muna, Fatima, and Jamila to attend the book presentation as well as the director-general of the Hodeida Health Office because he had to give the four women permission to travel to Sanaʿa and leave their jobs for a few days. While he was unable to attend the presentation himself, he permitted the four women to come. More than one hundred people attended the book presentation, among them government officials, staff of local and international nongovernmental organizations, and journalists. Hawa was willing to give a short speech, in which she briefly told the audience about her own involvement in the project, a discussant commented on the book, and I spoke about the background of the translation.

The book is now available in a number of bookstores in Egypt and Yemen, and I gave copies to everyone who participated in the research, or who in one way or another might be interested in reading the book. Forty books were distributed in Hodeida, among all the women I interviewed and people who had been involved in the project. Even though I had changed a number of sensitive parts in the book, I continued to worry about the effect of what I have written. But the reactions have thus far been limited. While everyone was happy to receive a copy, and some people even read the book, very few people have commented on its contents at the moment of writing.

Amsterdam
August 2006

Works Cited

Index

Works Cited

Abdulghani. Najiba A. et al. 1991. *Results of an Impact Study.* Hodeida: Hodeida Urban Primary Health Care Project.

Abu-Lughod, Lila. 1991. "Writing Against Culture." In *Recapturing Anthropology: Working in the Present,* edited by Richard G. Fox, 137–62. Santa Fe: School of American Research.

———. 1993. *Writing Women's Worlds: Bedouin Stories.* Berkeley: Univ. of California Press.

———. 1998a. "Feminist Longings and Postcolonial Conditions." In *Remaking Women: Feminism and Modernity in the Middle East,* edited by Lila Abu-Lughod, 3–31. Princeton, N.J.: Princeton Univ. Press.

———, ed. 1998b. *Remaking Women: Feminism and Modernity in the Middle East.* Princeton, N.J.: Princeton Univ. Press.

Abu-Nasr, Julinda, Nabil F. Khoury, and Henry T. Azzam, eds. 1985. *Women, Employment and Development in the Arab World.* Berlin/New York/Amsterdam: Mouton Publishers.

Addleton, J. 1991. "The Impact of the Gulf War on Migration and Remittances in Asia and the Middle East." *International Migration* 29, no. 4:509–21.

Adra, Najwa. 1983. *The Impact of Male Migration on Women's Roles in Agriculture in the Yemen Arab Republic.* Report prepared for the Inter-country Experts Meeting on Women in Food Production, Amman, Oct. 22–26.

Afshar, Haleh, and Stephanie Barrientos. 1999. "Introduction: Women, Globalization, and Fragmentation." In *Women, Globalization, and Fragmentation in the Developing World,* edited by Haleh Afshar and Stephanie Barrientos, 1–17. London: Macmillan.

Afshar, Haleh, and Carolyne Dennis, eds. 1992. *Women and Adjustment Policies in the Third World.* London: Macmillan.

AIV. 2002. *Integration of Gender Equality: A Matter of Responsibility. Commitment and Quality.* The Hague: Advisory Council on International Affairs.

Al-Dubai, Khalid Yasin. 2000. "Health Sector Reform in Yemen: Will It Lead to an Equitable, Efficient, and Effective Health Care System?" Master's thesis, Royal Tropical Institute, Amsterdam.

Ali, Kamran Asdar. 2002. *Planning the Family in Egypt: New Bodies, New Selves.* Austin: Univ. of Texas Press.

Al-Mughni, Haya. 2001. *Women in Kuwait: The Politics of Gender.* London: Saqi Books.

Altorki, Soraya. 1986. *Women in Saudi Arabia: Ideology and Behavior Among the Elite.* New York: Columbia Univ. Press.

Arce, Alberto, and Norman Long. 2000. "Reconfiguring Modernity and Development from an Anthropological Perspective." In *Anthropology, Development, and Modernities: Exploring Discourses, Counter-Tendencies and Violence,* edited by Alberto Arce and Norman Long, 1–31. London and New York: Routledge.

Arnold, David. 1993. *Colonizing the Body: State Medicine and Epidemic Disease in Nineteenth-Century India.* Berkeley: Univ. of California Press.

Badran, Margot. 1995. *Feminists, Islam, and Nation: Gender and the Making of Modern Egypt.* Princeton, N.J.: Princeton University Press.

———. 1998. "Unifying Women: Feminist Pasts and Presents in Yemen." *Gender & History* 10, no. 3:498–518.

Barnett, Tony. 1977. *The Gezira Scheme: An Illusion of Development.* London: Frank Cass.

Bastien, Joseph W. 1990. "Community Health Workers in Bolivia: Adapting to Traditional Roles in the Andean Community." *Social Science and Medicine* 30, no. 3:281–87.

Behar, Ruth, and Deborah Gordon, eds. 1995. *Women Writing Culture.* Berkeley: Univ. of California Press.

Benmayor, Rina, and Andor Skotnes. 1994. "Some Reflections on Migration and Identity." In *International Yearbook of Oral History and Life Stories: Migration and Identity,* edited by Rina Benmayor and Andor Skotnes, 1–18. Oxford: Oxford Univ. Press.

Bernal, Victoria. 1994. "Gender, Culture and Capitalism: Women and the Remaking of Islamic 'Tradition' in a Sudanese Village." *Comparative Study of Society and History* 36, no. 1:36–67.

———. 1997. "Islam, Transnational Culture, and Modernity in Rural Sudan." In *Gendered Encounters: Challenging Cultural Boundaries and Social*

Hierarchies in Africa, edited by M. Grosz-Ngaté and O. H. Kokole, 131–51. New York and London: Routledge.

Bertaux, Daniel. 1981. "Introduction." In *Biography and Society: The Life-History Approach in the Social Sciences*, edited by Daniel Bertaux, 5–15. Beverly Hills: Sage.

Bornstein, A. 1974. *Food and Society in the Yemen Arab Republic*. Rome: FAO.

Brettell, Caroline B., ed. 1993. *When They Read What We Write: The Politics of Ethnography*. Westport, Conn. and London: Bergin & Garvey.

Buitelaar, Marjo. 1990. *Women and Change III: Report on a Mission Concerning Childbirth Practices and Women's Activities in Ghulail, Hodeida*. Nijmegen: Public Health Consultants.

Buringa, Joke. 1986. *The Inhabitants of al-Ghulail: Some Background Data*. Hodeida: Hodeida Health Improvement and Waste Disposal Project.

———. 1988a. "Ervaringen als vrouwelijke antropoloog met ontwikkelings-samenwerking in een Arabische kontekst." Presentation at the Anthropological Sociological Centre, Univ. of Amsterdam, Nov. 4.

———. 1988b. *Yemeni Women in Transition: How Development Cooperation Could Fit In*. The Hague: Directorate General for International Cooperation.

Burrowes, Robert D. 1987. *The Yemen Arab Republic: The Politics of Development, 1962–1986*. Boulder, Colo.: Westview Press.

Carapico, Sheila. 1993a. "The Economic Dimension of Yemen Unity." *Middle East Report* 184 (Sept.–Oct.): 9–14.

———. 1993b. "Elections and Mass Politics in Yemen." *Middle East Report* 185 (Nov.–Dec.): 2–6.

———. 1996. "Gender and Status Inequalities in Yemen: Honour, Economics, and Politics." In *Patriarchy and Economic Development: Women's Positions at the End of the Twentieth Century*, edited by Valentine M. Moghadam, 80–98. Oxford: Clarendon Press.

———. 1998. *Civil Society in Yemen: The Political Economy of Activism in Modern Arabia*. Cambridge: Cambridge Univ. Press.

———. 2001. "The Dialectics of Fashion: Gender and Politics in Yemen." In *Women and Power in the Middle East*, edited by Suad Joseph and Susan Slyomovics, 183–90. Philadelphia: Univ. of Pennsylvania Press.

Carapico, Sheila, and Cynthia Myntti. 1991. "Change in North Yemen 1977–1989: A Tale of Two Families." *Middle East Report*, May–June, 24–29.

Carapico, Sheila, and Anna Wuerth. 2000. "Passports and Passages: Tests of Yemeni Women's Citizenship Rights." In *Gender and Citizenship in the Middle East*, edited by Suad Joseph, 261–71. Syracuse: Syracuse Univ. Press.

Cassels, A. 1995. "Health Sector Reform: Key Issues in Less Developed Countries." *Journal of International Development* 7, no. 3:329–47.

Central Statistical Organization (CSO), Yemen, and Macro International Inc. (MI). 1998. *Yemen Demographic and Maternal and Child Health Survey 1997.* Calverton, Md.: CSO and MI.

Clark, Janine. 2004. *Islam, Charity, and Activism: Middle Class Networks and Social Welfare in Egypt, Jordan, and Yemen.* Indianapolis: Indiana Univ. Press.

Clifford, James. 1986. "Introduction: Partial Truths." In *Writing Culture: The Poetics and Politics of Ethnography,* edited by James Clifford and George Marcus, 1–26. Berkeley: Univ. of California Press.

Clifford, James, and George Marcus, eds. 1986. *Writing Culture: The Poetics and Politics of Ethnography.* Berkeley: Univ. of California Press.

Crewe, Emma, and Elizabeth Harrison. 1998. *Whose Development? An Ethnography of Aid.* London and New York: Croom Helm.

Crush, Jonathan, ed. 1995. *Power of Development.* London and New York: Routledge.

Cunningham, Robert B., and Yasin K. Sarayrah. 1993. *Wasta: The Hidden Force in Middle Eastern Society.* Westport, Conn.: Praeger.

Dahlgren, Susanne. 2004. *Contesting Realities: Morality, Propriety, and the Public Sphere in Aden, Yemen.* Research Reports, no. 243, Department of Sociology. Helsinki: Helsinki Univ. Printing House.

Davis, Dona L. 1993. "Unintended Consequences: The Myth of 'The Return' in Anthropological Fieldwork." In *When They Read What We Write: The Politics of Ethnography,* edited by Caroline B. Brettell, 27–35. Westport, Conn. and London: Bergin & Garvey.

de Regt, Marina. 1997. "Community Participation in the Squatter Areas of Hodeidah, Yemen." *Sharqiyyat* 9, no. 2:124–38.

de Regt, Marina, et al. 1996. *The Impact of Literacy Classes for Women in HUPHC Centres: A Small-Scale Study.* Hodeidah: Hodeidah Urban Primary Health Care Programme.

de Regt, Marina, and Ali M. Ghailan. 2007. "Housing and Health Care in the City of Hodeidah." In *Yemen into the Twenty-first Century: Continuity and Change* edited by Kamil A. Mahdi, Anna Weurth, and Helen Lackner. Reading, U.K.: Ithaca Press.

Destremau, Blandine. 1990. *Femmes du Yémen.* Paris: Editions Peuples du Monde.

———. 2001. "The Emergence of a Domestic Labour Market in Yemen: A Study on Sana'a." Paper for the conference Domestic Service and Mobility: Labour, Livelihoods, and Lifestyles, Amsterdam, Feb. 5–7.

Detalle, Renaud. 1993. "The Yemeni Elections Up Close." *Middle East Report* 185 (Nov.–Dec.): 8–12.

———. 1997. "Ajuster sans douleur? La méthode yéménite." *Monde Arabe Maghreb-Machrek* 155:20–36.

DGIS. 1975. *Netherlands Development Cooperation 1975, Development Cooperation Information.* The Hague: Department of the Ministry of Foreign Affairs.

———. 1983. Formulation Report, Hodeida Health Improvement and Waste Disposal Project, The Hague.

———. 1987. "Do Not Forget Me!" De Nederlandse Ontwikkelingssamenwerking en de positieverbetering van vrouwen in Noord-Jemen. Rapport van een identifikatie missie, The Hague.

———. 1988. Beleidsplan voor de ontwikkelingssamenwerking met Noord-Jemen voor de periode 1989–1992, The Hague.

———. 1989. "Women and Health: Policy on an Operational Footing: Main Points and Checklist." Sector Papers Women and Development, no. 3, The Hague.

Donnison, Jean. 1977. *Midwives and Medical Men: A History of Inter-Professional Rivalries and Women's Rights.* London: Heinemann.

Dorsky, Susan. 1986. *Women of 'Amran: A Middle Eastern Ethnographic Study.* Salt Lake City: Univ. of Utah Press.

Dorsky, Susan, and Thomas B. Stevenson. 1995. "Childhood and Education in Highland North Yemen." In *Children in the Muslim Middle East,* edited by Elizabeth Warnock Fernea, 309–24. Austin: Univ. of Texas Press.

Doumato, Eleanor Abdella. 2000. *Getting God's Ear: Women, Islam and Healing in Saudi Arabia and the Gulf.* New York: Columbia Univ. Press.

Dresch, Paul. 1993. *Tribes, Government and History in Yemen.* Oxford: Clarendon Press.

———. 2000. *A History of Modern Yemen.* Cambridge: Cambridge Univ. Press.

Dresch, Paul, and Bernard Haykel. 1995. "Stereotypes and Political Styles: Islamists and Tribesfolk in Yemen." *International Journal of Middle East Studies* 27:405–31.

Dwyer, Daisy, and Judith Bruce, eds. 1988. *A Home Divided: Women and Income in the Third World.* Stanford: Stanford Univ. Press.

El-Messiri, Sawsan. 1978. "Self-Images of Traditional Urban Women in Cairo." In *Women in the Muslim World,* edited by Lois Beck and Nikki Keddie, 522–40. Cambridge, Mass.: Harvard Univ. Press.

El-Sanabary, Nagat. 1993. "The Education and Contribution of Women Health Care Professionals in Saudi Arabia: The Case of Nursing." *Social Science and Medicine* 37, no. 11:1331–43.

Ertürk, Yakin. 1994. "Implication of Labour Displacement for Production Relations in Yemen." In *Population Displacement and Resettlement: Development and Conflict in the Middle East,* edited by Seteney Shami, 107–20. New York: Center for Migration Studies.

Escobar, Arturo. 1984. "Discourse and Power in Development: Michel Foucault and the Relevance of His Work to the Third World." *Alternatives* 10:377–400.

———. 1991. "Anthropology and the Development Encounter: The Making and Marketing of Development Anthropology." *American Ethnologist* 18, no. 4:16–40.

———. 1995. *Encountering Development: The Making and Unmaking of the Third World.* Princeton, N.J.: Princeton Univ. Press.

ESCWA Secretariat. 1993/1994. "International and Return Migration: The Experience of Yemen." *Population Bulletin of ESCWA,* no. 41/42:107–151.

Fabian, Johannes. 2001. *Anthropology with an Attitude: Critical Essays.* Stanford: Stanford Univ. Press

Fahmy, Khaled. 1998. "Women, Medicine, and Power in Nineteenth-Century Egypt." In *Remaking Women: Feminism and Modernity in the Middle East,* edited by Lila Abu-Lughod, 35–72. Princeton, N.J.: Princeton Univ. Press.

Fayein, Claudie. 1955. *Une Française Médecin au Yémen.* Paris: Rene Julliard.

Ferguson, James. 1990. *The Anti-Politics Machine: "Development," Depoliticization, and Bureaucratic Power in Lesotho.* Cambridge: Cambridge Univ. Press.

Findlay, Allan M. 1994. "Return to Yemen: The End of the Old Migration Order in the Arab World." In *Population Migration and the Changing World Order,* edited by W. T. S. Gould and A. M. Findlay, 205–24. Chichester, U.K.: John Wiley & Sons.

Foucault, Michel. 1975. *The Birth of the Clinic: An Archeology of Medical Perception.* New York: Vintage.

Freeman, Carla. 2000. *High Tech and High Heels in the Global Economy: Women, Work, and Pink-Collar Identities in the Caribbean.* Durham and London: Duke Univ. Press.

Gerholm, Tomas. 1977. *Market, Mosque, and Mafraj: Social Inequality in a Yemeni Town*. Stockholm: Univ. of Stockholm.

Gluck, Sherna Berger, and Daphne Patai, eds. 1991. *Women's Words: The Feminist Practice of Oral History*. New York and London: Routledge.

Grillo, R. D. 1997. "Discourses of Development: The View from Anthropology." In *Discourses of Development: Anthropological Perspectives*, edited by R. D. Grillo and R. L. Stirrat, 1–34. Oxford: Berg.

Halliday, Fred. 1974. *Arabia Without Sultans*. Harmondsworth, U.K.: Penguin Books.

Haraway, Donna L. 1991, "Situated Knowledges: The Science Question in Feminism and the Privilege of Partial Perspective." In *Simians, Cyborgs, and Women: The Reinvention of Nature*, edited by Donna L. Haraway, 183–201. New York: Routledge.

Hardon, Anita, et al. 2002. *Health, Nutrition, and Population: Dutch Support to Programmes and Projects in Yemen 1995–1999*. Working Document, Policy and Operations Evaluation Department. The Hague: Ministry of Foreign Affairs.

Hassan, Abdul-karim, and Ebtisam Yahiya Amer. 1997. *An Evaluation of the Role of Female Health Guides*. Sana'a: OXFAM.

Hébert, Mary. 1987. *Population and Health among the Residents of al-Baydha', al-Mughtaribeen, Madinat al-Umal, Madinat al-Riyadhia, and Za'afran: The Results of a Rapid Appraisal*. Hodeida: Hodeida Urban Primary Health Care Project.

Herrmann, Jens. 1979. *Ambition and Reality: Planning for Health and Basic Health Services in the Yemen Arab Republic*. Frankfurt: Verlag Peter Lang.

Hijab, Nadia. 1988. *Womanpower: The Arab Debate on Women at Work*. Cambridge: Cambridge Univ. Press.

———. 2001. "Women and Work in the Arab World." In *Women and Power in the Middle East*, edited by Suad Joseph and Susan Slyomovics, 41–51. Philadelphia: Univ. of Pennsylvania Press.

Hilhorst, Dorothea. 2003. *The Real World of NGOs: Discourses, Diversity, and Development*. London and New York: Zed Books.

Hindess, B. 1986. "Actors and Social Relations." In *Sociological Theory in Transition*, edited by M. I. Wadell and S. P. Turner, 113–26. Boston: Allen and Unwin.

Ho, Engseng. 1997. "Hadhramis Abroad in Hadhramaut: The Muwalladun." In *Hadrami Traders, Scholars, and Statesmen in the Indian Ocean, 1750s–1960s*, edited by U. Freitag and W. G. Clarence-Smith, 131–46. Leiden: Brill.

Hobart, Mark, ed. 1993. *An Anthropological Critique of Development: The Growth of Ignorance.* London and New York: Routledge.

Hodeida Health Improvement and Waste Disposal Project. 1984. Plan of Operations.

Hodeida Health Office. 1993. Urban Health Development Plan. Hodeida.

Hodeida Urban Primary Health Care Project (HUPHC). 1987. Project Formulation Document.

———. 1991. Proposal Urban Primary Health Care 1992–1997.

———. 1995. Manual Urban PHC/MCH.

Hoeck, Eva. 1962. *Doctor Amongst the Bedouins.* London: Robert Hale Limited.

Hoodfar, Homa. 1997. "Devices and Desires: Population Policy and Gender Roles in the Islamic Republic." In *Political Islam: Essays from Middle East Report,* edited by Joel Beinin and Joe Stork, 220–33. Berkeley: Univ. of California Press.

———. 1998. *Volunteer Health Workers in Iran as Social Activists: Can "Governmental Non-Governmental Organisations" Be Agents of Democratisation?* WLUML Occasional Paper no. 10, Dec.

———. 1999. *Between Marriage and the Market: Intimate Politics and Survival in Cairo.* Cairo: American Univ. in Cairo Press.

Ibrahim, Barbara Lethem. 1985. "Family Strategies: A Perspective on Women's Entry to the Labor Force in Egypt." In *Arab Society: Social Science Perspectives,* edited by Nicholas S. Hopkins and Saad Eddin Ibrahim, 257–67. Cairo: American Univ. in Cairo Press.

Jansen, Willy. 1987. *Women Without Men: Gender and Marginality in an Algerian Town.* Leiden: Brill.

Jansen, Willy, et al. 1993. *Women in Development in Muslim Countries: Negotiating a Better Future.* Nijmegen: Center for Women's Studies, Katholieke Universiteit Nijmegen.

Justice, Judith. 1986. *Policies, Plans, and People: Culture and Health Development in Nepal.* Berkeley: Univ. of California Press.

Kanaaneh, Rhoda Ann. 2002. *Birthing the Nation: Strategies of Palestinian Women in Israel.* Berkeley: Univ. of California Press.

Kandiyoti, Deniz, ed. 1991. *Women, Islam, and the State.* Philadelphia: Temple Univ. Press.

———. 2001. "The Politics of Gender and the Conundrums of Citizenship." In *Women and Power in the Middle East,* edited by Suad Joseph and Susan Slyomovics, 52–58. Philadelphia: Univ. of Pennsylvania Press.

Kempe, Annica. 1994. *The Quality of Maternal and Neonatal Health Service in Yemen: Seen Through Women's Eyes.* Sana'a: Radda Barnen.

Kennedy, John G. 1987. *The Flower of Paradise: The Institutionalized Use of the Drug Qat in North Yemen.* Dordrecht: D. Reidel Publishing.

Koninklijk Instituut voor de Tropen. 1989. *Evaluation Report, Hodeida Urban Primary Health Care Project, Yemen Arab Republic.* Amsterdam: Koninklijk Instituut voor de Tropen.

Kuhnke, Laverne. 1990. *Lives at Risk: Public Health in Nineteenth-Century Egypt.* Berkeley and Los Angeles: Univ. of California Press.

Lackner, Helen. 1995. "Women and Development in the Republic of Yemen." In *Gender and Development in the Arab World: Women's Economic Participation: Patterns and Policies,* edited by Nabil F. Khoury and Valentine M. Moghadam, 71–96. London: Zed Books.

Long, Norman. 1992. "Introduction." In *Battlefields of Knowledge: The Interlocking of Theory and Practice in Social Research and Development,* edited by Norman Long and Ann Long, 3–15. London and New York: Routledge.

Long, Norman, and Ann Long, eds. 1992. *Battlefields of Knowledge: The Interlocking of Theory and Practice in Social Research and Development.* London and New York: Routledge.

Longva, Anh Nga. 1997. *Walls Built on Sand: Migration, Exclusion, and Society in Kuwait.* Boulder, Colo.: Westview Press.

Lucet, Marc. 1995. "Les rapatriés de la crise du Golfe au Yémen: Hodeida quatre ans après." *Monde Arabe Maghreb Machrek* 148 (Apr.–June): 128–42.

Macdonald, John J. 1994. *Primary Health Care: Medicine in Its Place.* London: Earthscan Publications.

Macleod, Arlene Elowe. 1991. *Accommodating Protest: Working Women, the New Veiling, and Change in Cairo.* New York: Columbia Univ. Press.

Makhlouf, Carla. 1979. *Changing Veils: Women and Modernisation in North Yemen.* London: Croom Helm.

Marcus, George E., and Michael M. J. Fisher, eds. 1986. *Anthropology as Cultural Critique: An Experimental Moment in the Human Sciences.* Chicago: Univ. of Chicago Press.

Martin, Charlotte. 2001. *Gender Mainstreaming Strategy Paper for the Health Sector Reform Programme, Republic of Yemen.* Amsterdam: Koninklijk Instituut voor de Tropen.

Meneley, Anne. 1996. *Tournaments of Value: Sociability and Hierarchy in a Yemeni Town.* Toronto: Univ. of Toronto Press.

Messick, Brinkley. 1983. "Legal Documents and the Concept of 'Restricted Literacy' in a Traditional Society." *International Journal of Social Languages* 42:41–52.

———. 1993. *The Calligraphic State: Textual Domination and History in a Muslim Society.* Berkeley: Univ. of California Press.

Meyer, Günter. 1986. *Arbeitsemigration, Binnenwanderung und Wirtschaftsentwicklung in der Arabischen Republik Jemen.* Wiesbaden: Dr. Ludwig Reichert Verlag.

———. 1989. *Transformation of the Society in the Yemen Arab Republic Through Migration.* Berlin: Berliner Institut for Verleichende Sozialforschung.

Mies, Maria. 1983. "Towards a Methodology for Feminist Research." In *Theories of Women's Studies,* edited by Gloria Bowles and Renate Duelli Klein, 117–39. London: Routledge and Kegan Paul.

Ministry of Public Health. 1996. National Plan for Training 3670 Community Midwives During the Period 1996–2001. Sana'a.

———. 1999. Implementation Plan for Health Sector Reform in Yemen: Guidelines for the MoPH HSR Implementation Task Force. Sana'a.

Mitchell, Timothy. 2002. *Rule of Experts: Egypt, Techno-Politics, Modernity.* Berkeley: Univ. of California Press.

Moghadam, Valentine M. 1993. *Modernizing Women: Gender and Social Change in the Middle East.* Boulder, Colo., and London: Lynne Rienner Publishers.

———, ed. 1994. *Identity Politics and Women: Cultural Reassertions and Feminisms in International Perspective.* Boulder, Colo.: Westview Press.

———. 1995. "The Political Economy of Female Employment in the Arab Region." In *Gender and Development in the Arab World: Women's Economic Participation: Patterns and Policies,* edited by Nabil F. Khoury and Valentine M. Moghadam, 6–34. London: Zed Books.

Molyneux, Maxine. 1982. *State Policies and the Position of Women Workers in the People's Democratic Republic of Yemen, 1967–77.* Geneva: ILO.

———. 1995. "Women's Rights and Political Contingency: The Case of Yemen, 1990–1994." *Middle East Journal* 49, no. 3:418–31.

Moors, Annelies. 1995. *Women, Property, and Islam: Palestinian Experiences, 1920–1990.* Cambridge: Cambridge Univ. Press.

———. 1999. "Debating Islamic Family Law: Legal Texts and Social Practices." In *A Social History of Women and Gender in the Modern Middle East,* edited by Margaret L. Meriwether and Judith E. Tucker, 141–75. Boulder, Colo.: Westview Press.

————. 2003. "Islam and Fashion on the Streets of Sana'a, Yemen." *Etnofoor* 16, no. 2:41–56.

Morris, Timothy. 1991. *The Despairing Developer: Diary of an Aid Worker in the Middle East*. London and New York: I. B. Tauris.

Moser, Caroline. 1989. "Gender Planning in the Third World: Meeting Practical and Strategic Gender Needs." *World Development* 17, no. 11:1799–825.

Mundy, Martha. 1983. "Sana'a Dress, 1020–75." In *Sana'a: An Arabian Islamic City*, edited by R. B. Serjeant and Ronald Lewcock, 529–41. London: World of Islam Festival Trust.

————. 1985. "Agricultural Development in the Yemeni Tihama: The Past Ten Years." In *Economy, Society, and Culture in Contemporary Yemen*, edited by B. R. Pridham, 22–40. London: Croom Helm.

————. 1995. *Domestic Government: Kinship, Community, and Polity in North Yemen*. London and New York: I. B. Tauris.

Myntti, Cynthia. 1984. "Yemeni Workers Abroad: The Impact on Women." *Middle East Report*, June, 11–16.

————. 1985. "Women, Work, Population, and Development in the Yemen Arab Republic." In *Women, Employment, and Development in the Arab World*, edited by J. Abu Nasr, N. F. Khoury, and H. T. Azzam, 39–58. Berlin: Mouton Publishers.

Najmabadi, Afsaneh. 1993. "Veiled Discourse—Unveiled Bodies." *Feminist Studies* 19, no. 3:487–518.

Nelson, Cynthia. 1974. "Public and Private Politics: Women in the Middle Eastern World." *American Ethnologist* 1:551–63.

Nientied, P., and F. Öry. 1991. *Mission Report of Pre-identification Mission to Hodeida*. Rotterdam: Institute for Housing and Urban Development Studies; Amsterdam: Koninklijk Instituut voor de Tropen.

Oldham, Linda, et al. 1993. Final Report on a Consultancy to the Netherlands Embassy and the UNDP Assessing the Potential for Women's Economic Programming in the Returnee Communities of Hodeida, Yemen.

Olmsted, Jennifer. 2005. "Is Paid Work the (Only) Answer? Neoliberalism, Arab Women's Well-Being and the Social Contract." *Journal of Middle East Women's Studies* 1, no. 2:112–39.

Ong, Aihwa. 1987. *Spirits of Resistance and Capitalist Discipline: Factory Women in Malaysia*. New York: State Univ. of New York Press.

Packard, Randall. 1997. "Visions of Postwar Health and Development and Their Impact on Public Health Interventions in the Developing World." In *International Development and the Social Sciences: Essays on the History and Politics of Knowledge*, edited by Frederick Cooper and Randall Packard, 93–115. Berkeley: Univ. of California Press.

Paluch, Marta, ed. 2001. *Yemeni Voices: Women Tell Their Stories.* Sanaʻa: The British Council.

Penney, Debra S. 2000. "Meeting Women's Health Needs in Yemen: A Midwifery Perspective." *Journal of Midwifery & Women's Health* 45, no. 1:72–78.

Personal Narratives Group. 1989. *Interpreting Women's Lives: Feminist Theory and Personal Narratives.* Bloomington and Indianapolis: Indiana Univ. Press.

Peterson, J. E. 1982. *Yemen: The Search for a Modern State.* London: Croom Helm.

Pigg, Stacy Leigh. 1992. "Inventing Social Categories Through Place: Social Representations and Development in Nepal." *Comparative Study of Society and History* 34, no. 3:491–513.

———. 1997. "Found in Most Traditional Societies: Traditional Medical Practitioners Between Culture and Development." In *International Development and the Social Sciences: Essays on the History and Politics of Knowledge*, edited by Frederick Cooper and Randall Packard, 259–90. Berkeley: Univ. of California Press.

Pizurki, Helena, et al. 1987. *Women as Providers of Health Care.* Geneva: WHO.

Pollert, Anna. 1981. *Girls, Wives, Factory Lives.* London and Basingstoke: Macmillan.

Porter, Doug, Bryant Allen, and Gaye Thompson. 1991. *Development in Practice: Paved with Good Intentions.* London and New York: Routledge.

Qassim, Taher Ali. 1994. *Ana Shahaat (I Am a Beggar). A Report on the Living Standards in Hodeidah City for Hodeidah Urban Primary Health Care Project.* The Hague: Directorate General of International Cooperation, Ministry of Foreign Affairs.

Rabo, Annika. 1986. *Change on the Euphrates: Villagers, Townsmen, and the Employees in Northeast Syria.* Stockholm: Stockholm Studies in Social Anthropology.

Rai, Shirin M. 2002. *Gender and the Political Economy of Development: From Nationalism to Globalization.* Cambridge: Polity Press.

Ramirez-Valles, Jesus. 1997. "Women Community Health Workers: A Case Study of Feminine Identities and Health Education in a Northern Mexican City." Ph.D. dissertation, Univ. of Michigan, Ann Arbor.

Rassam, Amal. 1984. "Towards a Theoretical Framework for the Study of Women in the Arab World." In *Social Science Research and Women in the Arab World*. Paris: Unesco.

Rathgeber, Eva M. 1990. "WID, WAD, GAD: Trends in Research and Practice." *Journal of Developing Areas* 24 (July): 489–502.

Robinson, Sheila A., and Donald E. Larsen. 1990. "The Relative Influence of the Community and the Health System on Work Performance: A Case Study of Community Health Workers in Colombia." *Social Science and Medicine* 30, no. 10:1041–8.

Rofel, Lisa. 1999. *Other Modernities: Gendered Yearnings in China After Socialism*. Berkeley: Univ. of California Press.

Rosenfeld, Maya. 2002. "Power Structure, Agency, and Family in a Palestinian Refugee Camp." *International Journal of Middle East Studies* 34, no. 3:519–51.

Rossi-Espagnet, A. 1984. *Primary Health Care in Urban Areas: Reaching the Urban Poor in Developing Countries*. Geneva: World Health Organization/UNICEF.

Sachs, Wolfgang, ed. 1992. *The Development Dictionary: A Guide to Knowledge as Power*. London and New Jersey: Zed Books.

Salaff, Janet W. 1981. *Working Daughters of Hong Kong: Filial Piety or Power in the Family?* Cambridge: Cambridge Univ. Press.

Salib, Dalia. 1998. "Re-imagining the Nursing Profession." *Ru'ya*, no. 11:16–17.

Scheepers, Lidwien M. 1991. "Jidda: The Traditional Midwife of Yemen?" *Social Science and Medicine* 33, no. 8:959–62.

Segall, Malcolm, and Glen Williams. 1983. "Primary Health Care in Democratic Yemen: Evolution of Policy and Political Commitment." In *Practising Health for All*, edited by David Morley, Jon E. Rohde, and Glen Williams, 300–316. Oxford: Oxford Univ. Press.

Seif, Huda A. 1995. "Contextualizing Gender and Labor: Class, Ethnicity, and Global Politics in the Yemeni Socio-Economy." In *Women's Rights, Human Rights: International Feminist Perspectives*, edited by Julie Peters and Andrea Wolper, 289–300. New York: Routledge.

Shami, Seteney. 1997. "Domesticity Reconfigured: Women in Squatter Areas of Amman." In *Organizing Women: Formal and Informal Women's Groups in the Middle East*, edited by Dawn Chatty and Annika Rabo, 81–99. Oxford and New York: Berg.

Shepherd McClain, Carol, ed. 1989. *Women as Healers: Cross-Cultural Perspectives.* New Brunswick and London: Rutgers Univ. Press.

Sidel, Victor W., and Ruth Sidel. 1975. "The Health Care Delivery System of the People's Republic of China." In *Practising Health for All*, edited by David Morley, Jon E. Rohde, and Glen Williams, 1–12. Oxford: Oxford Univ. Press.

Singerman, Diane. 1995. *Avenues of Participation: Family, Politics, and Networks in Urban Quarters of Cairo.* Princeton, N.J.: Princeton Univ. Press.

Stark, Ruth. 1985. "Lay Workers in Primary Health Care: Victims in the Process of Social Transformation." *Social Science and Medicine* 20, no. 3:269–75.

Stephen, W. J. 1992. *Primary Health Care in the Arab World.* Somerset: Somerset House.

Stevenson, Thomas B. 1985. *Social Change in a Yemeni Highlands Town.* Salt Lake City: Univ. of Utah Press.

———. 1993. "Yemeni Workers Come Home: Reabsorbing One Million Migrants." *Middle East Report*, Mar.–Apr., 15–20.

Stolba, Soheir, et al. 1998. *Hodeidah Primary Health Systems Support Project Appraisal Report: Background Paper.* Fair Oaks, Calif.: International Health and Development Associates.

Stone, Francine, ed. 1985. *Studies on the Tihamah: The Report of the Tihamah Expedition 1982 and Related Papers.* Harlow: Longman.

Stone, Linda. 1986. "Primary Health Care for Whom? Village Perspectives from Nepal." *Social Science and Medicine* 22, no. 3:293–302.

———. 1989. "Cultural Crossroads of Community Participation in Development: A Case from Nepal." *Human Organization* 48, no. 3:206–13.

Stookey, Robert W. 1978. *Yemen: The Politics of the Yemen Arab Republic.* Boulder, Colo.: Westview Press.

Swanson, Jon C. 1979. *Emigration and Economic Development: The Case of the Yemen Arab Republic.* Boulder, Colo.: Westview Press.

Towler, Jean, and Joan Bramall. 1986. *Midwives in History and Society.* London: Croom Helm.

Tucker, Judith. 1985. *Women in Nineteenth-Century Egypt.* Cambridge: Cambridge Univ. Press.

UNDP. 2002. *Arab Human Development Report 2002: Creating Opportunities for Future Generations.* New York: UNDP/RBAS.

UNICEF. 1993. *The Situation of Children and Women in the Republic of Yemen 1992.* Sana'a: UNICEF.

———. 1998. *Children and Women in Yemen: A Situational Analysis.* Sanaʻa: UNICEF.

Van der Geest, Sjaak. 1986. "Health Care as Politics: "Missed Chances" in Rural Cameroon." In *State and Local Community in Africa*, edited by Wim van Binsbergen, Filip Reyntjens, and Gerti Hesseling, 241–60. Brussels: CEDAF/ASDOC.

Van der Geest, Sjaak, Johan D. Speckmann, and Pieter Streefland. 1990. "Primary Health Care in a Multi-level Perspective: Towards a Research Agenda." *Social Science and Medicine* 30, no. 9:1025–34.

Van Hear, Nicholas. 1994. "The Socio-economic Impact of the Involuntary Mass Return to Yemen in 1990." *Journal of Refugee Studies* 7, no. 1:18–38.

Vaughan, Megan. 1991. *Curing Their Ills: Colonial Power and African Illness.* Stanford: Stanford Univ. Press.

Villareal, Magdalena. 1994. *Wielding and Yielding: Power, Subordination, and Gender Identity in the Context of a Mexican Development Project.* Wageningen: Thesis.

vom Bruck, Gabriela. 1988. "Re-defining Identity: Women in Sanaʻa." In *Yemen: 3000 Years of Art and Civilisation in Arabia Felix*, edited by Werner Daum, 396–400. Innsbruck: Penguin.

———. 1996. "Being Worthy of Protection: The Dialectics of Gender Attributes in Yemen." *Social Anthropology* 4, no. 2:145–62.

Walters, Delores M. 1987. "Perceptions of Social Inequality in the Yemen Arab Republic." Ph.D. dissertation, New York Univ. Ann Arbor: University Microfilm International.

———. 1998. "Invisible Survivors: Women and Diversity in the Transitional Economy of Yemen." In *Middle Eastern Women and the Invisible Economy*, edited by Richard A. Lobban Jr., 74–97. Gainesville: Univ. Press of Florida.

———. 2001. "Women, Healthcare, and Social Reform in Yemen." In *Feminism and Antiracism: International Struggles for Justice*, edited by France Winddance Twine and Kathleen M. Blee, 71–93. New York and London: New York Univ. Press.

Wedeen, Lisa. 2003. "Seeing like a Citizen, Acting like a State: Exemplary Events in Unified Yemen." *Comparative Studies in Society and History* 45, no. 4:680–713.

Weir, Shelagh. 1985. *Qat in Yemen: Consumption and Social Change.* London: British Museum Publications.

———. 1997. "A Clash of Fundamentalisms: Wahhabism in Yemen." *Middle East Report*, July–Sept., 22–26.

Wenner, Manfred W. 1991. *The Yemen Arab Republic: Development and Change in an Ancient Land*. Boulder, Colo.: Westview Press.

Wolf, Diane Lauren. 1992. *Factory Daughters: Gender, Household Dynamics, and Rural Industrialization in Java*. Berkeley: Univ. of California Press.

Worm, Ilse. 1998. "Women's Health and Politics in Yemen." Paper presented at the International Conference on Yemen, Univ. of Exeter, U.K.

Würth, Anna. 2003. "Stalled Reform: Family Law in Post-Unification Yemen." *Islamic Law and Society* 10, no. 1:12–33.

Youssef, Nadia Haggag. 1974. *Women and Work in Developing Societies*. Berkeley: Univ. of California Press.

Yuval-Davis, Nira, and Floya Anthias, eds. 1989. *Woman—Nation—State*. Basingstoke and London: Macmillan.

Zabarah, Mohammed Ahmad. 1982. *Yemen: Traditionalism vs. Modernity*. New York: Praeger.

Index

Italic page number denotes illustration.